Interpreting the Epistle to the Hebrews

Guides to New Testament Exegesis
Scot McKnight, General Editor

Interpreting the Epistle to the Hebrews

Andrew H. Trotter, Jr.

Baker Books

A Division of Baker Book House Co
Grand Rapids, Michigan 49516

© 1997 by Andrew H. Trotter, Jr.

Published by Baker Books
a division of Baker Book House Company
P.O. Box 6287, Grand Rapids, MI 49516-6287

Printed in the United States of America

Library of Congress Cataloging-in-Publication Data

Trotter, Andrew H., 1950–
    Interpreting the Epistle to the Hebrews / Andrew H. Trotter, Jr.
        p.   cm. — (Guides to New Testament exegesis ; 6)
    Includes bibliographical references.
    ISBN 0-8010-2095-6 (pbk.)
    1. Bible N.T. Hebrews—Criticism, interpretation, etc. I. Title.
II. Series.
BS2775.2.T76   1997
227′.8706—dc21   96-51940

For information about academic books, resources for Christian leaders, and all new releases available from Baker Book House, visit our web site:
http://www.bakerbooks.com

To my wife, Marie

But if the while I think on thee, dear friend,
All losses are restor'd, and sorrows end.

Contents

An expanded table of contents appears on pp. 21–24.

Editor's Preface

The New Testament is composed of four literary types (genres): the Gospels, the Acts of the Apostles, the Letters, and the Apocalypse. Each genre is distinct, and, as has been made abundantly clear by contemporary scholars, each requires different sensitivities, principles, and methods of interpretation. Applying the same method to different genres will often lead to serious misunderstandings. Consequently, students need manuals that will introduce them both to the specific nature of a particular genre and to basic principles for exegeting that genre.

The Guides to New Testament Exegesis series has been specifically designed to meet this need. These guides have been written, not for specialists, but for college religion majors, seminarians, and pastors who have had at least one year of Greek. Methods and principles may change, but the language of the New Testament remains the same. God chose to speak to people in Greek; serious students of the New Testament must learn to love that language in order better to understand the Word of God.

These guides have a practical aim. Each guide presents various views of scholars on particular issues. Yet the ultimate goal of each is to provide methods and principles for interpreting the New Testament. Abstract discussions have their proper place, but not in this series; these guides are intended for concrete application to the New Testament text. Various scholars, specializing in particular areas of New Testament study, offer students their own methods and principles for interpreting specific genres of the New Testament. Such diversity provides a broader perspective for the student. Each volume concludes with a bibliography of essential works for further study.

Although different genres require different methods and principles, a basic exegetical approach that can be adapted to various genres is also essential. Therefore, an introductory volume to the series covers the general methods and principles applicable to any genre. The individual exegetical guides will then introduce the student to more specific procedures for a particular genre.

The vision for this series comes from Gordon Fee's introduction to New Testament exegesis.[1] Without minimizing the important contribution Fee has made to New Testament study, this series goes beyond what he has presented, by providing exegetical handbooks for each of the genres of the New Testament.[2]

Finally, this series is dedicated to our teachers and students, in thanksgiving and hope. Our prayer is that God may use these books to lead his people into truth, love, and peace.

Scot McKnight

---

1. *New Testament Exegesis: A Handbook for Students and Pastors*, rev. ed. (Louisville: Westminster/John Knox, 1993).

2. A Helpful introduction to the various genres of the New Testament is David E. Aune, *The New Testament in Its Literary Environment*, Library of Early Christianity 8 (Philadelphia: Westminster, 1987).

Preface

My interest in doing a book on Hebrews stems from many sources. One of the first courses I took in seminary was an exegetical study of the epistle, and I have had a great personal love for it ever since. I have taught it in a variety of ways within a variety of contexts, some more academic than others, and have never failed to be stimulated toward more faithful discipleship each time I have done so. I have always had an insatiable intellectual curiosity about hermeneutics, and no book in the New Testament presents more interesting and crucial challenges for interpretation than this one. So to be asked to do a volume in this series is both a great honor and a great joy. My chief desire is that threefold hope that all Christians have for any of their endeavors: that it in some small way may bring honor to the Father's name, further his kingdom purposes, and add to the accomplishment of his will.

Two comments for those who are reading the preface in order to decide whether they will read the book. First, my introduction extensively defines my audience, purposes, and plans for this book, so let me gently ask you to turn to those pages for help with your decision. Second, this is not a commentary in the sense in which that word is used today, so if you are looking for one, let me direct you elsewhere. Writing at this moment in 1997, I would suggest the commentaries by Attridge, Bruce, Ellingworth, Hagner, and Lane as superior to the others, though an inspection of these works will reveal that they differ widely among themselves in audience, intention, and attention to personal application and academic scholarship.

I have far too many people to thank than is possible to do in such a small space. First on any list, though, should be my editors, Scot McKnight, the editor of this series, and Jim Weaver and Wells Turner at Baker. They suffered more than they deserved at my hands and served me exceptionally well in return. My hearty thanks for all the ways each of them improved this book, while I can safely say that any faults in this work rest squarely on my shoulders. Thanks are due to the Maclellan Foundation for making possible a short sabbatical in Cambridge so that the project could be pushed along. Thanks, too, to the people at Tyndale House for their assistance during that time. Thanks to those colleagues, students, and friends who have read parts of this manuscript at all its different stages and for the valuable suggestions they made along the way. The deepest thanks for anything I do, humanly speaking, go to my wife, Marie, my parents, Andy and Hazel Trotter, and my children, Andrew, Christopher, and Michael, who have given me more love, support, and joy than any man could merit.

I have seen more than one author's preface include apologies to children who frequently asked during the writing of the book, "When is Daddy going to be finished?" This book has taken so long from start to finish that my children have all grown up and moved away during that time. Maybe they asked about it in former days, but they gave up long ago if they did. My apology is aimed at others—at those editors, colleagues, family members, employers, students, and ultimately readers whose lives have been made at least somewhat uncomfortable by the book's delay. At least it finally got done.

Abbreviations

LXX   Septuagint

NA[27]   *Novum Testamentum Graece.* Ed. Barbara Aland et al. 27th rev. ed. Stuttgart: Deutsche Bibelgesellschaft, 1993.

NIV   New International Version

NRSV   New Revised Standard Version

NT   New Testament

OT   Old Testament

UBS[4]   *The Greek New Testament.* Ed. Barbara Aland et al. 4th corrected ed. Stuttgart: Deutsche Bibelgesellschaft/ United Bible Societies, 1994.

Introduction

The Task at Hand

This book has been prepared with the serious student of Hebrews in mind. There are many Bible study guides available today for the person without the ability to work in the original languages of Scripture, and, though they are of varying quality, many of them are outstanding. These books are joined by a great number of reference works that are produced for lay people: study Bibles, Bible dictionaries, concordances, and other books designed to open up the words and world of the Bible for those who really want to understand it. Again, the quality of these works varies, but lay people (I mean those without any formal training in exegesis and biblical languages) are well served with guides to deepening their understanding of the Bible.

On the other hand, the plethora of advanced level work for scholars that continues to pour forth in this age of personal computers and laser printers is astounding and may actually be causing more problems for scholars than it is helping them. Biblical studies researchers, for instance, have become increasingly atomistic in their work because trying to think broadly about a range of texts requires so much reading in secondary literature that many do not feel adequate to the task. Nevertheless, the point is made: there are more than enough books to keep the scholars occupied.

What seems to be lacking today are books for those who are in the middle: the pastor or the lay student of the Scriptures who have callings to preach or teach the Bible. They want and need to know it well enough to study it at a deep level, but they have far too many other elements to their callings to be able to do a Ph.D. in biblical studies. These two groups who share so much in common are expected to be teachers and preachers of the Word of God but simply do not have the time to be experts. Their level of expertise must be high because they recognize they are handling the Word of life; they have sheep coming to them to eat and drink the meat and milk of Scripture in order to be nourished by its rich truths, and they are responsible for feeding them. This is a great burden. It is for them that this book is offered.

I have said that the book is for the serious student, and I have tried to communicate something of what that means, but let me say a little of what it does *not* mean. First, serious does not mean advanced. The model for the book is the person who has had one year of Greek; often, a person who has never taken Greek but who has learned enough to be able to use some of the Greek tools will be helped by the book too. Even these boundaries include a wide range of people, some with exceptional skills and deep experience of exegesis, others with very little experience or skill who are just beginning their training in the great enterprise of biblical interpretation. The former will think that at times the book reads like an instruction manual I once saw for a telephone: "Pick up receiver. Listen for dial tone. Dial number." Only a child would need a book to tell them that. On the other hand, the latter group will sometimes think they have in hand directions for programming a VCR to record four shows over the next year and a half, some of them repeating, others only on once, all of them on different channels and different days of the week—only Ph.D.s in physics need apply. My hope is that neither group will feel that way very often, but I expect it will happen. And even when it does, it will help the experienced student to be exposed once again to some of the "basics," and the beginner will find that the difficult parts of the book will become clearer with time.

Serious also does not mean morbidly academic. We will have fun at times in this book—in everyday language, with relevant illustrations—and while that may offend some, I believe pastors and lay people benefit more from books that are easy and enjoyable to read and at least *try* to be funny, than they do from the turgid, funereal prose of the typical textbook. Again, I hope this approach will sacrifice nothing of real worth. There is a substantial benefit, for instance, in acquiring a technical vocabulary for any discipline, and we have not shied away from using that vocabulary. But I am trying to avoid being so technical that only a few "chosen ones" can read and benefit from the book. In the interest of accomplishing this goal, reference to purely academic journals or foreign language materials has been kept to a minimum.

Lastly, serious *does* mean willing to work. It takes time and effort to acquire any new skill, and biblical exegesis is no exception. Americans seem to be oriented much more toward activity than our counterparts in other areas of the world, and that makes a mental task like exegesis tougher for us than for others. We simply do not have the patience to reflect, to weigh one idea against another, to discuss with others what a biblical text may or may not mean. We want an answer, and we want it now. But serious students cannot afford to work that way, because the task they have before them is simply too complex to allow them to do so. Research into anything is a painstaking task, full of false trails and the need to stick to the job at hand. Exegetical research must be done with discipline and resolve, which eventually produces results—like the miner who, after many years of digging in the hard, unyielding ground, discovers the mother lode.

The rewards are great. Research into the cultural, historical, linguistic, and literary background of any piece of literature is bound to be helpful, but when a document was written in so alien a culture, at so great a historical distance, in so different a language, employing genres that are so radically foreign to us as the NT was, it becomes essential to investigate all these areas of knowledge in order to understand the book at all, much less to comprehend it well enough to teach it. But the silver lining to this cloud is that the returns are so satisfying. As serious study opens whole new windows onto the landscape that is the Word of God, the student of Scripture becomes more and more deeply aware of how powerful and beautiful are the vistas it gives of the world, of people, and of God himself—in short of life in all its immeasurable richness. Such views yield a joy in experiencing the mystery of the depths of the riches of God that cannot be had without the hard work required to achieve them. To change the metaphor, without the hard work of climbing the mountain, no amount of looking at a picture postcard of the same view will produce the same effect.

Overview

So what will our mountain climbing involve? What techniques will we have to master, and what equipment will take us to the top? Who are to be our guides? What sort of training will be necessary to endure the rigors of the journey? We will begin with what is most important: the notion of context.

Reading a text in context should always be the guiding principle for exegesis. To begin this task, chapter 1 will look at the historical and cultural context of the epistle, asking the questions "To whom was Hebrews written? When and for what kind of situation?" Rationale will be given for why the answers to all these questions are helpful, if not absolutely necessary, for good exegesis, but in a nutshell, we ask them so that we may better know the author and particularly his intended audience.[1] To know them better helps us to know what sort of people they were, and knowing that helps us relate them and their concerns to similar people and concerns today. The instructions in Hebrews, for instance, for those who resist submitting to their leaders have very timely and important relevance to those today who will not bow to authority unless it tells them to do what they already want to do. Such has never been the Christian view of authority and never will be; Hebrews will have much to say to those people. Similarly, to know something of the situation of these people, the *Sitz im Leben* as the Germans would say, points us to solutions for similar situations in life today. When we are being persecuted, for instance, albeit "not yet to the shedding of blood," we can take comfort and gain instruction from the words written so long ago to this struggling and fearful community. In short, to know the audience for a text gives us the opportunity to strive to duplicate their experience, if only intellectually, to become that audience in a way, so that we may lay a foundation for understanding what we should hear God saying to us in our age and our context.

In chapter 2 we tackle the difficult problem of authorship, recognizing that, if we can know who the author was, we will be able to understand the text better. By knowing something of what sort of person he was, what else he wrote, how he thought, etc.—so the idea goes—we will understand our text better, since all texts, at least the kind we find in our Bibles, are in part the result of human personality and experience. The more we know of the human being who wrote the text, the more we will understand why he chose to say this or

---

1. I use the masculine pronoun to refer to the author because the self-reference at Heb. 11:32 clearly defines the author as male (i.e., the gender of the participle δι-ηγούμενον is masculine).

that, to develop this theme or that one, and to use this metaphor or avoid that idea. Unfortunately, we will find that both the *Sitz im Leben* and the authorship of Hebrews are still shrouded in mystery, and though we know a lot from the text itself and the questions are clearly worth investigating, what we know for certain about the circumstances surrounding the production of Hebrews is limited.

After *Sitz im Leben* and authorship, we move to the study of the form of the book itself, its literary genre and structure. Here we will find ourselves on more solid ground, though large questions still remain and are regularly debated about both the epistle's genre and structure. Nevertheless, we will make some suggestions about exegesis and the way to perform it in relation to Hebrews because of its being a sermon with an epistolary twist and because of its connection to other ancient forms of writing and speaking and the characteristics it shares with them. We will also try to demonstrate the usefulness of understanding the structure of the book, particularly for preaching and teaching that book to others.

We conclude part 1 with a discussion of how we go about establishing the text so that we have something to study, and we will focus in some detail on the all-important and all-too-often-neglected art of textual criticism. I hope to show how textual criticism can yield a number of helpful preaching points for the expositor, so the discipline has a very practical side. But the theological rationale for learning to do some textual criticism ourselves is even more compelling: Do we really want to be teaching and preaching something as the Word of God when there is no good reason to think that it is?

In part 2, we will go from looking outside the text for its historical, cultural, social, and literary context to looking at the building blocks of the text itself—to the words and ideas that make it what it is. In the next three chapters, we come to the heart and soul of exegesis: the analysis of vocabulary, grammar, and style—in short, the study of the words of the text itself. Here the combination of looking at the practical use of tools (of which there are many) and at the theoretical study of the philosophy of language and how it works will help us develop skill at reading a text in a thoughtful and useful way. Word study in its lexical, grammatical, and stylistic modes will be the focus of these chapters. Without a clear grasp of these essentials, one can never really properly know the meaning of a text. While we will find it necessary in places to go over some rather old ground, the "bare bones" treatment of these avenues of study—combined with a concentration on the issues of vocabulary, grammar, and style particular to Hebrews—should make the chapters essential to anyone who wants to understand Hebrews well.

The last element of context for the exegete is theological context. Chapter 9 will attempt to "frame" Hebrews in such a way that its main themes are clarified. Then the reader can work with the particulars of a specific passage with some understanding of what the author was trying to get at in the whole of the book. Admittedly, this task will be even more subjective than others in the book, but it must be done; no one reads a text without bringing to it some theological presuppositions about that text. The best I can do is offer my suggestions and the reasons and evidence for their truthfulness and begin a dialogue with you, the reader, that will bring us as close as possible to the truths that are found in the text so that we may preach and teach it with boldness.

And after all, teaching and preaching Hebrews is the goal. Though there are no chapters specifically dedicated to preaching and teaching Hebrews, the entire book will in some sense focus on the attempt to "deliver the goods" to the people. I recognize that all that we have done in these chapters is for naught, if we do not know how to communicate it to the assembly-line worker and the lawyer, to the nurse and the farmer. These chapters will be our attempt at learning how to make first-century, priestly, OT-saturated Hebrews into the "word of exhortation" it should be for the twentieth-century salesman and computer programmer.

In the absence of a specific discussion of teaching and preaching the book, however, it might be wise to make a few remarks. Communication theory and linguistics have dominated a century in which God and man have both been declared passé. Thinkers in the West have for too long felt that all we have is our ability to communicate with each other, and so philosophy and literature departments all over this country and Europe have spent inordinate amounts of time discussing and thinking about language, its contours and programs. From structuralism through deconstruction to post-modernism, all the movements have had their theories of language, and all have influenced the way we view communication. Preachers and teachers of the Word of God must dialogue with these modern-day contributions, and while we will find much more dross than gold, the exercise and the insights will be worth the effort. Perhaps the best book with which to start is Anthony Thiselton's *The Two Horizons: New Testament Hermeneutics and Philosophical Description.*[2] Well-researched and thorough, if a little difficult to read sometimes, this book provides the sort of insight into modern communication theory that all preachers should analyze and know, if they wish to make their preaching relevant "both to the Jew and the Greek, to the wise and the foolish" of today's congregation.

To make a distinction between teaching and preaching is to open oneself up to unfavorable criticism, and rightly so, since the difference is not one that is clearly drawn in Scripture. But a practical distinction can and should be made in what we do in our churches today. We make the distinction in order to distinguish what the pastor does before the congregation in most churches on Sunday morning (preaching) from what all Christians do in a variety of contexts seven days a week (teaching), and we will try to make helpful comments about one or the other or both along the way. There are so many truths to teach and preach from the Book of Hebrews that it almost seems futile to begin to explicate them. Yet if we took the approach that we will not write anything if we cannot be comprehensive, we would never begin.

Expanded Table of Contents

---

2. Grand Rapids: Eerdmans, 1980.

Part 1

The Background of Hebrews

I love to travel. More precisely, I love to take trips to go to see strange, far away places and visit famous castles and museums and see paintings and *objects d'art* about which I have heard or read. I often find, though, that when I get there, the object I looked forward so much to seeing does not live up to my expectations. I discover that I enjoyed *planning* to see the view much more than I did the view itself. Like Wordsworth in the Lake District—who felt that the joy of planning, anticipating, and traveling to visit Coleridge in Keswick sometimes outstripped the actual event itself—I get wrapped up in the preparations for the event and enjoy those so much that I lose perspective and forget the purpose of the planning. It is not really the fault of the object of my desire; the object is just as attractive, or interesting as it is supposed to be. No, the problem is that I have put so much time and effort into the planning and preparation that the visit is anticlimactic; when I finally arrive and sit down by the fire—like Wordsworth with Coleridge—I have no energy left for discourse with my fellow poet.

The same can happen with the study of Scripture. The preliminary matters we will discuss in this section, which are so helpful to a proper understanding of the text, can never be allowed so to dominate our investigations that they swallow it up. If, for instance, we allow a particular view of the authorship of Hebrews to control how we think about the text, we may not have sufficient energy and discipline to listen to the text itself and will miss the meaning waiting there for us.

So our investigations in this section need to be taken with a grain of salt. They are useful—we might even say essential—for proper exegesis, but our conclusions will nevertheless be tentative and must be recognized as such. We regard them as preliminary to the meatier aspects of exegesis; they help answer certain questions (whether positively or with the true scholar's answer of "I simply don't know"), questions that by their nature must precede exegesis: Who are the "Hebrews" to whom the epistle is addressed? Who wrote this epistle? What was the author's purpose? Who received it and when? What kind of literature is this? These are all questions that constantly push themselves to the front before and during the study of a passage, and these are the questions we will ask in the next five chapters.

1

Historical and Cultural Context

To know the author of an epistle, when it was written, its geographical destination, and something about its readership helps modern day readers to relate the teaching of that epistle more clearly and more consistently to their own concerns. This principle, known as reading a work in its historical and cultural context, occupies the place of primary importance in the interpretation of any writing. Literary genre, style, and grammatical and structural context are perhaps equally important but are often more easily ascertained. This is particularly true in the case of Hebrews, where so many of the answers about historical and cultural context are inconclusive.

Nevertheless, to know the answers to these questions, even in a tentative form, is necessary for us to continue with the process of interpretation. We ask the questions so that we may better know the author and, particularly, his intended audience. To know them better, though not thoroughly, helps us at least to know more about what sort of people they were, and to know that helps us better relate them and their concerns to similar people and concerns today. Therefore even with all the obstacles in our way keeping us from knowing for certain the circumstances in which and to which Hebrews was written, we must find out what we can.

The question of authorship is so large that we have devoted a whole chapter to it. The present chapter will deal primarily with the destination, date, and readers of the epistle. The text of the book itself offers the most evidence concerning the last of these elements, and so we will begin with the question of the readers of the epistle. While dating the epistle is a risky endeavor, we nevertheless will be helped more in determining the destination of the epistle by first tentatively dating it. Thus we will next concern ourselves with the date of the epistle and then look at its destination.

Who Were Those Guys?

A famous line from one of my favorite films, *Butch Cassidy and the Sundance Kid*, expresses the frustration of the scholar when trying to figure out the anonymous audience of a biblical book. In the movie, Butch and Sundance begin their flight from lawmen with a cocky and self-assured attitude, promising their mutual friend Ellie that they will shortly be back after shaking their trackers. Starting well, and using every trick they know to evade the trackers, they find that their pursuers are relentless, and they can never seem to make good their escape. In exasperation, they begin to ask the question "Who *are* those guys?" since the trackers never flag in their mission. In the film, Butch and Sundance eventually jump off a cliff and effect their escape. Though the analogy isn't perfect, the frustration Butch and Sundance felt is a lot like that of the scholar trying to pursue the elusive audience of Hebrews. As the pursuers rather than the pursued, we are still asking today: Who *were* those guys?[1]

Ideas about the readership of the epistle must be based first and foremost on the best evidence we have: the text of the epistle itself. The first evidence that the modern reader encounters is, of course, the title of the epistle, which would seem to indicate, in English at least, that the readers of the epistle were Jews. This has been widely disputed, however, for a number of reasons. Some question the meaning of the title itself. They have argued that the title should actually be translated, "against the Hebrews,"[2] but there seems little likelihood that the title could actually mean this. In fact, the title itself is somewhat irrelevant to our question, because it seems to

---

1. Those investigating the background of the Book of Hebrews sometimes wish that they could use the same trick as Butch and Sundance, but it's not as easy as jumping off a cliff!

2. See Paul Ellingworth, *The Epistle to the Hebrews: A Commentary on the Greek Text*, New International Greek Testament Commentary (Grand Rapids: Eerdmans, 1993), 21–22, who mentions this view in order to refute it but does not say where the suggestion comes from.

have been added much later and probably reflects a later writer's opinion about who the recipients were.

Much more important for our investigation are clues within the text itself. We may state conclusively that the epistle is written to Christians. They may be Christians who need warnings about their faithfulness, (cf., e.g., 5:11–6:19; 10:19–39), but these warning passages themselves make it quite clear that the author considers both his readers and himself to be among those who are of the community of faith in Christ (Heb. 6:9–10; 10:39). Two additional questions arise from the text about the recipients of Hebrews. Were they predominantly Jewish, Gentile, or a mixture of both? And are they members of the community in general, or a particular group within that community? The answers to these two questions will give us most of the information that we can reliably state about the readership of Hebrews.[3]

The interpreter of Hebrews might instinctively opt for a Jewish readership, not only because of the title of the book but because of what is immediately apparent upon reading the text: the OT is quoted on almost every page. It is clear that the author expected his readers to be acquainted with the OT in great detail, not only because he explicates it at some length but also because he leaves some questions unanswered and yet seems to expect his readers to dig up those answers for themselves (cf., e.g., Heb. 9:5). This argument, however, is not as watertight as it might at first seem. The gentile world in many quarters was well aware of the OT, particularly the LXX. Use of various rabbinical practices in the interpretation of Scripture in the Book of Hebrews (see below, chap. 9) is a stronger argument for Jewish readership, but still not conclusive since many of the techniques used in Hebrews were also found in the Hellenistic world as well. Even the extensive discussion of sacrifices and priests, while of course taking place within a Jewish context, does not settle the matter. These practices were widely employed in Hellenistic worship as well. To get ahead of ourselves a bit, if this epistle is destined for Rome, another argument against assuming an exclusively Jewish readership is that Jewish practices were known more widely in Rome than elsewhere in the

---

3. A third question, What is the readers' relationship to the author of the epistle? is answered best in the discussion of the authorship of the epistle (see chap. 2).

empire. Many Gentiles were well aware of Jewish sacrifices and customs, so any reference to these would not necessitate a Jewish readership.

On the other hand, it is difficult to see any evidence for a purely gentile audience. Some see a gentile background in the following:

1. reference to families sharing the same flesh and blood (Heb. 2:14) and children's duty to submit to their parents' discipline (Heb. 12:5–11);
2. the analogy of the field (Heb. 6:7–8);
3. the contrast between milk and solid food (Heb. 5:12–14);
4. the typological language concerning shadows and realities (Heb. 8:5; 9:23; 10:1);
5. the use of the word στοιχεῖα (Heb. 5:12); and
6. the exhortation to be faithful in marriage (Heb. 13:4).

But these are all references that both Jews and Gentiles would understand and cannot be used to argue for an exclusively gentile origin for the book. The use of typology in the large central section of the book (Hebrews 7–10) does not point to a gentile authorship either, as we know from the techniques attributed to Philo, a Jewish philosopher working in Alexandria who synthesized the Jewish faith with Greek philosophy. A final argument for gentile readership comes from the reference to "dead works" (Heb. 6:1; 9:14). Yet the author of Hebrews does not consider the works of Judaism to be alive either, as his calling those works a mere shadow makes abundantly clear (cf. Heb. 8:5; 9:23; 10:1). Hence, there is no conclusive evidence that any of the language used in Hebrews could be understood only by Gentiles.

The weight of evidence tends toward a congregation of mixed background. The very fact that the Jewish references could be understood by Gentiles and the gentile references could be understood by Jews is an initial, though not strong, indicator in this direction. Paul Ellingworth points to the recurring contrast between true worship and apostasy as pointing to "the likely setting of the epistle and the likely situation of its addressees."[4] While agreeing that the predominance of the OT probably indicates a

---

4. Ellingworth, *Hebrews*, 25.

large Jewish population in the community, he makes the point
that the author consistently avoids both distinctively Jewish and
distinctively gentile language in the discussion. In other words,
rather than describe the Jews as Pharisees or legalists (some equivalent of the "Judaizers" of Paul, cf. Gal. 1:7; 3:1–3) or the Gentiles
as "barbarians" or some equivalent (cf. Paul's description in Romans 1), he avoids describing them at all. This would perhaps suggest a mixed group of addressees, neither of whom he wanted to
offend by references to their backgrounds.

A second question is whether the author of Hebrews addressed
his epistle to a particular group or to the broader community of
Christians as a whole. Wherever the original readers of the Epistle
to the Hebrews may have been, they seem to be a subgroup within
the larger community of Christians in that place. A number of references within the text lead us to that conclusion. Perhaps foremost among this evidence is the extensive condemnation of the
readers in Heb. 5:12–14. There the author admits that he has much
to say about Melchizedek, but it is "hard to explain" (δυσερμήνευτος, Heb. 5:11). This is because his readers have "become dull in
understanding" (νωθροὶ γεγόνατε ταῖς ἀκοαῖς, Heb. 5:11), implying that they once understood more than they do at the present.
Amplifying this thought, the author goes on to say that they ought
by this time to be "teachers" (διδάσκαλοι, Heb. 5:12), but they now
need someone to teach them basic truths once again. It is hard to
believe that the author would address an entire community as
those that ought by now to be teachers; by definition the office of
teacher necessitates a much larger group to be taught. The contrast
between those who feed on milk and those who feed on solid food,
and the references to infancy and maturity, further support this
idea in the passage.

A second important passage that demonstrates Hebrews to be
addressed to a subgroup of the Christian community is found in
Hebrews 13. While most of the exhortations in this chapter are
general, several of them have to do with paying deference to the
recipients' leaders. Hence, Heb. 13:7 enjoins the readers to "remember" (μνημονεύετε) their leaders and extensively describes
the way in which they should remember them—as those who
"spoke the word of God" to them and as models to be imitated in
"faith" (πίστις) and "way of life" (ἀναστροφή). Moreover, in Heb.

13:17 the readers are enjoined to "obey your leaders and submit to their authority" (NIV). Once again, this idea is elaborated by describing the leaders as those who must give an account to God and keep watch over the souls of the readers. The author goes on to enjoin his readers to help their leaders in their oversight of them so that they may do it "with joy and not with sighing—for that would be harmful to you" (Heb. 13:17 NRSV). Last and perhaps most revealing, the readers are exhorted to "greet all your leaders and all the saints" (Heb. 13:24 NRSV). This distinguishes the readership of this epistle from the larger group of the community and not just from the leaders. Hence, the readers of this epistle seem to be some smaller subgroup of the larger community that has a particular need to hear what our author has to say to them.

A further indication that the readers are a subgroup of the whole is found at Heb. 10:25, where the readership is enjoined not to neglect meeting with other Christians. There the readers are encouraged to "consider how to provoke one another to love and good deeds, not neglecting to meet together, as is the habit of some, but encouraging one another" (Heb. 10:24–25 NRSV). The command points to a group that has either separated itself semipermanently or at the very least regularly separates itself from the community during worship. Our author sees this as a serious breach of the gospel and clearly condemns it, using it as a lead-in to perhaps the strongest warning of the epistle (Heb. 10:26–39).

It is fruitless to speculate much further about the character of this group. Many have accepted the judgment of Spicq that the readers constituted a group of converted priests from Jerusalem.[5] William Manson thought them to be former leaders of the church, who, having been kicked out of Rome during the persecution of Claudius in A.D. 49, now have returned to the community in Rome. They are no longer leaders, and they are having difficulty with their status as followers in the community.[6] Others have associated these with converts in the community at Qumran or other more well defined groups. All these suggestions have something to commend them, but their difficulties are just as great. While we

---

5. Ceslas Spicq, *L'Épître aux Hébreux*, 2 vols., Études bibliques (Paris: Gabalda, 1952–53), 1:226–42.

6. William Manson, *The Epistle to the Hebrews: An Historical and Theological Reconsideration*, 2d ed. (London: Hodder & Stoughton, 1953), passim.

will make some tentative suggestions concerning the date and place of the recipients of the epistle, we should see this epistle as addressed to a particular group within the community rather than to the community as a whole, and that is all we can say for sure about who they are.

When Were Those Guys?

Dating a NT book is a process of elimination, starting from the dates on both ends of a time line before and after which the book could not possibly have been written and moving toward the date on the line that seems to fit both the best internal and the best external evidence.[7] First, one looks for references to the book in other early Christian literature that can be dated with some certainty, in order to find a date after which it could not possibly have been written (the *terminus ad quem*). For instance, we are fortunate enough to have several clear references to Hebrews in *1 Clement*, traditionally dated ca. A.D. 96. Therefore, we know it was written prior to it, but the question is: How much prior? This is a much more difficult question to answer, but there is internal evidence that may at least give us some clues.

Only a few interpreters would date anything in the NT prior to ca. A.D. 45–50; only a very few documents could even qualify for a date that early.[8] Hebrews, however, could have been written prior to A.D. 70, perhaps long before. The evidence for this early date comprises several facts. First, all the discussion of the sacrificial system is done in the present tense, indicating to some that the sac-

---

7. Cf. John A. T. Robinson, *Redating the New Testament* (Philadelphia: Westminster, 1976), 1–12, for a superb discussion of the principles and biases that have gone into the dating schemes of many modern NT scholars. What began as a joke for Robinson turned into a serious scholarly passion until he became convinced that there was no good, objective reason to date anything in the NT after A.D. 70. While his conclusions have not been generally accepted, he has shown that no *proof* exists against his position.

8. The date before which anything in the NT *could* have been written (the *terminus a quo*) is of course ca. A.D. 30, the approximate date of Jesus' death, but the reasonable supposition that it took some time for the early church to recognize the need for written documents that could be kept and distributed causes almost all NT scholars to regard A.D. 45–50 as the earliest reasonable date for any NT writing. Even Robinson dates only 1 and 2 Thessalonians and James prior to A.D. 50.

rifices were still continuing and that the temple had not yet been destroyed (as it was in A.D. 70 during the Roman wars). This evidence is not as strong as it might at first appear, however, because the concept of tense in Greek is not so much time-oriented as it is aspect-oriented, and therefore it gives very little indication of time.[9] Even if it did reflect present time in this instance, as some scholars still contend, it would not prove conclusively a pre–A.D. 70 dating; others writing much later than the destruction of the temple used the present tense to describe the cultic phenomena that went on there.[10] The whole discussion, too, is something of an abstraction; our author discusses the sacrificial system only in its typological relation to the present sacrifice that Christ brings before the Father in heaven. The notions of history and of time take second place to the eternal sacrifice of our great High Priest, and, therefore, whether the temple and what went on there is a present or past reality is less significant than it otherwise might be. Given all these arguments against the relevance of the present tense in Hebrews to describe temple rituals, there is nevertheless a strong argument from silence that, if the author knew the temple had been destroyed, he would not have used the present tense, since the substance of his argument revolves around the old having passed away and the new having come.[11]

The reference to Timothy's release from prison in Heb. 13:23 appears to be relevant only to the 50s and possibly the early 60s A.D. But this connection assumes that the Timothy mentioned in Hebrews is the famous associate of Paul. Even if it is that Timothy, we have no knowledge of how long Timothy outlived Paul, and since Paul is not the author of the epistle in any case (see below), Timothy could easily have lived until the 80s or even early 90s. Thus this reference, too, is not as conclusive of an early date as we may at first glance imagine. Ellingworth relates that some have suggested the reference from Ps. 95:10 to forty years (Heb. 3:9–10)

---

9. Cf. D. A. Carson, Douglas J. Moo, and Leon Morris, *An Introduction to the New Testament* (Grand Rapids: Zondervan, 1992), 399–400.

10. Cf., e.g., Josephus *Antiquities* 4.102–87.

11. Carson et al. argue rightly that Josephus and others were not "engaged in a theological argument about their [the temple rituals, etc.] principial obsolescence, about their utter replacement by the corresponding realities of the new covenant; but that lies at the very heart of the argument in Hebrews" (*Introduction*, 399). See more below on this argument from silence.

may indicate that the author was writing forty years after the crucifixion. As he points out, this is a tentative guess at best, since the author only relates the forty years to the people of Israel and not to his present readers. A more direct reference to the forty years, connecting it to the "today" of the passage, would add more weight to this contention, but such a reference is lacking.

More important is the argument from silence—admittedly dangerous, but strong nevertheless—concerning the fact that the fall of Jerusalem and the destruction of the temple are not mentioned in the epistle. The argument that these physical realities are only shadows of a truer reality in heaven is so strong in the epistle that clear proof of that argument in the form of the events of A.D. 70 would seem too good for our author to omit, if it had already happened. But there is no mention of these events. It is true that the statements about the levitical sacrifices are based on OT rather than contemporary practice, even referring to the tabernacle rather than the temple; nevertheless, reference to some sort of present activity among the Jews in Jerusalem seems clearly to be intended. The lack of reference to the destruction of the temple is simply too hard to believe if Hebrews were written after the event. So it seems certain that it was written before A.D. 70.

But how far before A.D. 70? Two factors indicate that at least some time has passed since the readers first became Christians. We saw above that they are expected by our author to have reached a level of maturity beyond what they have actually attained (Heb. 5:12–14). This would indicate a period of some time for their spiritual lives to have developed since the gospel first came to them. Add to this the reference in Heb. 2:3, indicating that the community to which our author writes was evangelized by second generation Christians, and one must allow some time to have elapsed between the first spreading of the gospel and the founding of this community. However, neither of these arguments requires a date later than A.D. 55–60. The gospel spread so rapidly during the *Pax Romana* that one could easily speak of second generation communities within five to ten years after the beginning of Paul's evangelistic thrust in the late 40s or early 50s.

Most problematic for a very early dating are the references to the persecution of the community, especially since this persecution seems to have taken place a while before (cf. Heb. 10:32–34;

12:5). Here decisions we make about other aspects of the historical and cultural background of the epistle come into play. If, for instance, the community is assumed to be at Rome, then the persecutions under Claudius in A.D. 49 and Nero in A.D. 64 are important, as is the supposed persecution that took place under Domitian (A.D. 91–95). If, however, the epistle was written to Palestine, there were of course persecutions afflicting the Christian church from its inception at Pentecost, recorded as we know in the Book of Acts. We do not want to get too far ahead of ourselves, but it may be time to move to the question of where the recipients were. Tentatively, let us conclude, then, that there is good reason to date the epistle prior to the fall of the Jerusalem temple, somewhere in the mid-60s.

Where Were Those Guys?

Date, authorship, and the nature of the recipients all play a role in determining the place to which the epistle was written, but there is some slender evidence that comes from the text itself. This is found in the greeting that "those from Italy" (οἱ ἀπὸ τῆς Ἰτα–λίας, Heb. 13:24) give to the readers. The phrase can mean that those who are in Italy with the author are sending a greeting to the readership, implying that the author is in Italy surrounded by others who are also from that place. This would indicate a place of destination outside the borders of Italy. It can also mean, however, that those who are with the author somewhere outside Italy, but who come from Italy, are sending back greetings to the recipients. The latter is the more likely reading for this text. F. F. Bruce points out that the phrase is used in the first way in one of the papyri,[12] but here it is certainly the more natural reading to let ἀπό have its normal sense of separation. If the author wanted to say the former thing, he would probably have said "those who are in Italy with me" (οἱ ἐν τῇ Ἰταλίᾳ σὺν ἐμοί; cf., e.g., Gal. 2:3), and while this is another argument from silence, it is nevertheless a compelling one.

A complete determination of the destination of the epistle cannot be made on the basis of this one simple reference, however

---

12. F. F. Bruce, *The Epistle to the Hebrews*, rev. ed., New International Commentary on the New Testament (Grand Rapids: Eerdmans, 1990), 391 n. 132.

compelling it seems to be, but other indications point to a destination somewhere in Italy. Given that our knowledge of persecution in the early church is limited, there are nevertheless persecutions that fit both what we know of the community at Rome and the statements in Hebrews concerning the persecutions that the readers experienced. References to the loss of property, public exposure to abuse and persecution, and being imprisoned (Heb. 10:32–34) but not having suffered to the point of shedding blood (Heb. 12:4) perfectly fit the situation of the Christian community in Rome between A.D. 49 and A.D. 64—after the persecution of Claudius (a bloodless persecution so far as we know) and yet before the persecution of Nero (one in which members of the community suffered to the point of death). As we said above in reference to dating, much is being read between the lines here. Nevertheless, the details fit so well that until a better hypothesis enters the picture, we will work with this one.

There have been other ideas put forward. Some have seen Alexandria as a destination for the epistle, but this is based purely on the notion that the methods of interpretation, particularly the use of typology, in the epistle show an affinity for the works of Philo. This is true, but Alexandria is an unlikely destination since there the epistle was quite clearly, but also quite wrongly, first attributed to Paul.[13] This mistake would be difficult to understand if the epistle had originally come to readers in this area. The second suggested destination is Jewish Christians in Palestine, an idea supported by several commentators down through the years.[14] This is difficult, however, on many grounds, not least of which is the reference to the readers' generosity to others (Heb. 6:10; 10:34; 13:16), when we know from Paul's letters that the church in Jerusalem was so poor that it itself was in need of financial help (cf., e.g., Rom. 15:26).

We have stated that our conclusions must remain tentative, but a working hypothesis that one can employ for understanding the Book of Hebrews from a historical and cultural perspective is as follows: A small group of former leaders in the church have en-

---

13. This attribution was first made by Clement of Alexandria (cf. Eusebius *Ecclesiastical History* 6.14.1–4).

14. Cf., e.g., Philip E. Hughes, *A Commentary on the Epistle to the Hebrews* (Grand Rapids: Eerdmans, 1977), 15–19.

countered difficulties submitting to the current leadership. These
leaders had been persecuted in Rome and were forced to go un-
derground for a time during the persecution of Claudius in A.D. 49.
Surfacing again some time around A.D. 64, they rejected the new
leadership and now must be rebuked for their lack of devotion to
their new leaders, to the community in general, and ultimately to
Christ. They need a clearer and newer vision of him, perhaps because of doctrinal error in their midst in addition to their unwill-
ingness to submit to authority. To this situation the author of the
epistle wrote. But who was that author?

2

Authorship

Charlotte Brontë once wrote in a letter to her good friend William Smith Williams that, as far as she was concerned, to her critics she was "neither man nor woman—I come before you as an author only. It is the sole standard by which you have a right to judge me—the sole ground on which I accept your judgment."[1] But can any author reach such a high degree of objectivity that their economic and social background, their education, and, yes, even their sex do not matter at all in the reading and understanding of their work? For years it has been a commonplace of biblical interpretation that knowledge of an author—his or her social and economic background, influences, tendencies, etc.—is crucial to a proper interpretation of that author's work.[2] Of course the interpretation of a novel is very different from that of an epistle; the purposes, aims and goals of any nonfiction work are radically different from those of fiction. But even poetry has been judged by its

---

1. Charlotte Brontë to William Smith Williams, 16 August 1849, *The Brontës: Life and Letters*, ed. C. Shorter (New York: Haskell House, 1908), 2:64.

2. We will not engage the question here, but discussion about the "objectivity" of the text, independent of authorial intent, has been going on for some time in critical circles, particularly among critics of English literature (cf., e.g., the recent discussion by Umberto Eco, Richard Rorty, and others found in *Interpretation and Overinterpretation*, ed. Stefan Collini (Cambridge: Cambridge University Press, 1992). See particularly E. D. Hirsch, Jr., *Validity in Interpretation* (New Haven: Yale University Press, 1967) for the best defense of the importance of authorial intent for discovering meaning in texts and Grant R. Osborne, *The Hermeneutical Spiral: A Comprehensive Introduction to Biblical Interpretation* (Downers Grove, Ill.: InterVarsity, 1991), 366–96, for a good summary of the issues.

authors to be a work so unto itself that knowledge of the details of the author's life are not needed to understand the work.[3]

Is it essential for us to know much about the author of a work for us to understand that work? If it is, then we are in trouble when we turn to the Epistle to the Hebrews, for we do not, indeed *cannot*, know conclusively who its author is, since he is not named anywhere in the work. In fact Origen, one of the first church fathers ever to investigate the question of the authorship of the epistle, wrote what is the most famous, and probably the wisest, dictum on this subject: τίς δὲ ὁ γράψας τὴν ἐπιστολήν, τὸ μὲν ἀληθὲς θεὸς οἶδεν ("As to who wrote the epistle, only God knows for sure").[4]

To know the background of and influences upon the author of a work is helpful, but not essential to at least a basic understanding of a work, especially the Epistle to the Hebrews. This is so for at least two reasons, one that would apply to any writing, the second a reason that applies particularly in the case of Hebrews.

Language is a universal tool of communication, and if the communication is relatively simple (i.e., about well-known concepts using widely recognized vocabulary and symbols), then who is doing the communicating becomes less important. When a communication has a very narrowly defined code in which it is transmitted, understanding may depend on specific definitions or formulations that the particular person might use. Then knowledge of that person is essential. Such is the case at times in Hebrews, but by no means is it always so. The idea of the levitical priesthood, for example, and how Jesus might relate to it is not limited to a tiny group of people or some one person who would give this idea thoroughly new content. The levitical priesthood is as broadly known as Judaism itself; any Jewish person, and in fact many Gentiles, might have said what is said about it in Hebrews, so which one did so is somewhat irrelevant. And such is the case with the

---

3. William Wordsworth, for example, was reticent to give life details to one who requested them because, as he said, "Nothing could be more bare of entertainment or interest than a biographical notice of me . . . the date and place of my birth, and the places of my Education [are] correct—the date of my publications is easily procured—and beyond these I really see nothing that the world has to do with, in my life which has been so retired and uniform" (William Wordsworth, *Letters of William Wordsworth: A New Selection*, ed. Alan G. Hill [Oxford and New York: Oxford University Press, 1984], 277).

4. Eusebius *Ecclesiastical History* 6.25.14.

vast majority of Hebrews, while, on the other hand, there are some things we do not know that could probably be answered if we were certain of the identity of the epistle's author.

Second, to say that we do not know exactly *who* wrote the epistle is not the same thing as saying we know absolutely nothing about its author. In fact, as we shall see below, we know quite a bit about him and can use this information in making interpretative judgments with some confidence. As we build a picture of the author based on this evidence, we will find that we can differentiate him and his world from most people in the ancient world and give him a relatively definite background in Hellenistic Judaism that will yield quite a bit of exegetical fruit.

If we do not, and cannot, know exactly who he is, why will we spend time discussing the various alternatives that have been proposed on this subject in the history of Christian thought? That is a good question, and in another sort of book, perhaps the amount of time we will spend would be inappropriate. But we will look at the question in detail more as an exercise in gaining an understanding of, and an appreciation for, the *process* scholars go through in determining authorship of an ancient document than as an attempt to solve a problem that has been recognized as unsolvable since the earliest days of the church. The process of examining authorship is useful for several reasons. It develops our observational skills. It increases our historical knowledge of the epistle and its interpreters, introducing us to some of the most interesting characters in the story of the Christian church. It develops our ability to think logically about the text. All these are useful skills when it comes to learning how to do exegesis.

But still the question persists: How important is it for us in the twentieth century to know in detail the character and influences of a first-century author in order for us to understand his or her work? The question is unanswerable, of course, as are all questions that ask one to measure things that are not measurable. Suffice it to say that the church has benefited for almost two thousand years from this magisterial work without knowing with any more certainty than we do today who authored it. If Origen's famous dictum remains true forever, and there is no reason to think it will not, then we will continue nevertheless to benefit from the doctrine and ethics taught in this marvelous book, and it will continue to challenge us well into the twenty-first century to act and think in obedience to God.

What We Know of the Author of Hebrews

The author of Hebrews tells us much about himself in spite of neglecting to give us his name.[5] The most important thing that he tells us about himself is found in Heb. 2:3–4. In this passage, where he for the first time addresses the people to whom he is writing in a personal way, the author announces that the salvation of which he is speaking "was first announced by the Lord, [and] was confirmed to us by those who heard him" (ἥτις ἀρχὴν λαβοῦσα λαλεῖσθαι διὰ τοῦ κυρίου ὑπὸ τῶν ἀκουσάντων εἰς ἡμᾶς ἐβεβαιώθη NIV). This clear statement of secondary knowledge of the gospel message is an important factor in determining who wrote Hebrews, as we shall see below.

The language is very much like that of other passages in the NT that in fact argue for primary knowledge of the gospel on behalf of their authors. In Gal. 1:11–12, for instance, Paul makes it quite clear that he "did not receive it [the gospel] from any man, nor was I taught it; rather, I received it by revelation from Jesus Christ" (Gal. 1:12 NIV). Similarly, in 2 Peter 1:16–18 Peter says that he told his readers about the power and coming of our Lord Jesus Christ, that he himself was an "eyewitness" (ἐπόπτης) of his majesty, and that he had "heard this voice that came from heaven when we were with him on the sacred mountain" (NIV), referring to his experience at Christ's transfiguration (cf. Mark 9:2–8 = Matt. 17:1–8 = Luke 9:28–36). Perhaps an even more important parallel is found in 1 Peter 1:12 where Peter says that the gospel was revealed to the prophets when they wrote of the things "that have now been told you by those who have preached the gospel to you by the Holy Spirit sent from heaven" (NIV), making a clear distinction between himself, those to whom he is writing, and those who preached to them.

In a strikingly different way, the author of Hebrews places himself with his readers as a secondary recipient of the gospel. The statement "this salvation, which was first announced by the

---

5. We have already observed that the masculine participle διηγούμενον in Heb. 11:32 designates the author as male.

Lord, was confirmed to us" does not mean that the salvation was announced to them by the Lord, but is rather a historical statement about the good news having been brought by Christ, who was not only the content of the good news but the announcer of it. Thus it was not given to the readers and the author by revelation in the way that Paul speaks of receiving the gospel in Galatians 1.[6] Rather, the gospel "was confirmed" (ἐβεβαιώθη) to the author and his readers "by those who heard him" (ὑπὸ τῶν ἀκουσάντων). While almost all commentators have agreed that Paul and Peter would not have written in such a way, it is just as strongly argued that Barnabas would not have, an opinion for which there is little basis (see more below). Nevertheless, it seems impossible that anyone who would write this could have been one of the twelve apostles.

The author of Hebrews also tells us in the crucial verses at the end of the book that he knew Timothy, referring to him as "our brother Timothy" (Heb. 13:23). He intimates not only that he knows him but that he will go with him to see the readers if Timothy comes to him soon, implying that Timothy will be meeting with him in the near future. This is an important but often overlooked piece of evidence for the Pauline authorship of this epistle, though it can of course be interpreted in a variety of ways. In any case, it shows that he did not have only a passing knowledge of Timothy, but a very close knowledge of him. This evidence assumes that it refers to the same Timothy who was a compatriot of Paul and who was involved in the sending of at least six of his letters (2 Corinthians, Philippians, Colossians, 1 and 2 Thessalonians, and Philemon). It is sometimes implied that this may not be a reference to the biblical Timothy,[7] but the coincidence seems too great for the name to refer to someone other than the Timothy we know from the Pauline Epistles.

---

6. Ellingworth suggests that this does not mean that the author and readers "were Christians of the second or a later generation . . . , but it is in sharp contrast with Paul's claim . . ." (Paul Ellingworth, *The Epistle to the Hebrews: A Commentary on the Greek Text*, New International Greek Testament Commentary [Grand Rapids: Eerdmans, 1993], 7, cf. also p. 30).

7. Cf. Werner Georg Kümmel, *Introduction to the New Testament*, rev. ed. (Nashville: Abingdon, 1975), 401: "if indeed the well-known companion of Paul is intended."

Other evidence treated in more detail elsewhere may be mentioned. Our author states that he is dwelling with people who are "from Italy" (Heb. 13:24). He speaks of having written them only a brief letter, which is referred to as a "word of exhortation" (Heb. 13:22), pointing to the fact that he is a preacher of the gospel, an assumption that is not difficult to support from many other elements in this epistle (see the chapter on genre). He also writes, "I particularly urge you to pray, so that I may be restored to you soon," perhaps implying that he is in prison, but not necessarily so. These passages complete the use of the first person singular in the Book of Hebrews, but there is much else that we know of this author from the text itself.

The author of Hebrews was a well-educated man. The writing of Hebrews is easily the finest in the NT, both in its use of grammar and vocabulary, and in its style and knowledge of the conventions of Greek rhetoric.[8] The epistle's author had almost certainly received rhetorical training, as his use of everything from alliteration to diatribe will attest. He is familiar with philosophy—both Jewish and, to a lesser extent, Greek—in that he uses many Philonic terms and, to a lesser extent, Stoic ones.[9]

Our author is an exceptional scholar when it comes to the use of the OT Scriptures. He knows their content intimately, as can be seen from the long list of heroes of the faith (presented in Hebrews 11) referring to people from the earliest chapters of Genesis right through to the later prophetic and poetical writings. He interprets the Scripture in varying ways, too, all with equal degrees of facility, employing everything from an almost allegorical technique to straight literal application. Once again, his great knowledge of Greek is demonstrated by his extensive use of the text of the LXX, the Greek Bible, throughout the epistle.

The author's education is displayed not only in his use of well-known rhetorical techniques that were taught in the ancient world but also in his ability to do theology creatively. The many innovations in this epistle demonstrate an extremely active mind, one that could only be spurred by deep and intensive study of the

8. "The language of Hebrews constitutes the finest Greek in the NT . . ." (William L. Lane, *Hebrews*, Word Biblical Commentary [Dallas: Word, 1991], 1:xlix). Cf. Nigel Turner, *Style*, vol. 4 of *A Grammar of New Testament Greek*, by J. H. Moulton (Edinburgh: T. & T. Clark, 1976), 106–13.

9. Cf. Turner, *Style*, 107.

Scriptures. These innovations, shown in the arguments the author uses, also point to a high level of education. His has been said to possess "an architectural mind,"[10] and this is certainly correct. Our author states a thesis, develops it by way of analysis, departs from it for very well thought-out and structured reasons, and then comes back to it brilliantly, incorporating the themes of his digression into the subsequent argument. The structure of Hebrews is a complicated matter (see below, chap. 4), but even a quick read-through of Hebrews leaves the impression that the author has taken care in its construction.

The author of Hebrews also distinguishes himself by his intensely "religious" nature. All of the authors of the NT are religious in one sense, of course, in that they speak of God and man and the relation between the two, but we mean "religious" in the sense of showing an intense interest in the symbols and the cultic actions of religion. Here our author has no peer in the NT. Much of his writing centers on the priesthood, the sacrifices, the tabernacle, the feasts, and just about anything else that has to do with the religious life of the people of Israel and how it points to Christ. While he certainly uses other metaphors and ideas to communicate, the majority of his illustrations come from the cultic activity of Israel. While comparing the "religiousness" of the writers of the NT (in the truest and best sense of that word) would certainly be a mistake, one would nevertheless be hard-pressed to find a more "religious" person (in the sense we have defined above) in the history of Christendom.

The author of Hebrews is clearly a preacher with a pastoral heart. He shows that combination of toughness and tenderness that is so crucial in ministry. Even when his warnings are as stringent as any in the NT, he makes sure to encourage those whom he believes are on the right track. One example is Heb. 6:4–6, the famous "apostasy" passage. Having just rebuked his readers because they need to be taught again the "elementary teachings about Christ" (Heb. 6:1), he then warns them of the impossibility of returning to God if they "fall away." But he is quite clear that he believes none of them are as yet in this situation, for he goes on to say that he is "confident of better things in your case—things that accompany salvation" (Heb. 6:9 NIV). He goes on to remind them that God will not forget

10. Lane, *Hebrews*, 1:xlix.

their work and life and tells them that he only speaks to them in this way so that they will not "become lazy," but will "imitate those who through faith and patience inherit what has been promised" (Heb. 6:12 NIV). This "tough and tender" attitude displays itself in other places in the epistle as well (cf., e.g., Heb. 10:26–39).

The author also lets us know something about his relationship with his readers. While we cannot know the exact nature of that relationship, it is evident from the tone in which the epistle is written that he expects to be listened to as an authority in the community.[11] The author's exhortations reveal an intimate knowledge of problems taking place in the community. For instance, it would be unlikely that he would simply mention, with no specific instance in mind, something like 13:4: "Marriage should be honored by all, and the marriage bed kept pure, for God will judge the adulterer and all the sexually immoral" (NIV). While sexual immorality was a common problem in the early church, as evidenced by both Paul's letters and the other epistles in the NT, mention of it is usually kept to a word, unless the problem is a serious, specific one. This passage, while betraying no details of the problem (such as mentioning names or describing the situation so specifically that identification of the offenders would be clear to the readers), nevertheless seems to point to a specific situation known to the author and readers.

Even more certainly, the problem of obedience to leaders is clearly a difficulty for the community. At Heb. 13:17, the readers are enjoined one last time to obey their leaders and "submit to their authority," but this is not the first time that leadership is mentioned as a problem. Leadership concerns seem to underlie the statements at Heb. 5:11–6:3, 10:25–39, and 12:15 and 25. Other references to problems in the community that may reflect intimate knowledge of it are found scattered throughout the epistle, particularly chapter 13. He calls his readers "brothers" (Heb. 3:1, 12; 10:19; 13:22) and "dear friends" (Heb. 6:9). He speaks of "each of you" (Heb. 6:11), individualizing them, anticipates being restored to them (Heb. 13:19), and refers to *our* brother Timothy" (Heb. 13:23).

---

11. While this is an argument from silence, it does cause some problems for the argument that our author does not claim authority and so can be neither Paul nor Barnabas, both known as apostles in the church. Paul does not assert his authority when he does not need to but reserves that for those epistles where his authority is clearly being challenged.

As we study the Epistle to the Hebrews, it is important to remember that this author knows his readers intimately; otherwise, the esoteric opening of Hebrews 1 could be misinterpreted as "doctrine without life," as if the statements about Christ and the angels have no practical significance for our author but rather are only part of an abstract theological treatise. What we know of the author prevents our regarding him this way. Similarly, knowing that he is well educated and uses the Greek Scriptures helps us to understand his particular attitude toward the law and to discern whether his view is at odds with the apostle Paul's or complementary to it. This knowledge can be of great use at many other points in interpreting the epistle.

But this is not the end of the investigation of the authorship of Hebrews. We can go further and give some tentative, if not absolutely certain, conclusions as to who actually wrote the epistle.

Suggested Authors of Hebrews

The number of those proposed as possible authors for Hebrews probably exceeds that of any two NT books put together. The author's not being named in the text precludes us from saying anything with certainty about his identity, but the question still remains: Who wrote the epistle? This question has been particularly important in the history of the book's interpretation because it is tied so closely to the question of canonicity. In the writings of Eusebius of Caesarea, much of the discussion of the authorship of Hebrews revolves around the authority of the epistle and, therefore, its canonicity. In short, if it was written by Paul, it should be accepted as authoritative; if not, real questions remain about its acceptance into the canon.

But the question of the canonicity of Hebrews is secondary to our study. We are interested in the identity of the author, and we shall now look at three of the suggestions that have been put forward, in order to get some notion of how scholars work on these sorts of questions.[12] As we said above, in addition to uncovering further information about the possible authorship of Hebrews, the exercise

---

12. There are of course many other names that scholars have proposed over the years, but there is so little scholarly consensus on any of them that they do not merit attention here. For a relatively full account of the possibilities, cf. Donald Guthrie, *New Testament Introduction*, 4th ed. (Downers Grove, Ill.: InterVarsity, 1990), 668–82.

will be instructive for us, even if we cannot reach definite conclusions. Deciding the relative merits of these three common suggestions is pointless, so after looking at their strengths and weaknesses,
we will proceed to the question of the literary genre of the epistle.

Apollos

Martin Luther first mentioned the idea of Apollos as author of
the epistle, a proposal that has been widely accepted in the twentieth century.[13] The suggestion seems plausible, when one looks at
how many parallels there are between the NT figure of Apollos and
what we know from the text itself about the author of Hebrews. The
Book of Acts tells us that Apollos was a Jew, a native of Alexandria,
and a learned man with a firm knowledge of the Scriptures (Acts
18:24). The four major elements found in this description—that he
was (1) Jewish, (2) Alexandrian, (3) educated, and (4) knowledge-
able in the Scriptures—are all elements that fit well the picture of the
author of Hebrews that emerges from the text itself. The author was
certainly a Jew, he was educated (i.e., learned), and he had a fair
knowledge of the Scriptures. The connection with Alexandria arises
from the author's acquaintance with a variety of interpretative
methods used on the OT in educated circles in the ancient world, especially those of Philo of Alexandria. This also squares with his extensive knowledge and use of the LXX, since it was commonly used
in Alexandria.

In addition, we are told that Apollos had been "instructed in the
way of the Lord," and that "he spoke with great fervor and taught
about Jesus accurately" (Acts 18:25 NIV). This would indicate that he
had the kind of knowledge of the sacraments of Jewish ritual that
would allow him to develop the themes of Hebrews and that he had
the pastoral, kerygmatic heart that could both proclaim the Scriptures
fervently and yet teach them pastorally. We know too from Acts that
he was "a great help" (συμβάλλω) to those in Achaia who had believed, "proving from the Scriptures that Jesus was the Christ" (Acts
18:27–28 NIV). The Acts passage even describes Apollos as refuting
the Jews in public debate, certainly something that the author of Hebrews is very much concerned to do as he argues against a Jewish interpretation of the law and in favor of a specifically Christian one.

---

13. Cf. Ellingworth, *Hebrews*, 20–21.

Apollos is mentioned by Paul in almost the same breath with Timothy (1 Cor. 16:10–12), indicating a connection with Timothy that our author also had (Heb. 13:23). A more subtle but no less clear piece of evidence is that Apollos seems to have had the same kind of mind as our author; he was an eloquent man and argued successfully, suggesting that he thought in the same logical and erudite manner as the author of Hebrews (Acts 18:28).

The great problem with accepting Apollos as the author of the epistle is that he is not identified as such anywhere else in Christian literature prior to Martin Luther. Apollos was a well-known and well-liked figure in early Christian writing, and if he had indeed been the author of this epistle, it is difficult to believe that it would not have been mentioned somewhere. Nevertheless, it must be recognized that this is an argument from silence, and arguments from silence are sometimes not very sturdy planks upon which to stand. Other objections to Apollonian authorship also rely on silence: (1) nothing is explicitly mentioned about Apollos having a formal education or any link with Philonic methods of interpretation in Alexandria; this is only inferred from Acts 18:24–28. (2) We know of no other writings of Apollos, while the author of Hebrews is so comfortable with the written word that it is hard to believe he wrote nothing else. Many of the things that are said about Apollos could be said about hundreds of other people in the ancient world, but this says nothing more than that we don't know precisely who the author is. But Apollos is certainly distinctive among the candidates, and this suggestion remains one of the more likely ones that have been put forward.

Barnabas

From ancient times it has been suggested that Barnabas is the author of Hebrews. Some believe this to be the oldest attribution on record.[14] Tertullian (ca. A.D. 200) refers to "an epistle of Barnabas entitled 'to the Hebrews,' "[15] but it is difficult to tell much about this reference for several reasons. First, it seems to imply that his information was secondary, and therefore it would point back to a still earlier period in the second century when Barnabas was believed to be the author. Tertullian's language, however, is extremely difficult,

---

14. Guthrie, *Introduction*, 674.
15. *De Pudicitia* 20.

and so the idea that Barnabas's authorship was widely accepted from an early period cannot be accorded much weight. The second problem with this reference is that Tertullian could well be confusing the Epistle to the Hebrews with the well-known *Epistle of Barnabas*, a work commonly attributed to Barnabas though certainly not written by him. Also, no one else among the North African fathers seems to make this attribution, though later, Jerome (ca. A.D. 400) mentions it, and it has had advocates in the twentieth century.[16] Hebrews certainly has nothing in common with the *Epistle of Barnabas*; the two differ widely in both theology and style.[17] Therefore, though the attestation is early, it is not particularly strong.

The strongest basis for the connection between Barnabas and the author of Hebrews rests on parallels between the text itself and biographical details from Acts. Acts 4:36 describes Barnabas as a Levite, linking him with references in the epistle to the levitical cult. He is said to be from Cyprus, making him a Jew of the Diaspora and giving him more likely acquaintance with the LXX than a Palestinian Levite would have. Hebrews describes itself as "a word of encouragement" (λόγος τῆς παρακλήσεως, Heb. 13:22); this fits well with the interpretation of Barnabas's name, which is "son of encouragement" (υἱὸς παρακλήσεως, Acts 4:36). Lastly, Barnabas is said to have given some of his property and money for the gospel (Acts 4:37), which parallels the encouragement to the readers of Hebrews who "joyfully accepted the confiscation of [their] property, because [they] knew that [they themselves had better and lasting possessions" (Heb. 10:34 NIV). All of these are remarkable coincidences to say the least and give a strong basis for this conjecture.

A further argument in favor of Barnabas being the author of Hebrews is his connection with Paul. This connection argues for his authorship in two ways: (1) the epistle reflects Pauline ideas and (2) the author seems to assume that his authority will be recognized. Barnabas traveled with Paul on his missionary journeys, being much in favor of the gentile mission, and he would have been constantly exposed to Paul's preaching and therefore to his ideas (Acts 11:22–30; 13–14; 15, esp. vv. 2, 12, 22, 25–26, 35). Of

---

16. Ellingworth, *Hebrews*, 14.
17. Cf. Brooke Foss Westcott, *The Epistle to the Hebrews*, 3d ed. (London: Macmillan, 1909), lxxx–lxxxiv.

course, Barnabas broke with Paul and did not accompany him on his second missionary journey (Acts 15:36–40), and Paul also seems to fault him for his lack of fellowship with the Gentiles at Antioch (Gal. 2:13), though the reference there still reflects his great affection for Barnabas. But these negative references do not really hinder the likelihood that Barnabas was an interpreter of Paul for the Hebrews.

Even more important is the status Barnabas seems to be accorded vis-à-vis Paul. Both Paul (1 Cor. 9:6) and Luke (Acts 14:14) count Barnabas as an apostle, showing that he was on equal footing with Paul in the ministry to the Gentiles. In addition, the reception of Barnabas and Paul by the Gentiles at Lystra (Acts 14:8–18) shows that there was no doubt about their equal status in the minds of those who heard them. The recognition and respect accorded Barnabas could explain the kind of authority the author wields in the epistle and his readers' ready acceptance of this authority.

The arguments *against* the authorship of Barnabas seem weak. The strongest is that it is odd that not more of the early church acknowledged his authorship. But this could be due to the fact that the *Epistle of Barnabas* (which was wrongly attributed to him) contains a great deal of defective theology, which may have made others reluctant to attribute to Barnabas a clearly orthodox epistle like Hebrews. In addition, this once again is an argument from silence and so should be given less weight.

There is a second argument against Barnabas's authorship. Hebrews 2:3–4 indicates that the author sees himself as a lesser authority than the primary witnesses to Jesus. The problems with this argument are two-fold. First, Barnabas *was* a secondary witness to Christ as far as we know, since there is no reference to him knowing Jesus prior to his association with Paul in the Book of Acts. Therefore, he could easily have made the statement in Hebrews without any notion that it reflected a lack of authority. Second, he could claim to be an apostle, to have all the authority of the risen Christ behind his teaching, and still be a secondary witness. This is obvious in the case of the historical Barnabas: Luke and Paul both refer to him as an apostle, as we mentioned above, and yet no one thinks he was a primary witness to Jesus.

Perhaps the most telling argument against the authorship of Barnabas is connected with the question of the supposed readership of the epistle. If in fact the readers are in Rome, there is no evidence that Barnabas ever got there or would have had as intimate an acquaintance with that community as that reflected by the author of the epistle. This is, of course, another argument from silence. But it is a powerful one, since so much depends on a strong relationship with the community at Rome, and there simply is no evidence of such a relationship in the case of Barnabas. Of course, this does not mean that he *did not* have a strong relationship, simply that no evidence of it has come down to us in Christian history. The possibility of Barnabas being the author of Hebrews, therefore, has strong elements in its favor, and the opposing arguments are not convincing.

Paul

In the history of the discussion of the authorship of Hebrews, authorship by the apostle Paul still ranks as the most often supported hypothesis. Very few scholars in the twentieth century believe that Paul is the author, however, and they have good reasons for rejecting this view, but the idea certainly has enough substance historically to warrant serious investigation.

A discussion of Pauline authorship of Hebrews should probably begin with the external evidence, meaning the references made in early Christian literature connecting Paul with the epistle. In all background matters, of course, we are on much more solid ground with arguments based on texts and references we actually have in the ancient documents, as opposed to the more subjective arguments that modern scholars have come up with based on style, grammar, theology, and other elements. And the matter of authorship is no exception to this rule. So let us turn first to the references linking Paul to Hebrews in the early church fathers.

An important distinction, usually made when investigating a matter in the fathers of the church, is that between what is known as "Western" versus "Eastern" writings and their relative differences.[18] When we turn to the West, we find a very strange set of circumstances regarding the Epistle to the Hebrews and its au-

---

18. This is a distinction often made in discussions involving early church history but never clearly defined. At the risk of oversimplifying the matter, the Western fathers wrote predominantly in Latin and were loyal to the Bishop of Rome; the Eastern fathers wrote in Greek (or Syriac, Coptic, or another of the Eastern languages) and resisted the dominance of Rome.

thorship. The epistle was certainly known very early on, since Clement of Rome quotes it several times and refers to it as an authoritative source. Nevertheless, he does not mention authorship or carry on any discussion concerning the matter. In fact, there is virtually no discussion of the authorship of the epistle in the West until very late. Not surprisingly, the canon of Marcion (ca. A.D. 150) omits the epistle altogether, since Marcion was attempting to drive a wedge between what he considered to be the OT God of wrath and the NT God of love. Hebrews would be just the sort of book he would reject out of hand because of its favorable attitude to the OT and its willingness to portray Jesus as a high priest. The Muratorian Canon (ca. A.D. 185) omits the epistle also, though the poor textual condition of that canon may be the reason for this. As we saw above in our discussion of Barnabas as an author, the powerful church father Tertullian mentions the epistle, but this evidence is confused and so scant in any case that it does not afford us much information on any of the discussions that may have been taking place in his circles about the epistle's authorship.

It is not until the time of Augustine, Jerome, and Hilary of Poitiers (fourth century A.D.) that we get much discussion in the West of the authorship of Hebrews at all. Perhaps this silence and Tertullian's minimal use of the epistle points to a rejection of Hebrews as Pauline. For whatever reason, the Western fathers did not join in defending its authenticity. The case was far different in Alexandria, however.

Our chief source of information about the Alexandrian fathers and their use of Hebrews comes from Eusebius of Caesarea and his *Ecclesiastical History*. He quotes Clement of Alexandria (d. ca. A.D. 215), who refers to the opinion of Pantaenus (d. ca. A.D. 190), his predecessor as bishop, as favoring Pauline authorship.[19] Clement intimates that Pantaenus believed Paul to be the author and defends against the only problem he saw for Pauline authorship (anonymity) by saying that "Paul, through modesty, since he had been sent to the Gentiles, does not inscribe himself as an apostle of the Hebrews, both to give due deference to the Lord and because he wrote to the Hebrews also out of his abundance, being a preacher and apostle of the Gentiles." His point was that

---

19. *Ecclesiastical History* 6.14.2–4.

the Lord Jesus was the apostle to the Hebrews, so Paul does not make himself out to be one, especially since he was the apostle to the Gentiles.

Clement obviously does not buy this argument, for as he says earlier in the passage,[20] he regards Luke as the translator of a Hebrew original written by Paul. The epistle is therefore in the same style as the Book of Acts, and he hints that "the [title] 'Paul, an apostle' was naturally not prefixed." The second reason Clement believes Paul did not affix his name to the document is that he "very wisely did not repel them [the Jews] by putting his name," since he was the apostle to the Gentiles and had, in the Jews' eyes, turned his back on his Jewish heritage. Clement shows that he views Paul as the real author by elsewhere quoting Hebrews as being by Paul.[21]

Perhaps the most important Alexandrian to discuss Pauline authorship is the brilliant scholar Origen (ca. 185–254). Eusebius has an extensive discussion of Origen's views as well.[22] Origen states that the style is definitely not Paul's, pointing to the eloquence of the language of the epistle and the fact that it does not have the "rudeness of speech of the apostle" (τὸ ἐν λόγῳ ἰδιωτικὸν τοῦ ἀποστόλου) that Paul even characterizes himself as having (2 Cor. 11:6). Origen admits that the thoughts of the epistle are elevated (i.e., the theology is admirable and worthy of attribution to Paul), while the style is lacking. This leads him to the hypothesis that Hebrews was written by a disciple of Paul who was taking "short notes of what his master said" (σχολιογραφήσαντός τινος τὰ εἰρημένα ὑπὸ τοῦ διδασκάλου). Thus Origen is able to eat his cake and have it too. He states that though the epistle was not actually written by Paul, it is perfectly legitimate for any church to regard this epistle as Paul's. His final conclusion is, of course, that God alone knows who actually wrote it.

Lastly, it is important to note that Eusebius himself seems to accept the Epistle to the Hebrews as Pauline, while making it clear that there is much disagreement about this in the church.[23] As Ellingworth points out, however, Eusebius does refer at one

---

20. *Ecclesiastical History* 6.14.2.
21. Cf., e.g., *Stromata* 6.8.
22. *Ecclesiastical History* 6.25.11–13.
23. *Ecclesiastical History* 3.3.5.

point to "the letter to the Hebrews and the rest of Paul's letters."[24] He sees this as "suggesting some difference of status or circumstances."[25] Other church fathers, among them Epiphanius (ca. 315–403), Theodore of Mopsuestia (ca. 350–428), and Ephraem Syrus (ca. 306–373), refer to Pauline authorship but are less important in this discussion.[26]

The internal evidence concerning Pauline authorship is not scanty. Much has been written about the style and theology of Hebrews versus the style and theology of Paul, even from the earliest days of the church. But there are several direct statements that must be dealt with before we move on to such subjective matters. Perhaps the most important passage is Heb. 2:3–4. No author in the NT makes a stronger claim to his direct reception of the revelation of the gospel than Paul. In writing to the Galatians, he says "I want you to know, brothers, that the gospel I preached is not something that man made up. I did not receive it from any man, nor was I taught it; rather, I received it by revelation from Jesus Christ" (Gal. 1:11–12 NIV). It seems impossible that the author of this and similar statements (cf., e.g., 2 Cor. 12:1–7) could so easily place himself among those who learned of the gospel from someone else. As much as Paul may wish to identify with his readers, he would not have done so by minimizing his authority as an apostle.

A corollary to this objection is that Paul never fails to "sign" his other letters. The anonymity of Hebrews, while perhaps explainable on literary grounds (since in any case the epistle does not have a formal opening), nevertheless speaks strongly against Pauline authorship. The idea that Paul left the letter unsigned because he was the apostle to the Gentiles and did not want to undermine that work by having it become known that he was fraternizing—even through a letter—with Jews, is doubly wrong since it assumes something false both about Paul (i.e., the favoritism that he condemns in Peter, Gal. 2:11–21) and about the composition of the community reading the letter (see above, chap. 1).

---

24. *Ecclesiastical History* 2.17.12.

25. Ellingworth, *Hebrews*, 6.

26. Ibid. Ellingworth also gives a good summary of the manuscript tradition, which shows varying degrees of acceptance of the Pauline authorship of Hebrews. Sometimes the epistle is placed alongside Paul's epistles in a prominent place, at other times it is left out altogether, and at still other times it is found in a variety of places such as after Galatians or 2 Corinthians (ibid., 6–7).

Better is Clement of Alexandria's suggestion that Paul omitted his name out of deference to the true apostle to the Hebrews, the Lord Jesus, but this suggestion is unprovable and remains unconvincing.

Paul Ellingworth gives strong internal evidence of the difference between the vocabularies of Hebrews and the Pauline epistles that is overwhelmingly against the possibility of their being written by the same person.[27] There are differences in the terms related to knowledge and revelation; life and death; power, conflict, and judgment; the people of God; expressions of emotion; anthropological, ethical, and liturgical terms; divine names and titles; and references to the author's own situation and work. Perhaps chief among the differences is the lack of forensic language to describe salvation in Hebrews. Paul often uses δικαιοσύνη and its cognates to describe legal justification; the author of Hebrews, when he uses the word group, regularly does so to speak of ethical righteousness (i.e., obedience to God's will; cf., e.g., Heb. 1:9; 12:11).

Stylistically also, Hebrews is far from Paul. William Lane points both to the author's sentence-building techniques and to his distinctive imagery as just two of many stylistic and grammatical elements that separate the author of the epistle from Paul.[28] The classical smoothness with which the author makes transitions contrasts with Paul's rough, hiatic style, and the long, contrived periods of Hebrews—which approach the best of classical writing—are unlike Paul's equally long but often rambling and diffuse sentences. The judicious use of the genitive absolute in Hebrews, his variation of word order, and "his love of the pure nominal phrase and avoidance of the copula" have also been suggested as stylistic differences between our author and Paul.[29]

Last but not least, among the differences separating the author of Hebrews from Paul is theology. As D. Guthrie rightly points out, "it should be noted that differences from Paul do not amount to disagreements with Paul,"[30] and he provides a useful list of theological elements in Hebrews that could rightly be called Pauline.[31] But the differences in emphasis cannot be missed. The

---

27. Ibid., 7–12.
28. Lane, *Hebrews*, 1:xlix.
29. Cf. Turner, *Style*, 106–7.
30. Guthrie, *Introduction*, 673.
31. Ibid., 709–10.

author considers the resurrection to be among the *elementary* teachings of the faith (Heb. 6:2), stressing the *exaltation* of Christ to the right hand of the Father as his triumph over death (Heb. 9:24–27), while Paul clearly elevates the *resurrection* to that status (cf. Rom. 1:4). Paul focuses more on the forensic and redemptive aspects of the blood of Christ; Hebrews clearly stresses the cultic cleansing, sanctifying, and perfecting work of the sacrifice. The struggle between flesh and spirit and the individualism of Paul's teaching of union with Christ is absent from Hebrews, where faith means holding fast to the confession and adhering to rules of obedience and belief. Lastly, Paul refers to the new covenant only in passing (2 Cor. 3:6) and never speaks of Christ in terms of the high priesthood, but these ideas form the central thoughts of the Epistle to the Hebrews.[32]

Concluding Profile of the Author of Hebrews

We have argued above that a working hypothesis concerning the specific identity of the author is not necessary for doing good exegesis of the epistle. Among those known to us from the first century, the choice of possible authors seems effectively narrowed to Barnabas and Apollos, and the evidence for and against both is so balanced as to make it impossible to choose between the two. Whoever the author, we know that he was a second-generation Christian who knew his readers intimately. We know he had a pastoral heart and knew when to be direct, and when oblique, in his attempts to shepherd the flock. We know that he was an accomplished preacher, displaying a wide range of classical rhetorical devices for communicating his message. We know that he was a superb interpreter of Scripture, able to use a number of different hermeneutical methods to explicate the text. We know he was well educated, a writer who had a number of different literary genres at his command. But which genre did he use in penning this epistle? That is our next question.

---

32. Cf. ibid., 673, and Kümmel, *Introduction*, 395, for more examples of the differences between Paul's thought and Hebrews.

3

Genre

G*enre* is a fancy-sounding French word that simply means the type of literature a document is. Every day, without even thinking about it, we use different types of literature with different literary conventions and different hermeneutical rules. Let's see how many different kinds of literature an average person might encounter in the course of a normal day by following a typical Christian reader through her day.

Jane Reader wakes up, gets her coffee, and reaches for her Bible from which she reads a psalm to start off the day. Continuing her devotional time, she reads that day's entry from *My Utmost for His Highest* and then turns to the list she uses to aid her in prayer. After a shower, she goes downstairs and brings in the morning paper, leaving it on the table as she prepares breakfast. She reaches into the cupboard for the box of Pop-Tarts and puts one into the toaster in accordance with the instructions on the side of the box.

Jane reads the paper as she eats her breakfast, scanning articles on the front page about the president's continued battle with Congress over his new tax bill, a local department store opening, and a street juggler who stopped a runaway car and rescued a little girl in the process. She looks at the editorial page, carefully reading one editorial on a proposed new law to limit vagrancy on city streets. She then turns to the financial pages to find out what the Dow Jones Average was yesterday and to check on some of her stocks. Then it's on to the sports page to see how the Red Sox did last night, reading both the stories about the game and the box score and then moving on to a recap of the current women's tennis tournament. She finishes her quick browse of the *Daily Telegraph* with a look at what's on at the movies and her two favorite cartoon strips, "Calvin and Hobbes" and "The Far Side."

On to work. Pulling the car out of the garage, she drives down the street, noticing just in time the detour sign that directs her to a different freeway on-ramp. As she gets on the freeway, the homeless person with his hand-held sign saying "Food for Work" reminds her to say a quick prayer for him and to make a mental note of Saturday morning's monthly volunteer time at the Salvation Army. On the freeway she sees three billboards, reinforcing her decision to see *Jurassic Park* tomorrow night, to buy some suntan lotion, and to think about that new car again. As she pulls into the parking garage of her building, she checks the ticket spit out by the machine; they have been printing the wrong date on these tickets recently for some unknown reason. When she speaks to the attendant, she is reminded by the name sewn on his shirt to call him Ernie.

In the elevator, she absentmindedly reads the state certificate of operation as she waits for the elevator to stop at her floor. Stepping out of the elevator, she takes a quick glance at the daily notice board that reminds her of the visit that day of one of the company's most important clients and of a special lunch planned in the cafeteria for their guests. Arriving at her office, she begins to work through the stack of papers left on her desk at the close of work yesterday—memos, reports, summaries, sales figures, computer printouts, correspondence, phone messages. Reading these items takes her until lunchtime.

Her afternoon is taken up with meetings, phone calls, and more reading—this time a lengthier study done by a research facility on the possibility of developing a new product. In the late afternoon, Jane takes off early from work because she needs to do a little shopping. There she reads everything from labels to price tags to brochures containing descriptions of the dresses she is thinking about buying. After a quiet dinner with friends at her favorite restaurant, where reading the menu is always fun for her because she gets to work on her Italian, she goes home. When she finishes going through her mail—which consists of letters, advertising fliers, catalogs, news and literary magazines, and the ubiquitous direct-mail appeals—she sits down at the piano to play a little relaxing music before curling up with the latest John le Carré spy novel and going off to sleep.

How many different kinds of literature did Jane Reader encounter in one ordinary day? One could easily count as many as forty different kinds of literature, all of which she would read with different expectations, different responses, different levels of trust and interest. She reads everything from the highly technical research document, which perhaps only she and a handful of others could understand, to the common comic strip enjoyed by children and adults, rich and poor, black and white, male and female alike. She reads works with a highly developed grammatical structure and works with no thought for proper grammar—in fact some without even an alphabet (sheet music). Some items are almost entirely pictures, others have no pictures at all; some are highly personal, others completely impersonal; some are in her native language, others not; some strain to be as historically and scientifically accurate as possible, others make no pretense of being accurate in these senses.

All these different types of literature have been developed for the same purpose—to communicate something to someone. Their authors differ merely in the forms chosen for communicating and in what they seek to say. Writers choose their forms, expecting certain things of their readers. Authors of devotional books know their readers are going to understand that they are merely writing their opinion about what a certain passage or an experience meant to them. A writer of an advertisement desires from the reader a high level of interest and trust in the writer's truthful objectivity, as does the newspaper reporter. The author of a comic strip seeks to entertain and does not care about "truth" in a historical sense at all; ditto the novelist. Some seek to inform; some seek to persuade; all seek to communicate.

But readers would fail to understand the document and the message it seeks to communicate, if they failed to understand the type of literature it was. What an impossible situation Jane Reader would face in understanding anything, if she took "Calvin and Hobbes" as seriously as she does her business correspondence or, conversely, if she took her business correspondence as lightly as she takes "Calvin and Hobbes"! We all naturally, usually instinctively, interpret the various communications we receive every day with different sets of hermeneutical rules, looking at a passage of OT poetry with very different eyes than those with which we read newspaper reports. Knowing a document's literary genre forces us to read it differently than we would read a document of a different genre, and employing the proper rules for interpreting that document entails knowing the rules for rightly reading that genre. So what is the literary genre of the Book of Hebrews, and what are the rules for interpreting it?

The Sermon That Changed Its Name

Hebrews, unlike many of the writings of the NT, gives us an indication in the body of its own text as to what sort of document it is. Near the end of the epistle, the author asks his readers to "bear with my word of exhortation, for I have written to you briefly" (Heb. 13:22 NRSV). The two parts of this sentence are equally important for our understanding of Hebrews's genre: it is a document to be understood from both an oral and a written perspective. What are the implications of the dual nature of the book? First, we need to do a bit more to establish this dual nature.

The phrase "word of exhortation" (λόγος τῆς παρακλήσεως) could at first glance refer to either a spoken or a written message. This particular construction is found in the NT only here and at Acts 13:15, where Paul is invited by the synagogue officials to speak εἴ τίς ἐστιν ἐν ὑμῖν λόγος παρακλήσεως πρὸς τὸν λαόν. The implication from this passage, and from several other uses of language similar to this phrase in contemporary literature, is that it functions as "an idiomatic designation for the homily or edifying discourse that followed the public reading from the designated portions of Scripture in the hellenistic synagogues."[1] We will have to take seriously the fact that words were chosen, structures formed, and thoughts woven together in this book very largely with an oral presentation in mind. The ramifications of this for exegesis will be apparent shortly, but for now the important thing to note is that the descrip-

---

1. William L. Lane, *Hebrews*, Word Biblical Commentary (Dallas: Word, 1991), 2:568. Lane mentions 1 Macc. 10:24, 2 Macc. 7:24, 15:8–11, and particularly 1 Tim. 4:13. For further reading on this topic, see particularly the essay by Lawrence Wills, "The Form of the Sermon in Hellenistic Judaism and Early Christianity," *Harvard Theological Review* 77 (1984): 277–99, and the mostly positive response to it by C. Clifton Black II, "The Rhetorical Form of the Hellenistic Jewish and Early Christian Sermon: A Response to Lawrence Wills," *Harvard Theological Review* 81 (1988): 1–18.

tion λόγος τῆς παρακλήσεως in Heb. 13:22 indicates that Hebrews is primarily regarded by its author as a sermon, an exhortation to believe and to do the great truths spoken of in the epistle. In a variety of other ways, the epistle exhibits an essentially oral character. At Heb. 5:11, 6:9, 8:1, 13:6, and perhaps 12:5, the author self-consciously refers to his communication to the Hebrews, and the language he uses is that of verbal communication. In Heb. 5:11, he admits his inability to convey all that he would like to get across to them because they have become literally "dull in the ears" (νωθροὶ ταῖς ἀκοαῖς), and the language he uses to express his frustration apparently recalls the idea of a lengthy speech for which the speaker has no time available.[2] In 6:9, the author claims to "speak" (λαλεῖν) in a certain way. Similarly, in 8:1 and 13:6 the use of λέγειν seems to fit a verbal context better than a written one.[3] The strong emphasis throughout the epistle on God's *speaking* (cf., e.g., Heb. 1:1; 12:25–27) is another indication of the conscious orientation of the document toward oral communication rather than written.

The *Epistle* to the Hebrews, however, was obviously not simply a sermon, given once or twice and then lost forever in the mists of time. It is not even the transcription of a sermon, notes taken by a devoted disciple and put into rough written form.[4] We have known of the book since very early in the church's history, and always as an epistle. In its earliest manuscripts it is found in several different places within the Pauline corpus, but always connected with Paul's

---

2. Cf. Paul Ellingworth, *The Epistle to the Hebrews: A Commentary on the Greek Text*, New International Greek Testament Commentary (Grand Rapids: Eerdmans, 1993), 299, for many references in classical literature to phrases similar to πολὺς ἡμῖν ὁ λόγος which indicate orations. Cf. particularly Acts 15:32 and 20:2 where, according to Ellingworth, λόγος πολύς "means 'a long speech,' without any indication of quality or content."

3. Λέγειν is generally used to describe oral expression, though it can be used to refer to writing too (cf. Walter Bauer, *A Greek-English Lexicon of the NT and Other Early Christian Literature*, trans. and adapted by William F. Arndt and F. Wilbur Gingrich, 2d ed. rev. and augmented by F. Wilbur Gingrich and Frederick W. Danker [Chicago and London: University of Chicago Press, 1979], s.v. "λέγω"). Λαλεῖν, though sometimes used of the sounds inanimate objects make to "speak" (cf. the thunder and the trumpet in Rev. 10:4; 4:1), always refers to expressions aurally received and almost always to human speech.

4. Cf. the preservation of the *Discourses* of Epictetus (ca. A.D. 55–ca. A.D. 135) by Arrian (2d cent. A.D.) as an example of this practice, one that was quite common in NT times.

writings. The title "To the Hebrews" stands over its first page, just as Paul's epistles have headings like "To the Philippians" or "To the Thessalonians," and this, coupled with the fact that it is always found with Paul's letters in the manuscript tradition, accounts for why the church has always considered it an epistle.

There are also some internal considerations that point to its epistolary nature. In the same verse where the author calls his appeal a word of exhortation, he mentions that he has written to them briefly (διὰ βραχέων ἐπέστειλα ὑμῖν, 13:22). And it is clear from many passages in the book, that he knows his readers and their circumstances and is writing to address those circumstances, a common purpose of other NT epistles. He also mentions mutual acquaintances in the much-discussed statement "those from Italy greet you" (Heb. 13:24), a phrase that would hardly occur at the end of a sermon but seems to have been consciously added at the end of a written document.

Commentators often point out that the author was writing because he was not able to address his audience face to face. One of his last appeals to his readers is for prayer "so that I may be restored to you soon" (13:19 NIV). Hebrews, then, is an epistle, but it is fair to say that it is not a "true" epistle, at least in the Pauline fashion. Later we will discuss more of the differences and similarities between this epistle and those of Paul, but suffice it to say for now that Hebrews is not simply a transcript of a sermon but a consciously written document.

Given the combination of oral and written elements in the work, what are the chief characteristics of these two literary genres that make up Hebrews? How do they fit to make a unified whole? Is it more like a written sermon or more like a preached epistle? How can we recognize oral and epistolary elements so that we can isolate them, define their influence, and better interpret the epistle? Finally, how important is it to our understanding of the epistle to be able to answer these questions?

The issue of their importance aside, the simple fact is that answers to these questions are ultimately not to be found. Perhaps if we had audio tapes of this sermon,[5] we could compare the oral presentation with the epistle and say with confidence "This is

---

5. Or is it a *set* of short sermons or homilies? We cannot answer this question. The connecting devices that unify the book's argument and make it seem like one continuous sermon could well have been added after the original sermons were given (see chap. 4 on structure).

oral" and "This is written," but as it is we have only the written form, and distinguishing how our preacher/author may have differentiated one from the other is difficult. Since the final form of Hebrews is a written document, it is perhaps correct to say that oral elements are embedded in its writing, so that even some elements that we will discuss here were intended primarily for oral persuasion, whereas all now serve the ultimate purpose of written persuasion. For instance, one may speak of alliteration as a stylistic characteristic that primarily affects the hearer, while brachylogy (the use of a simple shorthand expression or ellipsis) seems to have greater effect on the reader. Neither, however, can be said to function exclusively so. We must also remember that Hebrews was probably intended to be read publicly and to be meditated on in private as well (though the ancients, even when reading privately, read aloud to themselves!). Hence the importance of viewing each element as contributing at both the oral and written levels. Both oral and written considerations bear upon this complex subject, but separating the two is virtually impossible.

Before moving on, however, we should deal with one question that might arise in discussing literary genre that can be answered relatively simply. The Epistle to the Hebrews is definitely *not* a translation of a document written in another language. There are many indicators of this, not least of which are its clear dependence on the Greek version of the OT, the Septuagint, for its OT quotations. It is unlikely that a translator, presumably translating a work that was using the Hebrew OT, would have changed the Hebrew verses to their LXX equivalents. While there are some relatively literal translations of the Masoretic Text (the best version of the Hebrew OT that we have) in the LXX, differences occur quite often and are varied enough to make it unlikely that the writer of Hebrews was using the MT. The author also makes some wordplays in Greek that would not have occurred to him in another language. Harold Attridge notes two: "the plays on ἀρχηγός at 2:10; 12:2; and the exploitation of the ambiguity of δια-θήκη at 9:16–17."[6] Add to this the classical style of the document, with its linguistically-based rhetorical elements (e.g., its numerous plays on Greek etymology; see below, chap. 8), and the idea that this is a translation becomes impossible.

---

6. Harold W. Attridge, *The Epistle to the Hebrews*, Hermeneia (Philadelphia: Fortress, 1989), 20 n. 141.

Sermonic Elements

In many ways a sermon in NT times was not like those we hear today. Sermon styles today are so various that it is probably impossible to standardize them, but one element that seems to be less important to modern preachers than to the ancients is memorability. The reason for this is simple: the availability of various media (print, audio and video tape, etc.) gives hearers more than one shot at what the preacher has to say. Certainly preachers today seek to persuade and make their preaching memorable, but easy access to sermons in book form, to say nothing of printed outlines, notes, and audio tapes, lessens the need the ancients felt for enabling their hearers to recall what was said. The following well-known quotation from Socrates may not express the opinion of everyone in the ancient world, especially in the first century, but it certainly reflects a much more widespread belief than one would find today: "If men learn [writing], it will implant forgetfulness in their souls; they will cease to exercise memory because they rely on that which is written, calling things to remembrance no longer from within themselves, but by means of external marks."[7] Socrates was concerned that if people learned writing, their ability to memorize would atrophy and something would be lost. These words have proved prophetic; people today probably do not instantly retain as much as they would if they did not know how to write. Ancient speakers employed a number of devices to help words and ideas stick in the heads of their listeners. The Epistle to the Hebrews reflects its oral character by using many of those devices.[8]

---

7. Plato *Phaedrus* 275.

8. Of course the rhetorical devices used by our author were not intended simply as an aid to memory. Persuasion was an even more important goal among speakers in the ancient world, and the conventions of rhetoric were used as much to convince the emotions and the mind as they were to create accurate memories of what had been said. As G. Kennedy has put it: "Rhetoric is that quality in discourse by which a speaker or writer seeks to accomplish his purposes. Choice and arrangement of words are one of the techniques employed, but what is known in rhetorical theory as 'invention'—the treatment of the subject matter, the use of evidence, the argumentation, and the control of emotion—is often of greater importance and is central to rhetorical theory as understood by Greeks and Romans" (George A. Kennedy, *New Testament Interpretation through Rhetorical Criticism* [Chapel Hill, N.C.: University of North Carolina Press, 1984], 3).

Rhetorical Elements Found in Hebrews

Element	Reference
Alliteration	Heb. 1:1
Anaphora	Heb. 11 (passim)
Antithesis	Heb. 7:18–21, 28; 10:11–12
Assonance	Heb. 10:26–27
Asyndeton	Heb. 11:33–34, 37
Brachylogy	Heb. 12:24
Chiasm	Heb. 7:23–24; 2:17
Diatribe	Heb. 3:16–18
Ellipsis	Heb. 12:25
Hendiadys	Heb. 5:2
Hyperbaton	Heb. 2:9
Isocolon	Heb. 1:3
Litotes	Heb. 4:15
Paranomasia	Heb. 5:8
Rhythm	
Reverse Paeon	Heb. 1:1
Anapest	Heb. 1:6
Iambus	Heb. 2:1
Trochee	Heb. 12:8

The elements of rhetoric are thoroughly discussed in a number of places in ancient literature.[9] Above is a list of rhetorical devices employed by our author, with references to examples in the Book of Hebrews. We will later look in some detail at many of those that deal with smaller units of language (words, phrases,

---

9. Cf., e.g., Aristotle (*Topica* and the *Ars Rhetorica*) and pseudo-Cicero (*Rhetorica ad Herennium*) and the bibliographical discussion in Kennedy, *Interpretation*, 161–62.

etc.) as examples of the style of our author (chap. 8). Several of these categories may be unfamiliar to the reader, but all are defined where they are discussed in detail, either here or in chapter 8. The full list is given above in order to provide some feel for the breadth of control the author/preacher had over what he was saying and the care he took to say it well and memorably. Here we will discuss two elements that deal with larger literary units (listed in boldface in the preceding table). The first, diatribe, actually comes close to being a literary genre in and of itself, while the other, rhythm, can affect much of a particular passage or section of a book.

Diatribe

The diatribe is an element of ancient rhetoric much talked about by ancient rhetoricians but curiously not analyzed and categorized in quite the same way that many other elements were.[10] Twentieth-century classical scholarship has often discussed the definition of the diatribe and its relationship to the writings of the NT, with the doctoral thesis of Rudolf Bultmann on Romans setting the pace on the subject.[11] More recently, though, the work of Stanley Stowers on the use of the diatribe in Romans has shown that both classical scholars and Bultmann have misunderstood the diatribe. Stowers maintains that it is not primarily "a form of mass propaganda which used various sorts of dialogical and rhetorical techniques in order to create interest and persuade the common man on the street." Rather, "the form of the diatribe and the way it functions presupposes a student-teacher relationship."[12] The form is suited to the philosophical school and is essentially oral and dialogical in nature, and Paul, according to Stowers, uses it frequently in Romans.

---

10. Cf. Kennedy, *Interpretation*, 155: "The diatribe is not a literary genre, in the sense of genre understood by classical grammarians and rhetoricians, but it does have some claims to be regarded as a form with distinctive traditions."

11. Published as Rudolf Bultmann, *Der Stil der paulinischen Predigt und die kynischstoische Diatribe* (Göttingen: Vandenhoeck & Ruprecht, 1910).

12. Stanley Kent Stowers, *The Diatribe and Paul's Letter to the Romans*, SBL Dissertation Series 57 (Chico, Calif.: Scholars Press, 1981), 175.

Basically, the diatribe is a technique for answering objections to an argument. The speaker makes a statement and then puts into the mouth of an imaginary interlocutor a question that seems relevant to that statement. He may pile several questions on top of each other, but he finally gives an answer to the question. The technique is effective in part because of its harshness; generally the one using the diatribe intends to mock or shame the student into a consideration of the truth. Because of its rough tone, scholars thought for a long time that it was a technique used against enemies or in large crowds where it could be assumed that opponents to the teacher lurked. But Stowers shows that this is not the case at all; the diatribe was used in one of the most intimate of teaching situations in the classical world—that of master and disciple.

As this works out in Romans, Stowers rightly hypothesizes that the many diatribes in the book reflect teaching Paul had given to those mentioned by name in Romans 16; in short, that they were his pupils. But what does this have to do with Hebrews? And where is the evidence that the author of Hebrews employed this technique?

To answer the first of these questions, we need go no further than the information we explored above in chapter 1. There we discovered that regardless of whether one thinks the community was more Jewish or more Hellenistic in nature, the author was quite well acquainted with these people. Hence he could feel comfortable chastising his "students" and using a technique that might be rough on occasion, without fear of damaging his relationship with them. We also noted that he characterizes his message to them as a "word of exhortation" (λόγος τῆς παρακλή-σεως), a term that reflects an oral presentation. The phrase does not inherently refer to a tough method of speaking, but it is striking that in the one other place it is used in the NT (Acts 13:15), Paul criticizes the Jews in Jerusalem who crucified Jesus (Acts 13:26–29), ending his speech with a strongly worded warning for the people he is addressing not to fulfill the words of the prophets as the Jews in Jerusalem did (Acts 13:40–41). Similarly, Hebrews is filled with warnings for its listeners/readers and in tone is generally more like a kick in the pants than a gentle arm around the shoulder.

In answer to the question of where the author employs this technique, we can note several passages in the book. Although the diatribe is not a predominant method of argumentation in Hebrews, it is used in 3:16–18 with a distinctive triple rhetorical question format.[13] In Heb. 3:15 the author quotes Ps. 95:7, referring back to the lengthier quotation of Ps. 95:7–11 in Heb. 3:7–11. He now picks up key phrases in that passage to ask a series of three rhetorical questions, which he answers with three more questions, all of which are probably based on Numbers 14.[14] Our purpose here is not to do a full-scale exegesis of what points the author of Hebrews was trying to make, but rather to indicate the method he used. He blasts away at them, probably in order to drive home the exceeding seriousness of rebellion and unbelief and the fact that no one is safe—even those who have led the community of belief in the past like at least some of his listeners/ readers.

This passage is not the only example of diatribe in the book. The author's repeated use of the rhetorical question in order to make a point, prove an assertion, or answer another question he has raised probably indicates that the diatribe is never far from his mind. As early as the first chapter, he uses the rhetorical question to open his defense of the deity of Jesus (1:5 [twice!]) and to close it again (1:13–14), thereby heightening the impact of the intervening material (1:6–12). While this would work well enough in a written document, the effect in an oral presentation would have been dramatic, and the pedagogical effect is undeniable.

Other rhetorical questions sprinkled throughout the work appear in similar teaching contexts and point toward the diatribal style. In 2:2–4, the author asks his question immediately after the conditional clause, diatribal style, and then extends the sentence by heaping up other reasons why we will not escape if we ignore God's great salvation. In 7:11 there is an imaginary interlocutor, a common device of diatribe. Many in our author's audience would

---

13. Cf. James Moffatt, *A Critical and Exegetical Commentary on the Epistle to the Hebrews*, International Critical Commentary (Edinburgh: T. & T. Clark, 1924), 48: "The pointed questions which now follow (vv. 16–18) are a favorite device of the diatribe style."

14. Cf. Attridge (*Hebrews*, 120) and, more confidently, Lane (*Hebrews*, 1:88).

RLowen

have questioned the claim that moral perfection could not be attained through the levitical priesthood, so he anticipates their question and answers it.[15] The importance of the diatribe for the author is indicated by his use of it here at a major transitional point in his argument, where he leaves the consideration of the Genesis material on Melchizedek (7:1–10) and begins to argue for the superiority of the "priest like Melchizedek." He has already prepared his audience for this theme twice before (5:10; 6:20). The question found at 10:2 is a straightforward rhetorical question containing no obvious diatribal element, but the author seems to return to the style near the end of the chapter at 10:29, where he issues some of his most severe warnings to the congregation. The *a fortiori* argument contained in the question, along with its harsh verbs (καταπατέω, ἡγέομαι κοινόν, ἐνυβρίζω), marks it as diatribe. Other rhetorical questions in the book may also indicate the style (cf., e.g., 12:7, 9).

The importance for the modern interpreter of recognizing our author's use of the diatribe does not rest with the form itself; the diatribe is a relatively insignificant part of the puzzle of the literary genre of Hebrews. Its significance is found, rather, in two facts to which the use of diatribe points. First, the diatribe is a part of the larger genre area of *ancient rhetoric*. Blindness to the fact that our author employs rhetorical technique at point after point in his epistle may cause us to miss the *persuasive* element in our author's approach to truth. Biblical exegetes and preachers should make no apology for the ancient author's penchant for polemical technique. The early Christians believed that what they were handling was the very λόγος τοῦ θεοῦ; it was crucial to them to use any means short of deceit to persuade their audience to believe (cf., e.g., John 20:31). Perhaps persuasive technique was even more important for the author of Hebrews since no less than salvation was at stake (Heb. 2:2–4; 5:12–14; 6:4–12; 10:26–39). We will have much more to say later about the general rhetorical techniques our author uses (see chap. 8 on the style of Hebrews).

The second significant factor about our author's use of diatribe is that diatribe is a sermonic or, more accurately, a teaching device. We spent a lot of time above emphasizing that Hebrews is an *oral*

---

15. Cf. Lane's excellent discussion (*Hebrews*, 1:180–81) of the eschatological, rather than ethical or cultic, nuance of τελείωσις in 7:11.

work, but it is worth restating now: Hebrews is as much a sermon as it is an epistle and must be understood as such. A second rhetorical device that demonstrates the importance of this element is the use of rhythm in Hebrews.

Rhythm

Rhythm is not the most involved and complicated subject in classical Greek oratory, but it is nevertheless too extensive a subject to cover completely here. We will define it and then look at a few of the many examples in Hebrews in order to demonstrate its importance for the interpreter. Commentators have long recognized that Hebrews "is distinguished, among the prose works of the primitive church, by its rhythmical cadences."[16]

Rhythm, when the word has to do with words and not music or general patterns, is "the pattern of recurrent strong and weak accents, long and short syllables, and vocalization and silence in speech."[17] The use of the technique is of course much more structured, formal, and repetitive in poetry than in a prose work like Hebrews. Indeed, according to one commentator, "The primary rule for using rhythms in prose is . . . negative. Monotony should be avoided and variety cultivated, and Hebrews clearly abides by that prescription."[18] Our author seems to be acquainted with the oratorical rhythmical structures made popular by Isocrates in the fourth century B.C., though he handles them freely.[19]

Clear-cut instances of attention to rhythm abound in Hebrews. For example, the famous first four verses of the book, so full of literary devices, demonstrate a penchant for rhythmical balance in several places, so much so that the Nestle-Aland[27] text lays out verses 3 and 4 in a semipoetic fashion. This format is justified not only by the clear rhyming effect of phrases like τῆς ὑποστάσεως αὐτοῦ / τῆς δυνάμεως αὐτοῦ and ὃς ὢν ἀπαύγασμα / φέρων τε τὰ πάντα but also because of their rhythms:[20]

---

16. Moffatt, *Hebrews*, lvi.
17. *Random House Webster's College Dictionary* (New York: Random House, 1992), s.v. "rhythm."
18. Attridge, *Hebrews*, 20.
19. Moffatt, *Hebrews*, lvi.
20. The symbols ‾ and ˘ stand respectively for stressed and unstressed syllables.

Phrase	Rhythm Pattern	Comment
τῆς ὑποστάσεως αὐτοῦ τῆς δυνάμεως αὐτοῦ	‾ ˘ ˘ ‾ ˘ ˘ ˘ ‾ ‾ ˘ ‾ ˘ ˘ ˘	One unstressed beat is the only difference between the two.
ὃς ὢν ἀπαύγασμα φέρων τε τὰ πάντα	˘ ˘ ˘ ‾ ˘ ˘ ‾ ˘ ˘ ˘ ˘ ˘	The inconsistencies are due to minor, barely pronounced syllables like the -μα at the end of ἀπαύγασμα.

The opening words of the book are an indication not only of the author's interest in rhythm but also of his inventiveness with the convention. Πολυμερῶς, with its rhythmic pattern of ˘ ˘ ˘ ‾, is a paeon—a pattern of any combination of four syllables, three unstressed and one stressed. Aristotle suggests the use of a paeon for the opening of a rhythmic passage. But Aristotle suggested a paeon with the opposite pattern of ‾ ˘ ˘ ˘ for opening a phrase, the one our author uses for *closing* a phrase![21] To emphasize the point that the author of Hebrews was interested in doing something out of the ordinary, he repeats the pattern in the second word of the opening pair and throws in some alliteration for good measure.[22] To demonstrate the principle of variation mentioned above, Moffatt points out that our author might begin a period with any number of combinations of anapests, trochees, and iambuses.[23]

Another favorite use of rhythm surfaces in the author's penchant for beginning a new sentence, or even a new paragraph, with the same rhythmical structure with which he ended the last,

---

21. Aristotle *Rhetoric* 3.8.6. This has been inaccurately called a "reverse" paeon. In fact a paeon is a pattern of any combination of three unstressed syllables and one stressed one.

22. Πολυτρόπως by itself does not follow the ˘ ˘ ˘ ‾ pattern, but coupled with the preceding καί the word has exactly the same rhythm with a meaningless unstressed syllable added on the end: ˘ ˘ ˘ ‾ ˘. See Heb. 3:1, 7:10, 12:25, and 13:20 for other examples of this form of paeon opening a sentence.

23. Moffatt, *Hebrews*, lvi. Anapest, trochee, and iambus are poetic terms used to designate three different types of metric feet: anapest (three syllables = ˘ ˘ ‾), trochee (two syllables = ‾ ˘), iambus (two syllables = ˘ ‾). The reader unfamiliar with the technical terminology of poetic rhythm or meter should consult W. Thrall, A. Hibbard, C. H. Holman, eds., *A Handbook to Literature*, rev. ed. (New York: Odyssey Press, 1960), or other similar handbook of English literature.

contributing to the sense of smoothness for which he is noted.[24] A good example of this occurs at the end of Heb. 4:11 and the beginning of Heb. 4:12. There the rhythms of the last clause of 4:11, emphasizing in the negative the example of the Israelites who fell through their unbelief, are parallel to those of the first few words of 4:12, emphasizing the life and power of the word of God.[25] Other similar parallels, though with some departure from precise parallel, are found at 7:21 and 22, 8:13 and 9:1, and 10:10 and 11.

This parallelism of rhythm has practical significance for interpretation of the epistle. One might think that rhetorical form might take precedence over careful theological statement, but the opposite is the case. In order to make connections between thoughts that may not be apparent on the surface, he not only uses rational argument but also literary device. The verses mentioned above are an example. In Heb. 4:11–12, the author uses a negative encouragement (don't fall as the people of Israel did) and a positive encouragement (the word of God is living and active) to set the stage for the mention of Jesus, the high priest who can help us. The connection between the two is not readily apparent from their content, but the author makes that connection more obvious by his use of parallel rhythms.

From all this, it becomes apparent that close study of the use of rhythm in classical Greek would be invaluable for the twentieth-century interpreter of Hebrews. Unfortunately, we cannot even begin to do the subject justice here. But we can urge the reader to consider some of the implications of the fact that the author of Hebrews has taken such pains in the use of rhetorical techniques like diatribe and rhythm. The interpreter needs to gain a feel for what the author was trying to accomplish by this technique, to gain a feel for the *texture* of the text. It is a *literate* text, a polished work that demands from its interpreters care and attention to complex rhetorical and literary forms in order to be understood fully. It is a *polemical* text using techniques designed to persuade the heart, rather than dry, scientific language designed merely to inform or describe. The "poetry" and style of Hebrews, flowing from its oral character, must be stressed in any attempt to describe principles

---

24. Nigel Turner, *Style,* vol. 4 of *A Grammar of New Testament Greek,* by J. H. Moulton (Edinburgh: T. & T. Clark, 1976), 106: "He avoids all roughness."

25. Moffatt, *Hebrews,* lvi.

for understanding this book. That Hebrews comes to us in written form should force us to take its oral character all that much more into account. With this in mind, it is now time to try to understand the significance of its written character for interpretation.

Epistolary Elements

It is commonplace for any description of a biblical epistle to declare how different NT epistles are from modern letters. While modern letters, especially before the invention and widespread use of the telephone, convey all sorts of trivial, often personal information, the biblical epistle generally speaks to larger issues of theology and ethics. While conveying some necessary information about such things as the travels of Paul and Timothy (cf., e.g., Phil. 2:19–30), the primary purpose of a biblical epistle was to convey theological and ethical teaching.

Hebrews is no exception. "For all its oratory, Hebrews is no more than an epistle written in the exhortatory style, mingling theology and paraenesis in alternating sections, as distinct from Paul's method of keeping the theology and paraenesis apart. Nevertheless, Hebrews begins as a sermon and ends as an epistle."[26] As overstated as this opinion is, Nigel Turner nevertheless does capsule two characteristics that have allowed Christian writers through the ages to characterize Hebrews as an epistle: (1) the alternation of doctrine and exhortation and (2) the epistolary form of its ending. The first of these, however, does not fundamentally distinguish an epistle from a sermon; Hellenistic sermons and epistles alike interwove things to be believed (doctrine) with things to be done in light of those beliefs (ethics), as have all types of Christian teaching down through the ages for that matter. At times, though, Hebrews betrays some traces of editing that are the result of shaping an epistle from a sermon.

Hebrews as Epistolary Teaching

Despite all the rhetorical flourish with which Hebrews begins, it quickly settles into confronting the traditional task of an early Christian epistle, that of giving advice to a community that faces a problem of some sort. Paul, Clement, and others in the early

---

26. Turner, *Style*, 113.

church attempted to deal with such situations by writing letters with the right combination of doctrinal and ethical teaching to help solve the "problem." Of course the writer did this with one distinct disadvantage compared to the preacher: his absence from the situation. Whereas the preacher could speak directly to a situation and could clarify immediately and directly what he said, if misinterpreted, the writer had to try to anticipate any questions and misunderstandings and give responses to them. Rebuttal could only come to him by word of mouth some time, often a *long* time, later.

This need to anticipate audience response provides hints about the development of the book from its oral to its epistolary form. A small example of a written element seemingly added to the oral text in the book's movement from sermon to epistle is found in Heb. 2:14. There, apparently in order to explain more clearly whom Christ defeated, the author of Hebrews has added an appositive to what appears to have been the text of the original sermon. Where rhetorical elements are found in phrases like κα-ταργήσῃ . . . κράτος ἔχοντα and the repetition of θανάτου, the phrase τοῦτ᾽ ἔστιν τὸν διάβολον intrudes in a way that is didactic and explanatory at best, heavy and needless at worst. In any case, it indicates the sort of appositive that could be the result of a more reflective written form of the epistle, especially since it interrupts the flow of the oracular presentation of the material.

This example may extend further and encompass the whole last clause of the sentence (Heb. 2:15). There is a balance of negative and positive content between the clauses that speak of Christ "destroy[ing] the one who has the power of death" (negative) and "free[ing] those who all their lives were held in slavery by the fear of death" (positive; 2:14–15 NRSV), but scansion of the lines for parallel rhythms yields no discernible rhetorical elements. Surely the final clause of the sentence is part of the original sermon. It makes sense and rounds out the thought of the sentence, picking up on the identification of the children with Christ and their salvation by his action, a thought that is of course extended in the next few verses. The only question here is whether the rhetorical elements of a sermon, so discernible in other places, are present here or whether this particular language is more likely a part of the later written work.

This and other examples of the reworking of Hebrews into an epistle make the point: the interpreter must be aware that explanations and elucidations have been put into the text of the original sermon in order to anticipate difficulties and answer possible questions. Evidence that Hebrews was ultimately intended in its final form to be an epistle is found in more than these subtle changes in content, however. It is seen in its formal epistolary closing.

The Epistolary Closing of Hebrews

Paul's writings follow a fairly well-defined order of formal elements.[27] His salutation—an identification of himself, his colleague(s), and those to whom he is writing, along with some form of greeting, such as his unique χάρις ὑμῖν καὶ εἰρήνη (1 Thess. 1:1)—is lacking in Hebrews, as are his normal extended thanksgiving and reminiscence of ministry among his readers, his identification of a purpose for writing, and any specific reference to past visits by himself or colleagues. Instead, in Heb. 1:1–4 the reader finds a highly rhetorical opening, crying out to be read aloud because of its alliteration and assonance, its "developed sense of rhythm, the variation of meter, and the cultivation of those elements of a literary style that command the attention of the ear when read aloud. . . . The writer has cultivated the instincts of an orator, which are now brought into the service of preaching."[28]

Similarly, the body of the Epistle to the Hebrews does not parallel the typical epistle except, as we noted above, in its intermingling of teaching and exhortation. But since the so-called "body" of the Pauline epistle resists definite categorization anyway, it is hard to state dogmatically that Hebrews departs from a well-known or commonly followed formula.[29] Nevertheless, David Aune has surveyed five types of material found in central sections

---

27. For ancient letters in general see David E. Aune, *The New Testament in Its Literary Environment,* Library of Early Christianity 8 (Philadelphia: Westminster, 1987), 158–225, and for a fine summary of structural elements in Paul's epistles see Thomas R. Schreiner, *Interpreting the Pauline Epistles,* Guides to New Testament Exegesis (Grand Rapids: Baker, 1990), 25–31.

28. Lane, *Hebrews,* 1:5–6.

29. Aune, *Environment,* 188: "The central section (or body) of the letter is the section containing the information constituting the purpose for which the letter was written. It is also the section that has proven most resistant to formal analysis."

of early Christian letters,[30] and Hebrews includes none of them except what Aune calls "concluding paraenesis," material that more properly belongs to the formal category of the closing of an epistle. At Heb. 13:22–25, Hebrews does have a somewhat typical closing, highly reminiscent of Paul's. Almost no one disputes the epistolary nature of this unit of material nor that it had little to do with the eloquent sermon that was preached or to be read aloud to the congregation that received the letter. Many things in these brief verses point to their written character: (1) the author's reference to writing them briefly (13:22); (2) the pedantic information that Timothy has been set free and may be accompanying the author on his visit; (3) the ineloquent greetings to ἡγουμένους ὑμῶν καὶ πάντας τοὺς ἁγίους, with the similarly plain passing on of greetings from those with the author who are from Italy; (4) the standard closing reference to grace. All of these are standard elements of the NT epistle and are unknown to the first century exhortation.

The literary question whether Heb. 13:1–21 forms the exhortatory conclusion to the sermon or an epistolary addendum to the sermon remains unsolved, however.[31] The arguments for and against these two hypotheses are too extensive to treat sufficiently here. Suffice it to say that the weight of the evidence points to the chapter being an addition to the sermon, filling out some of its themes in typical epistolary fashion and adding a number of random reminders and warnings as something of an afterthought.[32] The last chapter is filled with ethical injunctions, a practice in which Paul sometimes engaged (cf., e.g., 2 Cor. 13:5–10), although he did not always do so and never so fully as the author of Hebrews.

---

30. They are: (1) internal transitional formulas, e.g., "I want you to know, brethren" (Phil. 1:12); (2) epistolary *topoi* (themes and motifs used in ancient letters), e.g., health or domestic events; (3) autobiographical statements, e.g., the lengthy Gal. 1:10–2:21; (4) travel plans, e.g., Rom. 15:14–33; and (5) concluding paraenesis, e.g., 1 Thess. 4:1–5:22. Aune, *Environment*, 188–91.

31. See Attridge, *Hebrews*, 384 n. 5, for the classic articles defending the notion that Heb. 13 is a later appendage.

32. Attridge, *Hebrews*, 384–85, and especially Lane, *Hebrews*, 2:491–507, argue eloquently for the "integrity" of chapter 13, meaning that chapter 13 formed part of the original composition of Hebrews. This is surely correct, if by "composition" one means the *epistle* as it was sent to its readers for the first time. But that has nothing to do with the question of whether it was part of the original *sermon*—a view that I find difficult to accept in light of the difference in content, style, and care of composition.

While the lack of connection between the content of the last chapter and the rest of the epistle has been overemphasized, there remain some standard ethical injunctions that would be puzzling in a sermon, though they fit the "tidying up" exercise at the end of an epistle quite well. For instance, while there is much in the epistle about leaders (13:7, 17) and suffering with Jesus our sacrificial Lamb (13:11–13), there is no prior mention of the marriage bed (13:4), hospitality to strangers (13:2), or even regulations about food (13:9),[33] all topics treated with equal stature in this chapter. The style of the last chapter is also much less poetic and eloquent than any section of the rest of the book, especially the hortatory sections. As Aune puts it: "Here the author relaxes the literary character of his Greek."[34] Lastly, while there are some flashes of the compositional brilliance of the earlier chapters, the chapter is largely a string of exhortations, with relatively little relation to each other or to what precedes. This looseness of character shows itself particularly clearly in the lack of connection between Heb. 13:1 and Hebrews 12.[35]

What does all this mean? So what if Hebrews is a complex literary form, basically a sermon but clearly reconstructed as an epistle? The question is not merely academic. For the twentieth-century reader it means that we cannot read Hebrews like we do *anything* from our era; it was even a unique document in the first century, much more so in ours. To summarize much of what we have written above, the rhetorical nature of Hebrews requires that we be particularly aware of the underlying Greek poetic devices used by the author and not attempt to press, for instance, the choosing of a particular word by the author on the basis of its content when evidence would indicate that the word was simply cho-

---

33. The reference in Heb. 9:10 to food and drink is inconsequential since it does not occur in an exhortation about abandoning or refraining from food regulations, nor does it give any hint that this was a concern among the congregation.

34. Aune, *Environment*, 213.

35. Even Lane, who staunchly defends the unity of chapter 13 with what precedes, can only say that the injunction of 13:1 (and its following "pairs" of injunctions) "evokes the exemplary stance that the community had assumed under harsh circumstances in the past (10:32–34)," saying only that it is "entirely appropriate that the sober recognition of the holiness of God in 12:28–29 should be followed by the admonition, 'Brotherly love must continue' " (*Hebrews*, 2:509). One must ask what ethical injunction would *not* be appropriate in those circumstances?

sen because it rhymed with another one. Second, we should be on the lookout for passages that were reworked by the author to anticipate questions or make fuller explanations and, conversely, for passages that do not seem to answer obvious questions—neither blaming such passages for not doing so nor, especially, trying to force such passages into answering questions they simply do not address. In sum, understanding the literary character of Hebrews should make us even more reticent than usual to build whole theologies on highly rhetorical and emotive passages like Heb. 6:4–6, since the wording of these passages is often dictated by literary rather than strictly theological concerns.

4

Structure

There is more to understanding a document than can be gained from simply understanding its literary genre. Lots of clues to understanding an author's thought can be discerned by asking a set of commonsense questions that reveal structures, emphases, transitions, and minor patterns in any piece of literature—whether it be Jane Reader's business letters or the sports stories in her morning newspaper. This process results in an outline of the structure of a document.[1]

Outlining is a common feature of exegesis at every level of training, from the simplest children's Bible study to the most complex doctoral analysis. The question of the proper outline of Hebrews has been the subject of a lot of study in recent years, and the difficulties raised by almost every attempt at delineating a structure for the book has caused one recent commentator to remark bluntly: "There is at the present time no consensus

---

1. There is some justification for thinking that a discussion of outlining should come after the discussion in chapter 5 on the textual criticism of Hebrews. After all, how can one outline a text before it has been established? Alternatively, one could argue that outlining should come before a discussion of literary genre. These questions deserve a longer, more complex answer, but the simple one is this: outlining is somewhat dialogical in nature. It cannot proceed without some understanding of the cultural, historical, and literary background of the text (see the preceding chapters), but at the same time it must form the overall basis for a detailed examination of the text (see the ensuing chapters). Perhaps in light of discoveries made during that examination, we will revise our outline, but we must start the exegesis of particular texts with at least a general picture of where the author is going.

regarding the literary structure of Hebrews."[2] The most recent approach has freely, and probably rightly, acknowledged that a proper outline should take into account the literary genre, rhetorical elements, and content of the book, with a weighting in favor of content.[3]

Much of the scholarly discussion moves in a technical sphere with subjects like discourse analysis, structuralism, and semantic theory making it difficult for all but the very few to understand. Such discussions are beyond the purview of this book, but there are a number of insights to be gained from working at outlining the book at any level.[4] We will discover some of them as we lay down principles for doing an outline ourselves. A few questions are in order before we begin.

Some Introductory Questions

First is the question of the usefulness of outlining itself. After all, why do we need to understand the overall structure of a book? Why not simply start studying the text sentence by sentence? If scholars have spent all this time studying the text in depth and cannot figure out for sure what the author was trying to do, why should we think we can? This is the same question we faced earlier when discussing authorship of the epistle. The answer is also similar to the one we gave there: we discover elements of the author's mind by going through the *process* of outlining, even if we can come to no final conclusion concerning the outline itself. There is no doubting the usefulness of knowing the overall argument of the book when interpreting some part of the text, and outlining helps us see the overall argument more clearly.

Second, some features of the structure of the book are obvious, and ignoring them would distort our perspective on the book. The warnings occurring at four places throughout the book (Heb. 2:1–4; 3:7–4:13; 5:11–6:12; 10:19–39), the several different comparisons

---

2. William L. Lane, *Hebrews*, Word Biblical Commentary (Dallas: Word, 1991), 1:lxxxviii.

3. Steve Stanley, "The Structure of Hebrews from Three Perspectives [Genre, Rhetoric, Content]," *Tyndale Bulletin* 45 (1994): 245, 270–71.

4. For interesting discussions of the relevant books and articles by Vanhoye, Dussaut, Guthrie, and others, see Stanley, "Structure," 245–71; Lane, *Hebrews*, 1:lxxx–xcviii; Paul Ellingworth, *The Epistle to the Hebrews: A Commentary on the Greek Text*, New International Greek Testament Commentary (Grand Rapids: Eerdmans, 1993), 50–58.

to Christ and how they are linked together in the mind of the author, the famous chapter on faith (Hebrews 11) and its place in the book—all these deserve some cohesive response from the reader. Otherwise, we are in grave danger of misunderstanding the message our author is giving to his readers.

On what should we focus in outlining the book: form or content? The answer to this question is relatively simple—neither. Why? Because form and content cannot be divided all that simply. Is it form or content when our author brings the text back around to a discussion of Melchizedek, as he does so very neatly at the end of Hebrews 6? Certainly this is a rhetorical device, intended to be felt by the audience hearing or reading it (form), but the teaching of Heb. 5:11–6:20 has also prepared us powerfully for the following discussion too; we are ready to hear who Melchizedek is and now know how important it is to the author that we pay attention (content).

Is it form or content when the readers of the letter are enjoined to "look unto Jesus, the pioneer and perfecter of our faith" at the beginning of chapter 12? The use of the word "pioneer" (ἀρχηγός) certainly brings the reader back to the earlier use of the word at Heb. 2:10, because it is such a rare word and stands out in both places (form), but the powerful phrases also emphasize the Jesus who in the central arguments of the book has been proved superior to all others (content). The question is ultimately unanswerable; form and content are so interwoven in this epistle that to differentiate greatly between them is futile.[5]

Similar to the dichotomy between form and content is the dichotomy between doctrine and ethics in Hebrews. This helpful distinction often forms the main dividing line in outlining a Pauline epistle; Ephesians is perhaps the best example with its clear division between chapters 1–3 and 4–6. Hebrews, too, has sometimes been outlined this way,[6] but such a division is far too

---

5. Ellingworth, primarily a linguist, insists "that the form and the meaning of a text operate on different, in principle independent, levels, and that little is to be gained by forcing a common meaning on an essentially formal feature." In the next sentence, though, he goes on to add: "It must, however, be admitted that the author himself probably did not make such a sharp distinction between form and meaning as a modern linguist would make . . ." (*Hebrews*, 57–58).

6. Cf. Donald Guthrie, *New Testament Introduction*, 4th ed. (Downers Grove, Ill.: InterVarsity, 1990), 717–21.

simple for this book. While warning passages and simple commands can be separated from doctrinal passages and straightforward doctrinal statements, these two elements are so interwoven throughout the text that a simple "doctrine, then ethics" or "doctrine is the foundation, ethics is the outworking" formula does not do justice to the text as it stands.

At the same time, there is a major difference between the form/content problem and the ethics/doctrine one. It is helpful and necessary to emphasize in the outline the fact that the author regularly "interrupts" a doctrinal section to provide paranaesis and then returns to the place he left off. But simply to claim that "doctrine and ethics are hopelessly mixed in Hebrews" is unwise. Most passages in the text are quite clearly ethical or doctrinal, and the author seems to have a clear purpose for keeping them distinct, but in developing the larger structure of the work, he skillfully interweaves them. I hope that what is sometimes a difficult line to draw can nevertheless be marked sufficiently in the outline prepared at the end of this section.

The Process of Outlining

Outlining is best done from the core of a work outward. One must first determine what the central teaching of a book is and then move to outline its elements in relation to that center and in relation to each other. How does one determine the main theme? There is no magic key to doing this. Probably many readers of this book learned the techniques of outlining in the first few years of their Christian life, and I know of no reason to depart from the simple techniques learned at that stage. Sometimes as we develop sophistication (yes, even in scriptural study!), we depart from the simple rather than building upon it, although that basis is fundamental to moving on to higher levels of understanding. Many books on Bible study go into great detail on outlining, so I will give just a few basic steps.

First, read through the book once, looking for three things. (1) Look for any statements that the author makes to his readers concerning the central purpose of the book. These may be very direct ("I am writing you because . . .") or less direct as here ("bear with my word of exhortation," Heb. 13:22). (2) Look for themes that recur so often that they cannot be missed. These should be obvious; if they seem too subtle to you, they probably are not the author's main point! The third thing to look for, however, is more subtle than the first two. (3) A main theme may not meet the two criteria above, and yet the author may point to it in a special way by giving it a place of prominence in the book stylistically. It may occur, for example, in the center of the work with the preceding argument leading up to it and the following argument explicating it. Nevertheless, the major theme should be clear enough to be recognized in a serious reading of the book.

From this material, decide what you think the main theme of the book is, and write it down in one sentence in your own words. The sentence should be relatively short and simple. While your sentence may show deference to important sub-themes, unless you simply cannot decide between two or three themes, *make clear the one idea the author is trying to get across to his readers.* You may have trouble doing this (particularly with Hebrews!), but work at it until you believe you know what the main theme of the book is.

Next, read the work and note any transitional elements that might be clues to the author's movement from one section to the next. Remember of course that the chapter and verse divisions in our Bibles are not always reliable guides to changes of this sort. Transitional words such as "therefore," "for," "however," and the like are good indicators of movement from one section to the next. As we will see below, Hebrews employs many devices not found in other books by which the author signals his intentions. One of the most important of these devices is called the *hook word*, a clearly substantial term or phrase that is used to link sections of text. A good example is the use of the word ἄγγελος in both Heb. 1:4 and 1:5. George H. Guthrie has discerned five different sorts of hook words operating in Hebrews.[7] Sometimes the author of Hebrews uses brief passages to link larger units together, having them serve either as the conclusion to one section and the introduction of the next or as

---

7. Lane, *Hebrews*, 1:xci–xciii. See also George H. Guthrie, *The Structure of Hebrews: A Text-Linguistic Analysis*, Novum Testamentum Supplement 73 (Leiden: Brill, 1994), 96–102.

a hinge between two passages, although belonging to neither.[8] The key to recognizing these special features is looking for similar concepts and/or vocabulary that seem to link two passages together.

Begin making an outline on your final reading. Of course any outline attempts to show connections among the various sections of a work, but an outline should also attempt to show the relation of the various sections to the main theme. To accomplish this, try to make the headings of each of your largest sections reflect the main theme in their wording. Lesser section headings may do this too, but it is more important that they reflect their relationship to the section in which they occur and derive their titles from it.

Outlining Hebrews

This simple model for outlining a book can be applied to Hebrews, but the reader should be warned that this task is not as simple as it is for some of the other books in the New Testament. We noted above that Hebrews presents special difficulties because of the complexity of its literary form. As one author noted about the Book of Revelation: "there are as many different outlines as there are interpreters."[9] What follows is my attempt at such an outline, along with explanation and justification at critical points.

The Main Theme of Hebrews

What in one sentence is the main theme of Hebrews? *Have faith in (by holding fast to and obeying) Jesus as the supreme, unique Son of God and priest of our faith.* Two words capsule the core of the purpose of Hebrews: Jesus and faith. From the opening sentence to the last

---

8. Guthrie calls these two uses "overlapping constituents" and "direct intermediary transitions" respectively (see Lane, *Hebrews*, 1:xciii–xcv, and Guthrie, "Structure," 102–11). Guthrie employs two other useful categories: "parallel introductions" and "woven intermediary transitions." The one example of a "parallel introduction" found in Lane is the similar wording in Heb. 5:1 and 8:3 that helps link Heb. 5:1–7:28 to Heb. 8:3–10:18. This link between the two passages enables the author to pick up his train of thought once again after leaving it briefly to deal with other matters. A "woven intermediary transition" is a cross between the "overlapping constituent" and the "direct intermediary transition"; themes from a preceding and a following section are woven together in the intermediary text to form a bridge between them. Lane offers Heb. 2:5–9 as an example.

9. J. Ramsey Michaels, *Interpreting the Book of Revelation*, Guides to New Testament Exegesis (Grand Rapids: Baker, 1992), 69.

command of the epistle, the author never seems to depart from a complex of truths revolving around these two ideas, and that complex can be further distilled into two subsets under each idea. The importance of holding fast or persevering in the faith (stated negatively, this means *not* apostatizing) is regularly stressed in the epistle, not only in the warning passages which are central to the purposes of the author but also, for example, in the commands to draw near to God (express and implied) found throughout the epistle (cf. Heb. 4:16; 7:19). The importance of obedience is shown in a variety of ways, from Christ's being the mediator of a new covenant (Heb. 9:15) to the straightforward commands for obedience found in the last chapter of the book (Heb. 13:1, 2, 3, 5, etc.). Faith is explicitly defined in the epistle (Heb. 11:1) and given an entire chapter full of illustrations. Either the command to believe or something equivalent is found from the earliest moments of the epistle (cf., e.g., Heb. 2:1; 3:1) until the end (cf. Heb. 13:15).

Just as our author's view of faith can be subdivided usefully into perseverance and obedience, so his view of Jesus divides between Jesus as Son of God and as priest. In chapter 9 we will demonstrate how pervasive these two themes are in the epistle, but suffice it to say now that throughout the book the author rarely departs from the theme of the sonship of Jesus. From the first few words where he proclaims the Son as God's final revelation of himself to man (Heb. 1:2) to the next to last chapter where he sets forth the Son as the supreme example for those who are sons of the grace of God's discipline (Heb. 12:2–3), the theme constantly vies for attention. And it alternates with the picture of Jesus as "merciful and faithful high priest" (Heb. 2:17). The sonship of Jesus is mentioned often early and mostly only implied late in the epistle; the opposite is true for his priesthood. As *high priest* he has "made purification for sins" (Heb. 1:3), but as *a priest after the order of Melchizedek* Jesus functions as the one through whom we "continually offer a sacrifice of praise to God" (Heb. 13:15 NRSV).

Two distinguishing characteristics of Jesus as Son and priest that are prominent in the epistle and should be included in the theme sentence are the uniqueness and the supremacy of his sonship and priesthood. Each of the contrasts of the epistle stresses that Jesus is unique vis-à-vis other possibilities for faith. Jesus is not just a better angel, "for to which of the angels did God ever say . . ." (Heb. 1:5).

He has more honor than Moses, just as the unique builder of the house is superior to the house itself (Heb. 3:3). He is the only high priest who is without sin (Heb. 4:15), and as the only source of eternal salvation was designated by a unique title: priest forever after the order of Melchizedek (Heb. 5:10; 6:20). He is the unique Son through whom God has spoken (Heb. 1:2) and the unique Jesus Messiah—the same yesterday, today, and forever—to whom glory is attributed forever and ever (Heb. 13:8, 21).

And yet in Hebrews his uniqueness is never completely divorced from anything known before or since. His uniqueness derives from his being the reality of things we know as imperfect and fleeting shadows in this life. Thus he is supreme over the angels as the one who, like them, has spoken the message of God (compare the use of λαλεῖν in Heb. 2:2 and 1:2), but he has spoken it finally. Like Moses, he rules and leads his people faithfully (Heb. 3:2, 5–6), but he leads them into the final promised sabbath rest. He is a high priest who, like other priests, had to have something to offer (Heb. 8:3) and ministers according to covenant regulations within a tabernacle (Heb. 9:1–15), but everything about his ministry is supreme over its shadowy counterpart: his sacrifice is permanent (Heb. 9:24–26), his covenant is forever (Heb. 7:22; 8:13; 9:15), and his tabernacle is the heavens (Heb. 9:24).

The Transitions of Hebrews

The first four verses of Hebrews 1 stand out plainly as an introduction. The γάρ of Heb. 1:5 points to the first division of the book. The key word ἄγγελος holds together the next nine verses, with the rhetorical question of Heb. 1:14 and the διὰ τοῦτο of Heb. 2:1 signaling a clear break, but at the same time a clear link, with the previous passage. A change of subject marks off Heb. 2:5–9 both from 2:1–4 and from the following passage, which no longer discusses Jesus in relation to angels but in relation to humanity. Hebrews 2:10–18 continues this discussion until in Heb. 3:1 another clear transition is marked by the word ὅθεν. The comparison between Jesus and Moses holds together Heb. 3:1–6 until Heb. 3:7, where the somewhat weak διό suggests a break. This assumption is confirmed by the development of the theme centering on the OT quotation "Today, if you hear his voice. . . ." This scriptural exegesis goes on until Heb. 3:19, where the summarizing καί ("So" in NRSV and NIV) combined with the contrastive οὖν of Heb. 4:1 signals a shift in thought. Hebrews 4:1–11 is really more of the same, and another complex scriptural exegesis follows until two powerful, independent statements at Heb. 4:12–13 prime the listener/reader for a major change of argument beginning at Heb. 4:14.

The mention of Jesus' priesthood at Heb. 4:14 harks back to Heb. 2:17 and 3:1, closing off the extensive teaching of Heb. 3:1–4:13 and unifying it. Having read the epistle and sensed that the exhortation to hold fast and to obey is central, as are the themes of the sonship and priesthood of Jesus, we are tempted, rightly, to mark Heb. 4:14–16 as a major transitional passage for the entire epistle. The verses mention prominently each of the elements of our main theme, both summing up the major ideas expressed in Heb. 1:5–4:13 and introducing those of Heb. 5:1–10:18.

Hebrews 5:1 moves from the exhortation of 4:16 into an explication of the earthly high priesthood, an explication that would continue clearly, logically, and virtually without a break until Heb. 7:28, were it not for Heb. 5:11–6:20. At Heb. 5:10 we see the power of the hook word for our author. He abruptly halts his straightforward teaching about Christ's priesthood, when he mentions Christ's having been designated "high priest according to the order of Melchizedek" (Heb. 5:10). At the repetition of the name Melchizedek (Heb. 5:6), he realizes that he is about to get into some very deep and complicated issues, and he dare not do so without a word of warning to his readers about their spiritual readiness for such teaching (Heb. 5:11–6:3). This leads him to the famous warning about not only losing the ability to teach others but falling away from the faith altogether (Heb. 6:4–8). The warning leads to an affirmation of the author's belief that his readers are bound for salvation, and he encourages them to persevere on the basis of God's faithfulness (Heb. 6:9–20). He then resumes the theme of Christ's priesthood (Heb. 6:20).

Hebrews 7:1–10 is the first half of the author's exegesis of Ps. 110:4b based on his reading of Gen. 14:18–20. It is self-contained, being both unified with Heb. 7:11–28 by content and separated from it by the movement from the historical to the theological. Hebrews 7:1–10 largely recounts facts about Melchizedek and compares him to Abraham and Levi, developing the theme of Melchizedek's superiority to both. Hebrews 7:11–28, prompted by the rhetorical question of verse 11, moves to the heart of the comparison between the Melchizedekian and the levitical priesthoods. One is permanent, perfect, and once for all; the other is temporary, weak, and in need of constant repetition.

The strong marker phrase κεφάλαιον δὲ ἐπὶ τοῖς λεγομένοις at Heb. 8:1 demonstrates the author's desire both to simplify and summarize and to move on to even more important issues. Hebrews 8:1–2 is an important, apex-like transitional statement with its references *back* to the very opening sentences of the book (Heb. 1:3) and *forward* to the closing ones of, if not the book, at least this long central section (Heb. 10:11–18). These verses serve to summarize the Son's appointment as high priest on our behalf ("seated at the right hand of the throne of the Majesty in the heavens," Heb. 8:1 NRSV) and provide as good a brief summary of the teaching of the first half of Hebrews as can be done. They also introduce a new idea that will be central to what follows: heaven as the sanctuary where this High Priest serves to make intercession for us. The description of this sanctuary includes two elements that will dominate the explanation of the following chapters: (1) the tabernacle of the heavens is the "true" (ἀληθινῆς) one and (2) it was set up by the Lord, not by humans.

Hebrews 8:3 introduces a short passage establishing that Jesus will offer a superior offering to that of the levitical priests. At Heb. 8:6 the author seems to digress slightly in order to explain an even more fundamental basis for superiority than that of the heavenly offering to the earthly ones. The superiority of the new covenant to the old covenant, as prophesied in Jer. 31:31–34, is the subject of Heb. 8:6–13 and forms a further basis for understanding the inherent superiority of the sacrifice of Christ to the earthly sacrifices. The μὲν οὖν of Heb. 9:1 signals the beginning of a long section, relatively unbroken, about that sacrifice, explaining that it

> takes place in heaven (Heb. 9:24);
> uses the blood, not of bulls and goats, but of the perfect Lamb of God (Heb. 9:12–14);
> makes Christ the mediator of a new covenant (Heb. 9:15);
> signifies the reality of Christ's ministry and covenant and the shadow-like character of all that went before (Heb. 10:1);
> is offered once for all (Heb. 9:25–26); and
> provides a perfect, eternal salvation for "those who are sanctified" (Heb. 10:14).

All this and more is developed in Heb. 9:1–10:18.

Hebrews 10:19–25 bears a resemblance to Heb. 4:14–16 in that it closes off the long section that precedes it by summarizing so many of that section's themes in a few short verses.[10] The heavenly tabernacle, sacrifice, and priesthood of Jesus are all explicitly mentioned and pressed into service for the salvation of believers, both cleansing from past sin and providing a basis for drawing near to God now. The section also encourages the reader to approach God "in full assurance of faith" (Heb. 10:22), to "hold fast to the confession of our hope without wavering" (Heb. 10:23), and to "consider how to provoke one another to love and good deeds" (Heb. 10:24 NRSV)—a three-fold injunction so illustrative of the content of the last three chapters of the book that some have seen it as a programmatic outline for it.[11] Thus, like Heb. 4:14–16, Heb. 10:19–25 at the same time summarizes the preceding major section and introduces the last major section of the epistle.

The negative command encapsulated in the participle of Heb. 10:25, warning his readers not to neglect meeting together (μὴ ἐγκαταλείποντες τὴν ἐπισυναγωγὴν ἑαυτῶν), seems to lead the author into a deeper, more serious warning in a manner similar to the one we discovered in the transition from Heb. 5:11–6:3 to Heb. 6:4–8. Hebrews 10:26–39 follows the same pattern as Heb. 6:4–20: after a strong statement of the terrible consequences of apostasy (Heb. 10:26–31), the author recounts the very good reasons why he considers them bound for better things (Heb. 10:32–34) and exhorts them to persevere on the basis of God's faithfulness (Heb. 10:35–39).

The hook word πίστις provides the transition into the next major section of the epistle, Heb. 11:1–40, the famous "Hall of Fame of Faith." Clearly bound together by the catch phrase "by faith" which occurs eighteen times in the chapter, the section now signals a major shift from doctrinal exposition to paraenesis. Hav-

---

10. On the basis of both verbal and conceptual parallels, some even see Heb. 10:19–22 as a conscious and direct echoing of Heb. 4:14–16 (cf., e.g., Ellingworth, *Hebrews*, 521).

11. Cf., e.g., James Swetnam, "Form and Content in Hebrews 7–13," *Biblica* 55 (1974): 333–48. Harold W. Attridge, *The Epistle to the Hebrews*, Hermeneia (Philadelphia: Fortress, 1989), 283, rightly points out that—while the three virtues of faith, hope, and love are highlighted in the next three chapters, and thus the three injunctions serve as an introduction to the chapters generally—to see these as providing an outline by which the last three chapters are structured is to force a separation between faith and hope that is artificial since the author so intimately links them in Heb. 11:1.

ing been encouraged throughout the epistle to hold fast and to obey, the readers are now taught *how* to do so. The examples of their ancestors who persevered in the faith will encourage them to remain as "those who have faith and so are saved" (Heb. 10:39 NRSV).

Hebrews 12:1, with its strong particle τοιγαροῦν, moves from the past to the present but continues the same exhortation to faith and perseverance by encouraging the readers to consider the supreme example of faithfulness and obedience, Jesus, so that they "may not grow weary or lose heart" (Heb. 12:3 NRSV). After a discourse on discipline and its purposes (Heb. 12:4–13) and a brief pastiche of commands (Heb. 12:14–17), the author begins to gather phrases and ideas from the entire sermon, bringing to mind everything from the angels mentioned in Hebrews 1–2 (Heb. 12:22) to the new covenant and better sacrifice of Hebrews 5–10 (Heb. 12:24) and the faithful saints just mentioned in chapter 11 (Heb. 12:23–24).

The separate nature of Heb. 13:1–25 is so apparent that many have thought it an addendum to the otherwise finished sermon. The summarizing character of Heb. 12:28–29 and the abrupt change in style found in Heb. 13:1ff. clearly mark chapter 13 off from what precedes. But the chapter in no way reads as a later addendum; it picks up on paraenesis scattered throughout the epistle, sometimes reemphasizing (Heb. 13:15–17), more often extending into new areas (Heb. 13:2, 4–5), the need for obedience to the supreme Son and Priest—a theme that has been present throughout the epistle. A brief epistolary conclusion finishes the letter (Heb. 13:20–25), and even here significant themes found throughout the epistle recur (cf. Heb. 13:20, 24).

An Outline with Titles

All that is now left to do is the actual outline with titles. Scholars have chosen to represent their outlines in as many different ways as the bases they have chosen for them. Although trying to organize an outline that makes very little distinction between form and content, I have nevertheless tried to reflect the author's movement back and forth between doctrinal and ethical exposition. Hence I have adopted a form attributed to G. Guthrie[12] that portrays the epistle in three col-

---

12. As found in Lane, *Hebrews*, 1:xcvi–xcvii; cf. Guthrie, "Structure," 144.

umns, though the divisions are somewhat different and the titles are entirely mine. The first column gives the reference to the passage with indention signaling subcategorization or dependence upon a previous passage. The second column gives the titles of passages that are *primarily* doctrinal, the third those that are *primarily* exhortatory.

Reference	Doctrine	Exhortation
1:1–4	Introduction	
1:5–4:13	The Superior Son	
1:5–14	The Son Is Superior to Angels	
2:1–4		Warning to Listen to God's Salvation
2:5–9	Jesus Made Lower Than Angels to Die	
2:10–18	Jesus Made Like His Brothers to Die	
3:1–6	The Son Is Superior to Moses	
3:7–19		Scripture on Believing and Obeying
4:1–11		Scripture on Entering the Rest Today
4:12–13	God's Word Judges	
4:14–16	Jesus Son and High Priest	Is to Be Held on to and Obeyed
5:1–10:18	Jesus the Unique High Priest	
5:1–10	Introduction to Priesthood of Jesus	
5:11–6:3		Warning about Slackness
6:4–8		Warning about Apostasy
6:9–20		Encouragement of God's Promise

Reference	Doctrine	Exhortation
7:1–10	Historical Exegesis about Melchizedek	
7:11–28	Theological Exegesis about Melchizedek	
8:1–2	Jesus the Priest of Heavenly Realities	
8:3–5	Jesus Has an Offering	
8:6–13	Jesus' Superior Covenant	
9:1–10:18	Jesus' Superior Offering and Tabernacle	
10:19–25		Draw Near, Hold Fast, Stir Up
10:26–13:19		Believe, Persevere, Obey
10:26–31		Warning about Apostasy
10:32–39		Persevere on the Promise of God
11:1–40	Examples of Faith	
12:1–3		Encouragement to Persevere
12:4–13	Teaching on Discipline	
12:14–17		Some Calls to Obedience
12:18–29	A Summary of the Sermon	A Summary of the Sermon
13:1–19		Godly Exhortations
13:20–25	Conclusion	

5

Greek Text

If you want to learn how to understand the details of the Epistle to the Hebrews, the first step is to get yourself a copy of the text. It sounds ludicrous, but it is nevertheless true: students who seek to understand Hebrews at a level where its deepest riches can be mined must settle on the text to be studied. Preparing for our exegetical task, then, requires us to do textual criticism.

Textual criticism, or the science of studying ancient copies of a book in order to determine the original text of that book, is one of those ugly blots on the NT requirements list guaranteed to elicit a groan from almost any student who must study it. The subject is thought to be too complicated, difficult, and boring. Besides, the typical pastor never seems to need it anyway, so why study it? Too many students do so only because it is demanded of them, and then they forget it along with their Greek New Testaments when they get out into the churches or schools and begin preaching and teaching. Leave the textual stuff to the scholars, they say, and let us get on with the real work!

What a shame. Our culture is crying out for people who will stand in the pulpit and declare the Word of the Lord with some measure of authority, while its teachers and preachers must themselves depend on someone else to determine which text actually *is* the Word of God and what that Word means. While we cannot all be textual critics of equal stature, those who desire to study Scripture and then to teach or preach its rich truths to others must be equipped to decide which texts are worthy of such study and exposition.[1]

---

1. We will go into some of the basics of textual criticism in this chapter: how mistakes were made, what sorts of witnesses we have to the text in the manuscripts we study, etc. For a more advanced look at textual criticism, see the essay by Michael W. Holmes, "New Testament Textual Criticism," in the introductory volume of this series, *Introducing New Testament Interpretation*, ed. Scot McKnight, Guides to New Testament Exegesis (Grand Rapids: Baker, 1989), 53–74.

Although a full explanation of the methods of textual criticism is beyond the scope of this chapter, many who are reading this will already know something about textual criticism anyway. We will focus on providing a simple way for students to understand the important textual problems in the Book of Hebrews.

The text of Hebrews is called by textual critics a very "stable" text. That is, there are not a great deal of variants going off in strange directions and creating uncertainty about the integrity of the text. Hebrews was circulated and copied as part of Paul's writings, and this may have something to do with its stability. It certainly is the reason we have so many early and good manuscripts witnessing to its text and assuring us that the text with which we are working is very close to the original.[2]

The table below is a guide to help the student work through the key textual variants in Hebrews. Carefully read the instructions at the beginning of the table; you should find that, even if you have not looked at your Greek NT in some time, you understand more than you thought you would. Some of the variants will directly affect the preaching and teaching of the Word, and some will do so only indirectly, but all are important as we seek to understand and faithfully defend God's Word.

Table of Important Textual Variants in Hebrews

The readings listed in the columns below are taken from the UBS[4] Greek NT because it is probably the Greek text most widely used by pastors and teachers in the United States today.[3] Most of the textual problems cited in this edition are listed below. Some additional problems are discussed as well; their references are marked with an asterisk (*). I have discussed almost all the problems Metzger mentions in his textual commentary.[4] Most of the variants for each problem are listed, but in the interests of space

---

2. For a listing of the principal manuscripts containing Hebrews and for a little more discussion of its text, see Harold W. Attridge, *The Epistle to the Hebrews,* Hermeneia (Philadelphia: Fortress, 1989), 32, and especially William L. Lane, *Hebrews,* Word Biblical Commentary (Dallas: Word, 1991), 1:clvi–clvii.

3. *The Greek New Testament,* ed. Barbara Aland et al., 4th corrected ed. (Stuttgart: Deutsche Bibelgesellschaft/United Bible Societies, 1994).

4. Bruce M. Metzger, *A Textual Commentary on the Greek New Testament,* 2d ed. (Stuttgart: Deutsche Bibelgesellschaft/United Bible Societies, 1994), 591–607.

and usefulness, some have been omitted and others have been combined using brackets in the text (see, e.g., 13:21 [2] below). The translation of the reading from the text is usually from the NRSV; if not, it is my own, as are the translations for the variants.

Column 4, Summary of Discussion, needs some explanation. Under three subcategories, I have listed certain helpful (I hope!) information. In the first subcategory, I have rated the theological and/or exegetical significance of each problem, using an A, B, or C rating. These ratings have nothing to do with the ratings in UBS[4], though I did get the idea there. Rather, they give guidance on how crucial a particular textual problem is for the interpreter. Sometimes the problem has theological significance; sometimes it is purely exegetical. The subcategory *Issue* either has a short phrase (e.g., Christology, Inerrancy of Scripture), because there is extensive discussion of that text in the last chapter of our book, or it has a brief explanation of the problem with no later discussion. *Suggested Reading* offers my recommendation of the best text.

Only textual problems rated A or B in UBS[4] are discussed in the body of the chapter, because of their importance or complexity. All these problems could have been discussed at greater length; the reader should check the major commentaries (especially Attridge and Lane) and Metzger's textual commentary for further information. The disputed words are in **bold print** (sometimes these appear in the text, more often in the variants). The remaining symbols are as follows:

txt = text
var = variant
 * = textual variant not found in UBS[4]
 A = great significance
 B = some significance
 C = little significance

Ref.	Possible Readings	Possible Translations	Summary of Discussion
1:3	txt: καθαρισμὸν τῶν ἁμαρτιῶν ποιησάμενος var: δι᾿ ἑαυτοῦ καθαρισμὸν τῶν ἁμαρτιῶν ποιησάμενος	txt: "when he had made purification for sins" var: "when **through himself** he had made purification for sins"	*Theological/Exegetical Significance:* C *Issue:* The middle voice for ποιησάμενος already points to Christ's sacrifice of himself (cf. 7:27; 9:14, 26); this scribal addition apparently sought to clarify the meaning of the relatively obscure middle voice. *Suggested Reading:* text
1:8	txt: καὶ ἡ ῥάβδος τῆς εὐθύτητος ῥάβδος τῆς βασιλείας σου var: καὶ ἡ ῥάβδος τῆς εὐθύτητος ῥάβδος τῆς βασιλείας αὐτοῦ	txt: "and the righteous scepter is the scepter of **your** kingdom" var: "and the righteous scepter is the scepter of **his** kingdom"	*Theological/Exegetical Significance:* C *Issue:* Αὐτοῦ makes no sense in the context and would represent a departure from both the Hebrew and the Greek versions of the OT text being cited here. There is no real difference theologically, since the kingdom is God's in either version. This is probably simply a transcriptional error. *Suggested Reading:* text
1:12	txt: ὡς ἱμάτιον καὶ ἀλλαγήσονται var: καὶ ἀλλαγήσονται	txt: "and **like clothing** they will be changed" var: "and they will be changed"	*Theological/Exegetical Significance:* C *Issue:* The author has added the words "like a garment" to the OT text, apparently "to emphasize that the metaphor of the garment is sustained" (Lane, *Hebrews,* 1:21–22 n. *h*). Scribes later tried to conform the text to the OT. *Suggested Reading:* text

2:7	*txt:* δόξῃ καὶ τιμῇ ἐστεφάνωσας αὐτόν, *var:* δόξῃ καὶ τιμῇ ἐστεφάνωσας αὐτόν, **καὶ κατέστησας αὐτὸν ἐπὶ τὰ ἔργα τῶν χειρῶν σου**	*txt:* "you have crowned him with glory and honor" *var:* "you have crowned him with glory and honor, **and set him over the works of your hands**"	*Theological/Exegetical Significance:* C *Issue:* The scribe probably felt that the quotation was incomplete and therefore added the extra phrase from the OT text. *Suggested Reading:* text
2:9	*txt:* ὅπως χάριτι θεοῦ ὑπὲρ παντὸς γεύσηται θανάτου *var:* ὅπως **χωρὶς** θεοῦ ὑπὲρ παντὸς γεύσηται θανάτου	*txt:* "so that by the grace of God he might taste death for everyone" *var:* "so that **without** God he might taste death for everyone"	*Theological/Exegetical Significance:* B *Issue:* Christology, work of Christ *Suggested Reading:* text
3:2	*txt:* ὡς καὶ Μωϋσῆς ἐν [ὅλῳ] τῷ οἴκῳ αὐτοῦ *var:* ὡς καὶ Μωϋσῆς ἐν τῷ οἴκῳ αὐτοῦ	*txt:* "just as Moses also 'was faithful in **all** God's house' " *var:* "just as Moses also 'was faithful in God's house' "	*Theological/Exegetical Significance:* C *Issue:* scribal conformity to a quotation from Num. 12:7, which appears also in Heb. 3:5, just a few verses later *Suggested Reading:* variant
3:6 (1)	*txt:* οὗ οἶκός ἐσμεν ἡμεῖς *var:* **ὅς** οἶκός ἐσμεν ἡμεῖς	*txt:* "whose house we are" *var:* "**which** house we are"	*Theological/Exegetical Significance:* B *Issue:* Christology *Suggested Reading:* text
3:6 (2)	*txt:* ἐάν[περ] τὴν παρρησίαν καὶ τὸ καύχημα τῆς ἐλπίδος κατάσχωμεν *var:* ἐάν[περ] τὴν παρρησίαν καὶ τὸ καύχημα τῆς ἐλπίδος **μέχρι τέλους βεβαίαν** κατάσχωμεν	*txt:* "if we hold fast the confidence and the pride that belong to hope" *var:* "if we hold fast the confidence and the pride that belong to hope **firm until the end**"	*Theological/Exegetical Significance:* C *Issue:* This variant shows an interest in the questions about perseverance raised by Heb. 6:4–6 and 10:26–30. The longer reading is not preferred in this case because it looks too much like a scribal insertion imitating Heb. 3:14. It does have extensive manuscript support, however. *Suggested Reading:* text

Ref.	Possible Readings	Possible Translations	Summary of Discussion
4:2	*txt*: μὴ συγκεκερασμένους τῇ πί-στει τοῖς ἀκούσασιν *var 1*: μὴ **συγκεκερασμένος** τῇ πίστει τοῖς ἀκούσασιν *var 2*: μὴ συγκεκερασμένους τῇ πίστει **τῶν ἀκουσάντων** *var 3*: μὴ συγκεκερασμένους τῇ πίστει τοῖς **ἀκουσθεῖσιν**	*txt*: "because they were not united by faith with those who listened" *var 1*: "**because it did not meet** with faith in the hearers" *var 2*: "because they were not unit-ed with the faith **of the hearers**" *var 3*: "since they were not united by faith **with the things that were heard**"	*Theological/Exegetical Significance*: B *Issue*: faith *Suggested Reading*: text
4:3	*txt*: εἰσερχόμεθα γὰρ εἰς [τὴν] κατάπαυσιν οἱ πιστεύσαντες *var 1*: εἰσερχόμεθα **οὖν** εἰς [τὴν] κατάπαυσιν οἱ πιστεύσαντες *var 2*: εἰσερχόμεθα **δὲ** εἰς [τὴν] κατάπαυσιν οἱ πιστεύσαντες *var 3*: **εἰσερχώμεθα** γὰρ εἰς [τὴν] κατάπαυσιν οἱ πιστεύσαντες *var 4*: **εἰσερχώμεθα οὖν** εἰς [τὴν] κατάπαυσιν οἱ πιστεύσαντες	*txt*: "For we who have believed en-ter that rest" *var 1*: "**Therefore** we who have be-lieved enter that rest" *var 2*: "**But** we who have believed enter that rest" *var 3*: "For **let us** who have be-lieved enter that rest" *var 4*: "**Therefore let us** who have believed **enter** that rest"	*Theological/Exegetical Significance*: C *Issue*: The wide variety of variants is explain-able either as unintentional scribal error or as assimilation to nearby verses (cf., e.g., the "therefore" of 4:1, 11, 14, 16). *Suggested Reading*: text
5:12	*txt*: πάλιν χρείαν ἔχετε τοῦ διδά-σκειν ὑμᾶς **τινὰ** τὰ στοιχεῖα τῆς ἀρχῆς τῶν λογίων τοῦ θεοῦ *var*: πάλιν χρείαν ἔχετε τοῦ διδάσκειν ὑμᾶς **τίνα** τὰ στοιχεῖα τῆς ἀρχῆς τῶν λογίων τοῦ θεοῦ	*txt*: "you need **someone** to teach you again the basic elements of the oracles of God" *var*: "you need to be taught again **which** are the basic elements of the oracles of God"	*Theological/Exegetical Significance*: B *Issue*: teachers vs. teaching *Suggested Reading*: text

Ref	Greek text	English translation	Theological/Exegetical Significance
6:2	txt: βαπτισμῶν διδαχῆς ἐπιθέσεώς τε χειρῶν var: βαπτισμῶν **διδαχὴν** ἐπιθέσεώς τε χειρῶν	txt: "**of** instruction about baptisms, of laying on of hands," var: "instruction about baptisms, laying on of hands,"	*Theological/Exegetical Significance:* B *Issue:* authority of teaching *Suggested Reading:* variant
6:3	txt: καὶ τοῦτο ποιήσομεν var: καὶ τοῦτο **ποιήσωμεν**	txt: "And we will do this" var: "And **let us do this**"	*Theological/Exegetical Significance:* C *Issue:* The future tense (ποιήσομεν) is more in accord with the phrase that follows ("if God permits") than is the awkward exhortation. In the first reading, one has almost a promise from the author to leave behind the "elemental things," in the second, an exhortation to do so. The weight of external evidence also favors the reading of the text. *Suggested Reading:* text
*7:13	txt: ἀφ' ἧς οὐδεὶς προσέσχηκεν τῷ θυσιαστηρίῳ var: ἀφ' ἧς οὐδεὶς **προσέσχεν** τῷ θυσιαστηρίῳ	txt: "from which no one has ever served at the altar" var: "from which no one ever **served** at the altar"	*Theological/Exegetical Significance:* C *Issue:* The difference here is a literary rather than a theological one. The perfect tense in the text reading forms a wordplay with the similar verb in the first part of the sentence. The variant destroys this paronomasia, a favorite device of the author. *Suggested Reading:* text
8:8	txt: μεμφόμενος γὰρ αὐτοὺς λέγει var: μεμφόμενος γὰρ **αὐτοῖς** λέγει	txt: "God finds fault with them when he says" var: "God finds fault when he says **to them**" (or possibly, "God finds fault **in them** when he says")	*Theological/Exegetical Significance:* A *Issue:* the author's view of the first covenant *Suggested Reading:* text

Ref.	Possible Readings	Possible Translations	Summary of Discussion
8:11	*txt:* καὶ οὐ μὴ διδάξωσιν ἕκαστος τὸν πολίτην αὐτοῦ *var:* καὶ οὐ μὴ διδάξωσιν ἕκαστος τὸν πλησίον αὐτοῦ	*txt:* "And each one shall not teach his fellow citizen" *var:* "And each one shall not teach his **neighbor**"	*Theological/Exegetical Significance:* C *Issue:* One variant of the LXX reads "neighbor," and apparently some scribes sought to bring the quotation in Hebrews into conformity with that OT text type. *Suggested Reading:* text
9:1	*txt:* Εἶχε μὲν οὖν [καὶ] ἡ πρώτη δικαιώματα λατρείας τό τε ἅγιον κοσμικόν. *var:* Εἶχε μὲν οὖν ἡ πρώτη δικαιώματα λατρείας τό τε ἅγιον κοσμικόν.	*txt:* "Now **even** the first covenant had regulations for worship and an earthly sanctuary." *var:* "Now the first covenant had regulations for worship and an earthly sanctuary."	*Theological/Exegetical Significance:* B *Issue:* the author's view of the first covenant *Suggested Reading:* text
*9:2	*txt:* καὶ ἡ πρόθεσις τῶν ἄρτων *var:* καὶ ἡ πρόθεσις τῶν ἄρτων καὶ τὸ χρυσοῦν θυμιαστήριον	*txt:* "and the bread of the Presence" *var:* "and the bread of the Presence **and the golden altar of incense**"	*Theological/Exegetical Significance:* B *Issue:* inerrancy of Scripture *Suggested Reading:* text
9:10	*txt:* καὶ διαφόροις βαπτισμοῖς, δικαιώματα σαρκὸς μέχρι καιροῦ διορθώσεως ἐπικείμενα. *var:* καὶ διαφόροις βαπτισμοῖς **καὶ δικαιώμασιν** σαρκὸς μέχρι καιροῦ διορθώσεως ἐπικείμενα	*txt:* "and various baptisms, regulations for the body imposed until the time comes to set things right" *var:* "and various baptisms **and regulations** for the body imposed until the time comes to set things right"	*Theological/Exegetical Significance:* C *Issue:* The change to the dative (δικαιώμασιν) was probably by attraction to the other datives in the verse. The other variants (not listed here) are either very poorly attested or make little sense. *Suggested Reading:* text

9:11	*txt:* ἀρχιερεὺς τῶν γενομένων ἀγαθῶν *var:* ἀρχιερεὺς τῶν **μελλόντων** ἀγαθῶν	*txt:* "a high priest of the good things that have happened" *var:* "a high priest of the good things **to come**"	*Theological/Exegetical Significance:* B *Issue:* Is a past or future event being discussed? *Suggested Reading:* text
9:14	*txt:* τὴν συνείδησιν ἡμῶν *var:* τὴν συνείδησιν **ὑμῶν**	*txt:* "**our** conscience" *var:* "**your** conscience"	*Theological/Exegetical Significance:* B *Issue:* exegetical *Suggested Reading:* text
9:19	*txt:* τὸ αἷμα τῶν μόσχων **καὶ τῶν τράγων** *var:* τὸ αἷμα τῶν μόσχον	*txt:* "the blood of calves **and goats**" *var:* "the blood of calves"	*Theological/Exegetical Significance:* C *Issue:* There is no sure way to know whether the passage should include "and goats." Scribes could have *omitted* it in order to conform the passage to Exod. 24:5, or they could have *added* it in order to conform it to Heb. 9:12. *Suggested Reading:* text
10:1 (1)	*txt:* **οὐκ αὐτὴν** τὴν εἰκόνα τῶν πραγμάτων *var:* καὶ τὴν εἰκόνα τῶν πραγμάτων	*txt:* "**not the true** form of these realities" *var:* "**and** the form of these realities"	*Theological/Exegetical Significance:* A *Issue:* the author's view of the first covenant *Suggested Reading:* text
10:1 (2)	*txt:* οὐδέποτε δύναται τοὺς προσερχομένους τελειῶσαι *var:* οὐδέποτε **δύνανται** τοὺς προσερχομένους τελειῶσαι	*txt:* "**it** can never make perfect those who approach" *var:* "**they** can never make perfect those who approach"	*Theological/Exegetical Significance:* C *Issue:* In either case the referent is the law. The singular reading agrees grammatically with its subject and the plural may have arisen because of the plural verb (προσφέρουσιν, "they offer") in the immediate context. *Suggested Reading:* text

Ref.	Possible Readings	Possible Translations	Summary of Discussion
10:11	*txt:* Καὶ πᾶς μὲν ἱερεὺς ἕστηκεν καθ᾽ ἡμέραν *var:* Καὶ πᾶς μὲν **ἀρχιερεὺς** ἕστηκεν καθ᾽ ἡμέραν	*txt:* "And every priest stands day after day" *var:* "And every **high priest** stands day after day"	*Theological/Exegetical Significance:* C *Issue:* The contrast with Christ in the passage overall probably prompted a scribe to elevate the status of the contrasting element from "priest" to "high priest." Of course the high priest did not stand day after day offering sacrifices on behalf of the people, so it is unlikely that the author of Hebrews, so well versed in sacrificial law, would make such an error. Ἱερεύς clearly has better external support too. *Suggested Reading:* text
10:34 (1)	*txt:* καὶ γὰρ τοῖς δεσμίοις συνεπαθήσατε *var:* καὶ γὰρ τοῖς **δεσμοῖς [μου]** συνεπαθήσατε	*txt:* "For you had compassion for those who were in prison" *var:* "For you had compassion for **[my] chains**"	*Theological/Exegetical Significance:* C *Issue:* The reading "[my] chains" seems to have arisen unintentionally when a scribe let an iota drop out of the word for prisoners and it became "chains." The external evidence is distributed widely among a number of variations of these two readings and is therefore inconclusive. *Suggested Reading:* text
10:34 (2)	*txt:* γινώσκοντες ἔχειν ἑαυτοὺς κρείττονα ὕπαρξιν καὶ μένουσαν *var:* γινώσκοντες ἔχειν ἐν ἑαυ-**τοῖς** κρείττονα ὕπαρξιν καὶ μένουσαν	*txt:* "knowing that you yourselves possessed something better and more lasting" *var:* "knowing that you possessed **among yourselves** something better and more lasting"	*Theological/Exegetical Significance:* C *Issue:* The second reading apparently arose from a misreading of the first in some manuscripts. The external evidence weighs heavily in favor of the text's reading. *Suggested Reading:* text

10:38	*txt:* ὁ δὲ δίκαιός **μου** ἐκ πίστεως ζήσεται *var 1:* ὁ δὲ δίκαιος ἐκ πίστεός **μου** ζήσεται *var 2:* ὁ δὲ δίκαιος ἐκ πίστεος ζήσεται	*txt:* "but **my** righteous one will live by faith" *var 1:* "but the righteous one will live by **my** faithfulness" *var 2:* "but the righteous one will live by faith"	*Theological/Exegetical Significance:* A *Issue:* faith *Suggested Reading:* text
*11:4 (1)	*txt:* Πίστει πλείονα θυσίαν Ἄβελ παρὰ Κάϊν προσήνεγκεν **τῷ θεῷ** *var:* Πίστει πλείονα θυσίαν Ἄβελ παρὰ Κάϊν προσήνεγκεν	*txt:* "By faith Abel offered **to God** a more acceptable sacrifice than Cain's" *var:* "By faith Abel offered a more acceptable sacrifice than Cain's"	*Theological/Exegetical Significance:* C *Issue:* The sacrifice is offered to God in either case. Strong external evidence argues for including the phrase "to God," though there are very good stylistic arguments for questioning this decision. *Suggested Reading:* text
*11:4 (2)	*txt:* μαρτυροῦντος ἐπὶ τοῖς δώροις αὐτοῦ τοῦ θεοῦ *var 1:* μαρτυροῦντος ἐπὶ τοῖς δώροις αὐτοῦ τῷ θεῷ *var 2:* μαρτυροῦντος ἐπὶ τοῖς δώροις αὐτῷ τοῦ θεοῦ	*txt:* "God himself giving approval to his gifts" *var 1:* "**he [God?]** himself giving approval of his gifts **to God**" *var 2:* "**God** giving approval of his gifts **to him**"	*Theological/Exegetical Significance:* C *Issue:* The problem is a thorny one since none of the readings makes very good sense, and all can be explained as scribal changes of one of the others. As Bruce Metzger says, the "least unsatisfactory reading appears to be αὐτοῦ τοῦ θεοῦ," the reading of the text. (Metzger discusses this variant in the first edition of his *Textual Commentary on the Greek New Testament* [Stuttgart: United Bible Societies, 1971], 671–72, but omits it from the second edition.) *Suggested Reading:* text

Ref.	Possible Readings	Possible Translations	Summary of Discussion
11:11	*txt:* Πίστει καὶ αὐτῇ Σάρρα στεῖρα δύναμιν εἰς καταβολὴν σπέρματος ἔλαβεν *var 1:* Πίστει καὶ αὐτῇ Σάρρα δύναμιν εἰς καταβολὴν σπέρματος ἔλαβεν *var 2:* Πίστει καὶ αὐτῇ Σάρρα ἡ στεῖρα δύναμιν εἰς καταβολὴν σπέρματος ἔλαβεν *var 3:* Πίστει καὶ αὐτῇ Σάρρα στεῖρα δύναμιν εἰς καταβολὴν σπέρματος ἔλαβεν *var 4:* Πίστει καὶ αὐτῇ Σάρρα στεῖρα οὖσα δύναμιν εἰς καταβολὴν σπέρματος ἔλαβεν	*txt:* "By faith he received power of procreation, **and Sarah herself was barren**" *var 1:* "By faith even (also?) Sarah herself received power of procreation" *var 2:* "By faith even (also?) Sarah herself, the barren one, received power of procreation" *var 3:* "By faith even (also?) barren Sarah herself received power of procreation" *var 4:* "By faith, Sarah herself also being barren, he received power of procreation"	*Theological/Exegetical Significance:* A *Issue:* role and significance of women *Suggested Reading:* text
11:37	*txt:* ἐλιθάσθησαν, ἐπρίσθησαν *var 1:* ἐλιθάσθησαν, ἐπρίσθησαν, **ἐπειράσθησαν** *var 2:* ἐλιθάσθησαν, **ἐπειράσθη-σαν**	*txt:* "They were stoned to death, they were sawn in two" *var 1:* "They were stoned to death, they were sawn in two, **they were tempted**" *var 2:* "They were stoned to death, **they were tempted**"	*Theological/Exegetical Significance:* B *Issue:* exegetical *Suggested Reading:* text

*11:39	*txt:* Καὶ **οὗτοι** πάντες μαρτυρηθέντες διὰ τῆς πίστεος οὐκ ἐκομίσαντο τὴν ἐπαγγελίαν *var:* καὶ πάντες μαρτυρηθέντες διὰ τῆς πίστεος οὐκ ἐκομίσαντο τὴν ἐπαγγελίαν	*txt:* "Yet all **these**, though they were commended for their faith, did not receive what was promised" *var:* "and although they all were commended for their faith, they did not receive what was promised"	*Theological/Exegetical Significance:* B *Issue:* exegetical *Suggested Reading:* text
12:1	*txt:* τὴν εὐπερίστατον ἁμαρτίαν *var:* τὴν **εὐπερίσπαστον** ἁμαρτίαν	*txt:* "the sin that clings so closely" *var:* "the sin that **so easily distracts**"	*Theological/Exegetical Significance:* C *Issue:* Which adjective was used? Though one very early manuscript uses the variant, the overwhelming majority of manuscripts, some of them very early, have the reading adopted in the text. *Suggested Reading:* text
12:3	*txt:* εἰς **ἑαυτόν** *var 1:* εἰς αὐτόν *var 2:* εἰς ἑαυτούς *var 3:* εἰς αὐτούς	*txt:* "against **himself**" *var 1:* "against himself" *var 2:* "against themselves" *var 3:* "against themselves"	*Theological/Exegetical Significance:* A *Issue:* Christology, sin, consequences for actions *Suggested Reading:* variant 3
12:18	*txt:* Οὐ γὰρ προσεληλύθατε ψηλαφωμένῳ *var:* Οὐ γὰρ προσεληλύθατε ψηλαφωμένῳ **ὄρει** [some MSS: ὄρει ψηλαφωμένῳ]	*txt:* "You have not come to something that can be touched" *var:* "You have not come to a **mountain** that can be touched"	*Theological/Exegetical Significance:* C *Issue:* scribal assimilation to 12:22 where the reference to Mt. Zion obviously contrasts with the present verse *Suggested Reading:* text

Ref.	Possible Readings	Possible Translations	Summary of Discussion
*13:6	txt: Κύριος ἐμοὶ βοηθός, [καὶ] οὐ φοβηθήσομαι var: Κύριος ἐμοὶ βοηθός, οὐ φοβηθήσομαι	txt: "The Lord is my helper, **and** I will not be afraid" var: "The Lord is my helper; I will not be afraid"	*Theological/Exegetical Significance:* C *Issue:* Absence of the "and" stresses a main thought of the book: the necessity to banish fear through meditation on, and acceptance of, God's sovereignty. Though most critical texts leave the "and" in the text in brackets, Lane states that it "almost certainly . . . was omitted in Hebrews" (*Hebrews*, 2:509 n. *u*). *Suggested Reading:* variant
13:15	txt: δι' αὐτοῦ [οὖν] var: δι' αὐτοῦ	txt: "Through him, **then**," var: "Through him"	*Theological/Exegetical Significance:* C *Issue:* The addition of οὖν seems to smooth the grammar somewhat. Bracketed text shows the almost complete equality of the two readings in the manuscripts. *Suggested Reading:* text
13:21 (1)	txt: ἐν παντὶ ἀγαθῷ var 1: ἐν ἔργῳ ἀγαθῷ var 2: ἐν παντὶ ἔργῳ ἀγαθῷ var 3: ἐν παντὶ ἔργῳ καὶ λόγῳ ἀγαθῷ	txt: "in everything good" var 1: "in good **work**" var 2: "in every good **work**" var 3: "in every good **work and word**"	*Theological/Exegetical Significance:* C *Issue:* The difference theologically is profound here, but all the readings except the text are highly suspect either on external or internal grounds. The last reading is an obvious assimilation to 2 Thess. 2:17. *Suggested Reading:* text

*13:21 (2)	txt: ποιῶν ἐν ἡμῖν τὸ εὐάρεστον ἐνώπιον αὐτοῦ var 1: **αὐτῷ** ποιῶν ἐν ἡμῖν τὸ εὐ-άρεστον ἐνώπιον αὐτοῦ var 2: ποιῶν **ἑαυτῷ** ἐν ἡμῖν τὸ εὐ-άρεστον ἐνώπιον αὐτοῦ var 3: **αὐτός}** ποιῶν ἐν ἡμῖν τὸ εὐάρεστον ἐνώπιον αὐτοῦ	txt: "working among us that which is pleasing in his sight" var 1: **"in him** working among us that which is pleasing in his sight" var 2: "working **in himself** among us that which is pleasing in his sight" var 3: **"He** is working among us that which is pleasing in his sight"	*Theological/Exegetical Significance:* C *Issue:* The reflexive pronoun is as awkward here in Greek as it is in English, and the other variants probably arose by mistake from the presence of the same word (αὐτοῦ) just prior to ποιῶν in the text. A few manuscripts have the nominative αὐτός, perhaps implying a cooper-ative working in the passage similar to that of Phil. 2:12–13. The best reading, however, is the short reading without the pronoun. *Suggested Reading:* text
13:21 (3)	txt: ποιῶν ἐν ἡμῖν τὸ εὐάρεστον ἐνώπιον αὐτοῦ var: ποιῶν ἐν **ὑμῖν** τὸ εὐάρεστον ἐνώπιον αὐτοῦ	txt: "working among us that which is pleasing in his sight" var: "working among **you** that which is pleasing in his sight"	*Theological/Exegetical Significance:* C *Issue:* The difference here is obvious: is the au-thor seeking to be inclusive or not? The stron-gest evidence supports the text; the variant arose because of the presence of ὑμᾶς earlier in the sentence. *Suggested Reading:* text
13:21 (4)	txt: ᾧ ἡ δόξα εἰς τοὺς αἰῶνας **[τῶν αἰώνων]** var: ᾧ ἡ δόξα εἰς τοὺς αἰῶνας	txt: "to whom be the glory forever **and ever**" var: "to whom be the glory for-ever"	*Theological/Exegetical Significance:* C *Issue:* The phrase "forever and ever" occurs twice in the Pastoral Epistles and twelve times in Revelation. The author was probably pat-terning his text after the traditions reflected in those occurrences. It was later shortened by copyists assimilating it to Heb. 13:8. *Suggested Reading:* text

Ref.	Possible Readings	Possible Translations	Summary of Discussion
13:25	*txt:* ἡ χάρις μετὰ πάντων ὑμῶν. *var:* ἡ χάρις μετὰ πάντων ὑμῶν. ἀμήν	*txt:* "Grace be with all of you." *var:* "Grace be with all of you. **Amen**"	*Theological/Exegetical Significance: C Issue:* As Metzger puts it, "The later liturgical use of the concluding words ('Grace be with all of you') must have made it difficult for scribes not to add ἀμήν when copying the epistle" (*Textual Commentary*, 2d ed., 607). *Suggested Reading:* text

Helpful Books on Textual Criticism

There are a number of books that can help you as you attempt to come to grips with the text of Hebrews. First, the essential tool is the Greek NT itself. Second, in addition to the standard critical commentaries, there are books that will help you make informed decisions about the text of Hebrews by discussing the textual problems outlined above, as well as others. Lastly, there are general works on textual criticism that will help you hone your skills and broaden your knowledge, should you become deeply interested in this branch of biblical study.

There are two standard critical editions of the Greek NT. These two editions share basically the same text, differing only very slightly in the way they punctuate the Greek text, but not differing at all in the readings they have chosen.

The Greek New Testament. Ed. Barbara Aland et al. 4th corrected ed. Stuttgart: Deutsche Bibelgesellschaft/United Bible Societies, 1994. (abbreviated UBS[4])

Novum Testamentum Graece. Ed. Barbara Aland et al. 27th rev. ed. Stuttgart: Deutsche Bibelgesellschaft, 1993. (abbreviated NA[27])

There are some basic differences between these two texts. UBS[4] records fewer textual variants but cites more evidence in support of each variant; NA[27] records many more variants but cites fewer witnesses in support of each variant. UBS[4] is the standard text for pastors and teachers who do not do a lot of close technical work with the text. It has large, readable type and rates the textual decisions it has made on a scale from "A" (very high amount of agreement among the members of the editorial committee on a reading's validity) to "D" (great uncertainty about the accuracy of a reading). NA[27] is preferred by scholars because so many more variants are listed, and if one takes the time to master its critical apparatus, the additional information it contains will yield some wonderful insights.

There are other works that can help you decide between textual variants in Hebrews by giving you the reasoning behind the selection of a particular reading.

F. W. Beare. "The Text of the Epistle to the Hebrews." *Journal of Biblical Literature* 63 (1944): 379–96.

Philip W. Comfort. *Early Manuscripts & Modern Translations of the New Testament.* Wheaton: Tyndale House, 1990; reprint, Grand Rapids: Baker, 1996. Pp. 164–71.

Bruce M. Metzger. *A Textual Commentary on the Greek New Testament.* 2d ed. Stuttgart: Deutsche Bibelgesellschaft/United Bible Societies, 1994. Pp. 591–607.

R. V. G. Tasker. "The Text of the 'Corpus Paulinum.' " *New Testament Studies* 1 (1954–55): 180–91.

Günther Zuntz. *The Text of the Epistles: A Disquisition upon the Corpus Paulinum.* The Schweich Lectures of the British Academy, 1946. London: Oxford University Press, 1953.

Do not forget, too, that some of the best helps for the discussion of difficult textual problems are the critical commentaries. Here are some helpful books for digging deeper into textual criticism.

Kurt Aland and Barbara Aland. *The Text of the New Testament: An Introduction to the Critical Editions and to the Theory and Practice of Modern Textual Criticism.* Trans. Erroll F. Rhodes. 2d ed. Grand Rapids: Eerdmans, 1989. This book is technical and should not be tackled by a beginner.

F. F. Bruce. *The Books and the Parchments.* Rev. ed. London: Marshall Pickering, 1991. The chapter on textual criticism in this book is superb as an introduction to textual criticism, though it is somewhat dated.

Jack Finegan. *Encountering New Testament Manuscripts: A Working Introduction to Textual Criticism.* Grand Rapids: Eerdmans, 1974. This can be somewhat heavy going, but it is fascinating.

J. Harold Greenlee. *Introduction to New Testament Textual Criticism.* Grand Rapids: Eerdmans, 1964. An excellent, standard introduction to the discipline.

J. Harold Greenlee. *Scribes, Scrolls, & Scripture: A Student's Guide to New Testament Textual Criticism.* Grand Rapids: Eerdmans, 1985. A very fine introduction for the layperson to the work of textual criticism.

Bruce M. Metzger. *The Text of the New Testament: Its Transmission, Corruption, and Restoration.* 3d, enlarged ed. New York

and Oxford: Oxford University Press, 1992. The standard
introduction to the discipline for many years. Newly up-
dated and completely revised, it cannot be beaten as both
an introduction to the subject and a resource for more advanced students.

Part 2

The Exegesis of Hebrews

The questions we approached in our first five chapters were necessary to the journey we are taking, but it was not always obvious how they were directly relevant to learning how to do exegesis of Hebrews. Now we turn to the text itself, and in the next four chapters, we will learn how to do exegesis from the center out as if we were looking at concentric circles of context. The central circle is the individual word. The next chapter will focus on how to do word studies in Hebrews. Then as we surround the *word* with the circles of *phrase, sentence,* and *paragraph,* we must study grammar, syntax, and style. Lastly, as we try to synthesize what we have learned from this rather technical exegesis, we will look at the theology of the book and round out the circle by coming to a fuller understanding of what the author was trying to do in his "word of exhortation."

6

Vocabulary

This may be a good time to take stock of how far we have come. We began by exploring the notion of context, our guiding principle for exegesis, and looked first at the historical and cultural context of the epistle: when was it written? to whom? to what kind of situation? Then we tackled the difficult problem of authorship, recognizing that if we could know who the author was, we would be better able to understand the text. We would then know what sort of person he was, what else he wrote, how he thought, etc. Unfortunately, we saw that the historical and cultural situation and the authorship of Hebrews are still shrouded in mystery, and though we can infer a lot from the text itself, we know little else about the circumstances surrounding the production of Hebrews.

After *Sitz im Leben* and authorship, we moved to the study of the form of the book itself, its literary genre and structure. Here we found ourselves on more solid ground, though questions still remain about the epistle's sources, genre, and structure. Nevertheless, we made some tentative suggestions about the exegesis of Hebrews, seeing it as a sermon with an epistolary twist having connections and shared characteristics with other ancient forms of writing. We closed part 1 by offering a table discussing some of the textual variants in Hebrews, establishing the text so that we have something to study.

In part 2, we move from looking outside the text for its historical, cultural, social, and literary context to looking at the text itself, to the words and ideas that make it what it is. We come to what is

in many ways the heart and soul of exegesis itself: the analysis of
vocabulary, grammar, and style—the study of the words of the
text. There is no good reason to go into detail concerning the philosophy and basic tasks of word study or grammatical and stylistic analysis in this chapter; these have been treated admirably in
other places.[1] We will only give a "bare bones" treatment of the
basics of these avenues of study, concentrating instead on the issues of vocabulary, grammar, and style particular to Hebrews.

Word Study in General

I can remember as a schoolboy going to hear a famous preacher
of the time. He spoke that evening on Acts 1:8: "But you will receive power when the Holy Spirit has come upon you; and you
will be my witnesses in Jerusalem, in all Judea and Samaria, and
to the ends of the earth" (NRSV). One of his chief points was that
the Holy Spirit's power was like dynamite, exploding into the
ancient world with a wonder-working might that was unlike
anything humans could devise. I was moved by his powerful
statement that the Holy Spirit is an explosive force in the
world—that where he is moving, things happen, and they happen in an exciting way.

But I was also disturbed. Didn't the Holy Spirit move in quiet
ways, too, gently moving hearts and minds to follow him? In addition to Pentecost in Acts, wasn't there an audience with Agrippa?
But my problem was this: the preacher based his claim squarely
on the statement of the Word of God, and his claim was that the
Holy Spirit's power equaled the explosive power of dynamite.
And what was the basis of his claim? He did not base his case on
the evidence of the stories in the rest of the Book of Acts, though
he certainly could have—the stories of Peter and John healing the

---

1. The introductory volume of the Guides to New Testament Exegesis series,
Introducing New Testament Interpretation, ed. Scot McKnight (Grand Rapids: Baker,
1989), contains two excellent essays by Darrell L. Bock (chap. 4: "New Testament
Word Analysis") and Scot McKnight (chap. 3: "New Testament Greek Grammatical Analysis") that are useful for the student who wants to know how to do vocabulary and grammatical analysis. Of course the relevant sections in Gordon D. Fee,
New Testament Exegesis: A Handbook for Students and Pastors, rev. ed. (Louisville:
Westminster/John Knox, 1993), are fundamental to their essays and to my present
chapter.

lame man or of Paul and Silas being delivered from prison, of Philip being directed to the Ethiopian eunuch's side and being snatched away again by the Spirit, of the conversion of Saul and the raising of Tabitha from the dead, and so on. Rather, he based it on the Greek word for "power" used in Acts 1:8 (δύναμις) from which the English word *dynamite* is derived. I can still recall him saying, "The Holy Spirit gives us God's power, God's 'dynamite,' to empower us to be explosive witnesses in the world for him." The problem is that Luke, the author of Acts, was simply using a word that meant no more than the basic idea of "ability," a word that is used in NT Greek for everything from the power to work miracles (cf., e.g., Acts 10:38) to the ability to bear up under persecution (2 Cor. 1:8) and the capacity for giving money (2 Cor. 8:3). The power of the Holy Spirit, even in Acts, is manifested in many different ways—some explosive, some not. Whatever Luke meant in using the word δύναμις, he certainly was not miraculously predicting the invention of dynamite, which, wrongly or rightly on my part, was part of the message I got!

The preacher of my story is by no means the only one making such mistakes today. Time and time again, preachers and teachers of the Word proclaim confidently, "As the original Greek says . . ." and then go on to commit a linguistic fallacy that sounds convincing to the untrained listener. Lay people trust the preacher to have done the homework and believe that deeper research into the original languages of Scripture will yield great riches, but they also are usually unable to discern whether or not the preacher is using good exegetical principles. When they hear preachers wielding the power of "the original languages," they are, to use a contemporary expression, wowed.

The seriousness of the bad exegetical technique used by preachers and teachers of the Word cannot be emphasized enough. The people of God look to their shepherds to feed and water them; too often, they are instead being slaughtered by the very hand they think is nourishing them. If the preceding words seem too harsh, there is a reason. In large measure, contemporary preachers and teachers are not totally to blame for their mistakes; in their interpretations, they are often only following the author of a commentary or study tool, who *they* hope has done the homework. Even the greatest scholars must depend on the research of others, so they likewise go to their books expecting to find gold and silver but come away with something that appears to be precious but is in fact fool's gold.

To break this chain of "trust in the experts," we can neither distrust them all and throw away our books nor throw up our hands in despair since we can never be skilled enough to write our own Greek grammar. Rather, we must work hard at Greek, reviewing some first principles over and over again until they become second nature, so that we feel confident enough in our abilities to disagree with the experts sometimes and to have good reasons for doing so. Admittedly, this will not be easy. As one author put it: "Exasperation and pain, with discipline, can give birth to a settled contentment [with one's abilities in Greek]."[2] Not an enthusiastic endorsement of language study, but a realistic one, and only advocated because language study is both necessary and worth the sacrifice it takes to do it.

As is often pointed out, word study is sadly misunderstood in much NT teaching and preaching today.[3] Word study probably yields the most, and the most devastating, errors of any that good-hearted but wrong-headed preachers make. Perhaps reviewing just a few of these errors will help the serious expositor of Scripture to avoid them. Here is a list of some of the most common errors.[4] Never assume that

1. a word always means what its root means (the etymological fallacy),
2. a word means everything it could mean in every place it occurs (illegitimate totality transfer),
3. a word's meaning in *later* history contributes significantly

---

2. McKnight, "Grammatical Analysis," 76.

3. Cf. Fee, *Exegesis*, 100–101; Bock, "Word Analysis," 110–12. Cf. also, D. A. Carson, *Exegetical Fallacies*, 2d ed. (Grand Rapids: Baker, 1996), and Moisés Silva, *Biblical Words and Their Meaning: An Introduction to Lexical Semantics*, rev. and expanded ed. (Grand Rapids: Zondervan, 1994), passim.

4. Many of these "errors" are errors of excess; in other words, there are times and places when these approaches can be rightly used to clarify a word's meaning. For instance, when a biblical author coins a term (i.e., creates a new word that has never been used before), the etymology of that word is probably very important for determining the meaning of it. For an example of this, see the discussion of μισθαποδοσία later in this chapter.

to its present meaning in a passage (semantic anachro-
nism),

4. a word's meaning in *earlier* history contributes significantly to its present meaning in a passage (semantic obsolescence),

5. a word always has only one meaning and means the same
thing in every passage (the prescriptive fallacy),

6. the study of any particular word is tantamount to a complete study of the idea that word represents (the word-
idea fallacy), and

7. a word always has a very specific, inherent meaning apart
from its context (the referential fallacy).[5]

Do not make the mistake of reading this list and thinking you
understand the error described, if you have not ever devoted serious study to these fallacies. They are not easily grasped and require a great deal of subtle thought. For instance, the referential
fallacy (fallacy 7 above) does *not* say that words have *no* meaning
apart from their context; every word defines at least one or more
semantic fields which differentiate it from thousands of other possible semantic fields. If this were not so, dictionaries would be an
impossibility and communication would be virtually impossible,
especially between those speaking different languages. But it *does*
say that even the most concrete referents, a name for instance, can
be seriously misunderstood without a context to determine its
meaning. A friend of mine who does not have a college education
once proved this point to me. In normal conversation, I mentioned
my studies at Cambridge University, to which he replied that he
too had gone to Cambridge . . . but only long enough to change
trains for Peterborough! Again, some study of words and language, and the way they work, will bring great reward.

But what are some of the *right things* to do with words? How
does one do vocabulary study and use the results in such a way
that the Word of God is made more understandable? Simply put,

---

5. Each of these mistakes is quite common and too complex to be explained in
detail here, but I cannot emphasize enough the importance of making sure that
you understand the error each of these brief statements describes and how to avoid
it. The books and articles listed in n. 3 above are excellent resources for finding out
about any of these fallacies that may be unfamiliar or confusing to you.

one asks the right questions. The first question one must ask is: Which words are worthy of particular study? The answer to this question requires that we divide the important words into two categories: (1) those words that are important for you the exegete and (2) those words that are important for the author.

Perhaps it is obvious to you that one should study terms that are important for the author, but at first glance it may seem illegitimate to study words *you* want to study. After all, aren't you then drifting away from the task of discovering what the author meant, the goal of exegesis, toward that of looking for what *you* want to find in the text? Not at all. To say that you are, confuses the setting of the parameters of a word study with the process of the word study itself. Words may be selected for study based on all sorts of motivations: the need of a congregation to hear teaching on a certain topic, your own desire to know what the Bible says about a certain subject, etc. The difference is this: after selecting the term you want to study, you are then obligated to find out what the *author* meant by that term in its biblical context. To do otherwise, simply to import your own theology or ideas into the word, is called *eisegesis*, the very opposite of exegesis; but your selecting the terms you want to study is merely using Scripture to find answers to the real questions you face.

So what sorts of words should you look for? Certainly the most important category of words are *theologically* or *ethically important* ones, such as παράβασις in Heb. 2:2 or σωτηρία in Heb. 2:3.[6] Words that are *unclear and yet seem important for understanding the meaning of the passage*, like the words in the phrase ὁ δι᾽ ἀγγέλων λαληθεὶς λόγος in Heb. 2:2, are often ones you should further investigate. Words that seem important to the author may stand out in the passage because of their *repetition* (e.g., εἰσέρχομαι or κατάπαυσις in

---

6. Fee, *Exegesis*, 101, has an important warning in this regard: "Make a note of those words known . . . to be theologically loaded. Do not necessarily assume you already know the meaning of ἐλπίς (hope), δικαιοσύνη (righteousness), ἀγάπη (love), χάρις (grace), etc. For example, what does 'hope' mean in Col. 1:27, or χάρις in 2 Cor. 1:15, or δικαιοσύνη in 1 Cor. 1:30? In these cases in particular it is important to know not only the word in general but also the context of the passage in particular." An excellent example of this in Hebrews is the word σωτηρία, salvation, found in Heb. 2:3. Context is particularly important for getting the right meaning there, yet salvation is such a well-known word to us, we tend to assume that we know what it means in this context.

Heb. 3:12–4:11) or the prominence given them by their *symbolic or metaphorical content* (ἀρχιερεύς in Heb. 4:14), their *position in a list* (all the words in the phrase θεμέλιον μετανοίας ἀπὸ νεκρῶν ἔργων in Heb. 6:1), their *inclusion in a summary sentence* (ὑπόστασις or ἔλεγχος in Heb. 11:1), or the use of some other means. *Extremely rare terms or terms that seem to have been coined by the author* (see the tables below) are also worthy of further attention.

After deciding which words are worthy of study, the exegete must ask the all-important question: What did the author mean by this term? Exegetes who ask this question, and ask it rigorously,[7] will avoid a multitude of sins. This involves asking questions like

> Does this term have any special significance in the immediate context?
> Does the author seem to have a fondness for the term in the rest of his writing?
> Does he point in the passage to any important associated concepts that force us to take note of the term?
> Does he give us any clues to his defining or treating the term in a special way?
> Is there a biblical, philosophical, or historical significance to the term that is important for understanding its use in this context?

Of course if the answer to any of these questions is yes, then a follow-up question is necessary: What is it that the author is trying to tell the reader by using this very special term? In other words, why did he use this word and not some other, and what did he mean by using it? These questions are necessary in order to determine whether one's understanding of the passage can be enriched by doing further study of the word. Answers to them can best be

---

7. By "rigorously," I do not mean that the interpreter should try to do the impossible. We cannot "reproduce what the author must have been thinking at a given point or why he wrote. Rather, the interpreter's goal is to ascertain what the writer wanted to communicate through the terms he chose for his message" (Bock, "Word Analysis," 98 n. 1). I do mean that as we proceed with the task of exegesis, we should never stray from the question and should come back to it over and over again, asking: "Is this really what the author meant?"

found by beginning to make use of some of the plethora of tools available today for word study.

Doing Word Studies

The process of word study, like most tasks in exegesis, is time consuming but rewarding. You will find many treasures as you begin to use the tools that are available to you, and you will bring immeasurable riches to those you teach from the fruit of these studies, as long as you use the tools wisely. Restraint is perhaps the first order of business at all times; remember, you are after the meaning the author intended as much as that is possible to find. You must adopt a healthy skepticism as you study, making sure that what you are learning is really useful to your listeners and not simply what you would like to find.

Word studies can be done for many purposes, as we saw above, but most purposes require the use of one of two types of word study: thematic study and expositional study. Most of the process for doing the two types of studies is the same, but they start from different places. In a thematic study, one is interested in what the Bible or, more likely, a portion of the Bible has to say about a particular theme or idea. For instance, a pastor might decide to preach a series on *righteousness*. To accomplish this task, one would need to do word studies that relate to this theme. Expositional study, on the other hand, may be done when a student of Scripture wants to know what a particular word means in a given passage. If asked to teach on Heb. 11:1, one would need to do an expositional study of words like ὑπόστασις and ἔλεγχος and perhaps others. But what tools and procedures should one use for these two types of study?

Thematic Word Studies

The first thing one needs to do in a thematic study (after choosing the theme, of course!) is to limit the range of the study. Very few themes can be meaningfully traced through the whole Bible. To do this properly on the level at which the pastor or teacher should operate would take years and far too much work to make the task a reasonable option. So, for instance, to take our idea of doing a study of the concept of *righteousness*, one might want to limit the study to its use in the NT (a still almost impossible task) or in Paul (daunting yet) or Hebrews (yes, now we are getting somewhere!). A series on "Righteousness in Hebrews" would not at all be impossible to handle.

We next move to the step of actually doing the word study. At this point, those who have done some biblical study might think: "Aha! I know what he's going to advocate next. He'll suggest that I take a concordance and look up all the occurrences in the Book of Hebrews of the word δικαιοσύνη, the Greek word for righteousness." Good guess, and I will certainly advocate that shortly, but there is an important step or two that many people miss to their detriment by turning straight to the concordance.

First, without really needing another book, except perhaps a Greek dictionary, you must list any verb, adjective, adverb, and any other noun that shares a root with the noun you have chosen to study. These four parts of speech will often, if not always, be important elements for studying any concept in depth. The more concrete and specific the object, the less it is likely that all four parts of speech will be represented (there is no related adjective, adverb, or verb to be studied if your word study is "Abraham in the Book of Hebrews"!), but usually you will need to look up all four. In our case, the verb δικαιοῦν and the adverb δικαίως do not occur in Hebrews, but important verses would be missed if we did not look up the adjective δίκαιος and the related noun δικαίωμα.

Now are we ready for the concordance? Not yet! The first tool to be used in a thematic word study is not a concordance but a thesaurus or, better yet, the *New International Dictionary of New Testament Theology* or, best of all, the *Greek-English Lexicon of the New Testament: Based on Semantic Domains*. Don't be scared off by the titles! A thesaurus should be at every pastor's side already.[8] It lists synonyms for almost every word imaginable and is extremely useful when preparing sermons (or writing a book!). It helps you find just the right word to express an idea or to smooth out your style and give it some diversity. It can help us in our study of righteousness in Hebrews, because the idea of righteousness may be expressed by more than just the word δικαιοσύνη and its cognates. One thesau-

---

8. The best thesaurus is still the granddaddy of them all: *Roget's Thesaurus of English Words and Phrases*. Although many publishers offer this public-domain work, make sure to get a new one and to get the official version; there are many abridged and adapted editions out there, which are not as useful.

rus entry gave several other related concepts worthy of study—
holiness, purity, virtue, goodness, sanctity, and others. So word
studies on these and similar terms might be in order. Here one
must exercise some selectivity, since it would be impossible to
study every synonym for *righteousness*. Curiosity tempered with
common sense should guide the selection process.

But using a thesaurus can be cumbersome. After selecting the important linking concepts from the thesaurus, you must then find the
Greek word that best translates those concepts and begin doing concordance work on each of the words. Also, a thesaurus is by its nature overly full in its entries. Its purpose is to give as many options
as possible to the speaker or writer, and the time spent wading
through its offerings in the interests of exegesis can be better spent.
Thankfully, there are two excellent tools that can help cut short the
process. If you can afford either or both of these books, or have access to them through a seminary or college library, make use of
them and forget the thesaurus (for this purpose anyway).

Colin Brown, ed. *The New International Dictionary of New Testament
    Theology.* 4 vols. Grand Rapids: Zondervan, 1975–86. (abbrevi-
    ated *NIDNTT*)
Johannes P. Louw and Eugene A. Nida, eds. *Greek-English Lexicon
    of the New Testament: Based on Semantic Domains.* 2d ed. Vol. 1,
    Introduction & Domains; vol. 2, *Indices.* New York: United Bible
    Societies, 1989.

From *NIDNTT* and Louw and Nida's lexicon, you can get an
idea of the Greek words you will need to study in order to work
on the theme of righteousness in Hebrews. You may settle on the
nouns δικαιοσύνη, δικαίωμα ("regulation"), and εὐθύτης ("up-
rightness"); the adjectives δίκαιος, ἔνδικος ("right, just"), and
ἅγιος ("holy"); and the verb ἁγιάζειν ("to make holy"). How do
you then go about doing your research on these words? If you are
doing a thematic word study, it is now time to use the concordance to see when and where these words are used in Hebrews.
You then begin to study each occurrence in context, and it is at this
point that our two types of study, thematic and expositional, become one. When you begin to study words in their Scriptural contexts, you are doing expositional word study. Now a few words of
warning about this kind of study.

Expositional Word Studies

In an expositional word study, while the goal of discerning the author's meaning remains the same as in a thematic study, the steps taken are different. The parameters of the study are of course already set: one comes upon a word and wants to know what it means in its context. At this point it is crucial that we remember the fallacies listed above and carefully avoid them, while nevertheless employing the very books that could cause us to fall into their traps. Doing word study without going to the excesses denoted by those fallacies is both the challenge and the joy of word study. We cannot hope to reach the goal without plunging ahead. Like Odysseus, we must sail between Scylla and Charybdis; there is no other way home.

But isn't this a little melodramatic? All of this talk about danger and sailing between Scylla and Charybdis (or should it be racing between Tyrannosaurus and Velociraptor to use a more contemporary myth?!) is overly cautious. Provided we understand from the warnings above what we should not do, can't we just go ahead and complete our study, making sure to avoid those pitfalls?

This would be fine except for one thing: each fallacy listed above contains some truth and is the perfectly logical outcome, *not of the normal use of illegitimate categories for determining the meaning of a word, but rather of an excessive use of perfectly legitimate ones*. The meaning of a word in its context often does have something, if only very little, to do with its etymology (fallacy 1); it can have different shades of meaning or even double meanings in any particular use (fallacy 2); its later and earlier meanings can be pointers to its meaning in the NT (fallacies 3 and 4); a word does have at least some basic range of meanings that distinguish it from other words (fallacies 5 and 7); and one word and its cognates can be the overwhelmingly agreed upon conveyor of a particular idea (fallacy 6). So we must study our word both *diachronically* and *synchronically*, looking both at the history of the word with its usage and changes through time (diachronic) and at the literary relationships the word has, particularly in its context in Hebrews but also in related literature of the time (synchronic).[9] When the two approaches conflict, priority certainly must be given to the contempo-

---

9. For more on diachronic and synchronic analysis of words, see Silva, *Biblical Words*, passim. His treatment is very balanced, readable and yet thorough.

rary context of the word, but we throw the baby out with the bath water if we ignore a word's prior history and the insights we can gain from studying it.

So we come to the study of our word in context. The first order of business is to see where else in Hebrews the word is used. Concordances are the tools for that.

Using a Concordance

A concordance is an alphabetical listing of all of the words in a given text.[10] Under each word is a list of references where the word can be found in the text and usually a partial quotation of each reference. Some concordances contain other information, such as the total number of times a word occurs in the text or perhaps footnote and reference schemes that cross-reference the text with other texts or point out special phrases in which the word occurs regularly.[11]

Not too many years ago, discussing concordances was a very simple matter. If you used English, you used one of three concordances, each based on the Authorized, or King James, Version. They were painstakingly compiled by hand by three men named Young, Strong, and Cruden, and the old joke ran that if you were young, you used Young's; if you were strong, you used Strong's; and if you were . . . well, let's just say more people used Young's and Strong's than Cruden's. But in fact, Young's and Strong's concordances *were* better than Cruden's, because they devised ingenious ways of helping someone without any knowledge of the original languages of Scripture get at the different Greek and Hebrew words underlying the English translation. Under the main entry for each English word, Young subdivided the references based on the Hebrew or Greek word(s) lying behind that English word. Strong, on the other hand, listed all the references consecutively for each English word, regardless of the different underlying Greek or Hebrew word. Then he assigned a number to each Greek or Hebrew word and attached

---

10. There are concordances available not only for the Bible but for many bodies of ancient literature (e.g., the works of Josephus and Philo) as well as for some more modern ones (e.g., Shakespeare, Milton).

11. For example, the famous concordance for the Septuagint, Edwin Hatch and Henry A. Redpath, eds., *A Concordance to the Septuagint and the Other Greek Versions of the Old Testament, Including the Apocryphal Books.* 2 Vols. (Oxford: Clarendon, 1897; reprint, Grand Rapids: Baker, 1987), is painstakingly cross-referenced, giving the Hebrew word that lies behind each Greek word, when that can be determined.

it to the corresponding English word used to translate that Greek or Hebrew word. In an appendix he listed all the Greek and Hebrew words by their number and defined them. Both systems have been refined and incorporated into other concordances and word study tools over the years and are still used with profit by many today, as are the concordances themselves.

If you could read Greek, until relatively recently the only concordance option you had was Moulton and Geden. Today, however, there are several other Greek concordances available for the NT, but in addition to Moulton and Geden, there are really only two that the student should know about.

Kurt Aland, ed. *Vollständige Konkordanz zum griechischen Neuen Testament.* Band 1, Teil 1 *(A–Λ),* Teil 2 *(M–Ω);* Band 2, *Spezialübersichten.* Berlin and New York: Walter de Gruyter, 1978, 1983.

H. Bachmann and W. A. Slaby, eds. *Computer-Konkordanz zum Novum Testamentum Graece.* 2d ed. Berlin and New York: Walter de Gruyter, 1985.

W. F. Moulton, A. S. Geden, and H. K. Moulton, eds. *A Concordance to the Greek New Testament.* 5th ed. Edinburgh: T. & T. Clark, 1978.

The onset of computers has changed the world of biblical research, and we have not yet seen the end of the changes. Many of the best programs are still too expensive, complicated, and technical (and the lesser ones too deficient) for normal Bible study use, but that situation is changing fast. For now, however, the book remains the easiest and most sure method for doing concordance work on the NT.[12]

---

12. Gary M. Burge, *Interpreting the Gospel of John,* Guides to New Testament Exegesis (Grand Rapids: Baker, 1992), 132–34, has a very helpful summary of the programs that were available for both IBM and Macintosh computers as of 1992. For more-recent information on what is available for computer-aided biblical research, see Software for Theologians: A Selection (http://www.pitts.emory.edu/bob/theosoft.html). A few of the more popular programs are reviewed at Bible-Search Software for Scholarly Research (http://www.chorus.cycor.ca/hahne/reviews.html). For some cautions when using Bible-search software for scholarly research, see Harry Hahne, "Interpretive Implications of Using Bible-Search Software for New Testament Grammatical Analysis" (paper presented at the annual meeting of the Evangelical Theological Society, 24 November 1994); available online at http://www.chorus.cycor.ca/hahne/ntgram.html.

The use one makes of a concordance depends entirely on the user. You may use it simply to look up references, or you may use all the appendices and special features of the volume. As you use the concordance and begin to look at the way a particular word is used in other contexts, I suggest that you take notes—recording observations, questions, connections, and anything else that comes to mind from reading the text. You might want to use a sheet with two columns for each word you are researching—one column for the reference where the word is found and one for your notes.[13] This should help a great deal, but after doing what you can to understand the word in its context using only the text itself, you will probably find that you long for a little more knowledge of the word's history and its use in other contexts. That is the job of the Greek language dictionary.

Greek Lexicons and Their Relevance

If a word derives its meaning from its context, what good are dictionaries, especially the extensive multivolume works available to NT students today? Isn't this just so much fruitless effort—all these long, drawn out articles on the classical uses of a word, its meaning in other places in the NT, its use in the LXX, and the meanings of its Hebrew and Aramaic equivalents in the OT and in writings contemporary to the NT? In fact, worse than being useless, aren't studies like this damaging to biblical study, misleading one into thinking that a word has a "meaning" apart from its context and causing one to fall into one or more of the fallacies warned against above?

We attempted to answer this objection earlier. There we acknowledged briefly that if it came down to choosing between what a word seems to mean in its immediate context versus what it may have meant generally in the culture or in its etymology or history, then one should certainly choose contextual evidence over evidence from outside the text. Context determines the clearest, final meaning of a word, as I illustrated by the two ways one could take the phrase "go to Cambridge." But we also said that each of the fallacies mentioned above has a grain of truth in it and

---

13. Burge, *John*, 138–39, shows a three-column format you may want to follow in taking your notes. His center column includes word associations that any particular reference might display.

that to ignore all the extensive diachronic research when doing our Bible study would be a great mistake. Why is that?

The answer lies in the questions one naturally and rightly asks when one comes to a text to discover its meaning.[14] First of all, the reason one often consults a dictionary to find out the meaning of a word is because the context has failed us: we do not know what the word means, even though we have all the surrounding words, indeed the context of the entire book at our service. Something is lacking in the context that keeps understanding at bay; in fact, we often speak of the term "standing out" because it is not readily apparent to us how it fits with the rest of the sentence to produce a clear and reasonable thought.

The wondrous thing is that when we look up the word in a dictionary, the thought is often completed for us and suddenly the meaning of the sentence becomes clear. This confirms our suspicions: words *do* have some sort of discernible content that results from the history of their usage and development over time, meaning that has been assigned to that set of symbols—whether by convention, accident, or history—but meaning nevertheless. That content is certainly more limited than some think, and of course it can and does change over time, but nevertheless the word in its normal use[15] does define some range of ideas that distinguishes it from a huge number of other terms. If I use the word *mountain* without any context, the person who hears me may think of the Alps while I think of the Blue Ridge mountains of Virginia, but neither one of us thinks of a dog or an egg.

But is this the only useful function a dictionary serves? Do we only benefit from a brief listing of the possible meanings of words, just picking up enough meaning from the list to fit the word back

---

14. *Meaning* is one of those very difficult words that defies simple definition when one begins to analyze it closely. It is like the old saw about art: nobody can define it, but everybody knows what it is. Linguists rightly insist that every word has several different kinds of meaning. Bock, "Word Analysis," 100–103, has given an excellent, brief list and explanation of such different kinds of meaning as *encyclopedic meaning, significance meaning,* and *figurative meaning* with footnotes guiding the student to further discussion of this topic.

15. By "normal," I mean uses that pertain to what is usually called the "literal" sense of the word, rather than its "figurative" or "metaphorical" sense. A word can be made to mean virtually *anything* when it is used figuratively, but this is usually readily apparent to the hearer or reader.

into the context from which it came and discern its fuller content there? This is a more difficult question and depends on the word used, the intentions and typical literary conventions of the author, and even on the understanding of the community for which the author was writing and how they might have understood the word. If the word is a simple, straightforward signifier (like our word *mountain* in the last paragraph), often a simple dictionary definition is enough to understand it in its context and is all one should attempt to read into its meaning.

But if the word is a complex theological term, fraught with cultural or social meaning or often discussed and used in a wide range of writings, then we may need to know much more before we can understand it properly in its context. In a way, we are still only bringing a certain "dictionary definition" to the context, but that definition is much more rich and informed than a simple one- or two-word definition would imply. Here even the author's conscious intention recedes somewhat into the background. Paul did not use the word *holiness* in a vacuum but as a first-century Jewish Pharisee, shaped by the OT and first-century Judaistic practice. What would the word have meant to him—a meaning not even he was aware of but that we need consciously to address?

Of course we need to take into account his conscious intentions too. Most of the NT was not written haphazardly without any thought as to the words selected and the forms used. These men were handling the Word of Truth, and it is apparent that this often moved them carefully and consciously to select the words they used for just the right effect, because they understood the seriousness of their task.

The last reason the Greek dictionary is a book worth using for more than just basic meanings is that the words in the NT were used to communicate truth to different groups of people with all their various understandings and backgrounds. First-century audiences would have automatically understood certain things by the words the authors of the NT used, and if we are not aware of these nuances, we are in danger of missing what we need to know to interpret a passage properly.

Let's return to Hebrews and our word *righteousness* for a moment. The word could mean a lot of different things in the ancient world, and there were some relatively serious differences between a Jewish understanding of the term and a Hellenistic one. This distinction has sometimes been overdrawn, to be sure, but it nevertheless holds true that a pagan understanding of righteousness is something inherent to humans, related to their responsibility to others and to accepting their role in society and fulfilling it. It had "the idea of conformity to a standard . . . and the standard was primarily that of social obligation."[16] In Jewish thought, on the other hand, righteousness has to do with being rightly related to God—with understanding and holding covenant loyalty; loving God with all one's heart, mind, and strength; and being obedient to the covenant God had made through the law. It was a word that could be, and very often was, used to refer to God and his loyalty to his covenant promises and obligations, whereas in classical thought, it was a purely human characteristic.

Without grasping these and other important distinguishing aspects of the word, it is virtually impossible to understand some statements in Hebrews. In the quotation of Ps. 45:7 at Heb. 1:9 ("You have loved righteousness and hated wickedness"), the covenant promise of the Son's victory and enthronement is the focus of the psalm, within the context of the Son's also being God who reigns in covenant righteousness. The statement about Noah becoming "an heir of the righteousness that is according to faith" (Heb. 11:7) is a striking example that only makes sense within a Jewish context. Noah obeyed the warning God had given him because of his covenant loyalty to the statements of God which flowed from his relationship of trust in him. His covenant loyalty to God was so great that it clearly transcended his relationship to society, and therein the world was condemned (Heb. 11:7). If δικαιοσύνη had to do with social obligation here, the sentence would be meaningless.

So there are many reasons to use the resources that scholars have developed to explain the Greek language. In English there are five books—or more accurately in most cases, sets of books—that stand out among the many that scholars have compiled for understanding the words of the Greek NT. Each of them, with the possible exception of BAGD, is extremely easy to use, even if you have very little knowledge of Greek. But each has a different

---

16. Colin Brown, ed., *The New International Dictionary of New Testament Theology*, 4 vols. (Grand Rapids: Zondervan, 1975–86), 3:358.

enough twist in what they offer the student, that no one of them makes any of the others redundant. They are listed in alphabetical order by author or editor.

Horst Balz and Gerhard Schneider, eds. *Exegetical Dictionary of the New Testament*. 3 vols. Grand Rapids: Eerdmans, 1990–93. (abbreviated *EDNT*)

Walter Bauer. *A Greek-English Lexicon of the NT and other Early Christian Literature*. Trans. and adapted by William F. Arndt and F. Wilbur Gingrich. 2d ed. rev. and augmented by F. Wilbur Gingrich and Frederick W. Danker. Chicago and London: University of Chicago Press, 1979. (abbreviated BAGD)

Colin Brown, ed. *The New International Dictionary of New Testament Theology*. 4 vols. Grand Rapids: Zondervan, 1975–86. (abbreviated *NIDNTT*)

Gerhard Kittel and Gerhard Friedrich, eds. *Theological Dictionary of the New Testament*. Trans. by Geoffrey W. Bromiley. 10 vols. Grand Rapids: Eerdmans, 1964–76. (abbreviated *TDNT*)

Johannes P. Louw and Eugene A. Nida, eds. *Greek-English Lexicon of the New Testament: Based on Semantic Domains*. 2d ed. Vol. 1, *Introduction & Domains*; vol. 2, *Indices*. New York: United Bible Societies, 1989.

This is not the place to go into the particular use of each of these works.[17] Suffice it to say that BAGD and the one by Louw and Nida are basic lexicons, while the other three are multivolume encyclopedic dictionaries each with its own strengths and weaknesses. This distinction is not perfect since even the "basic" lexicons have a great deal of information and a number of advanced uses, but it is nevertheless a helpful one as we will see, if for no other reason than to distinguish the relatively small and inexpensive tools from the large and expensive ones. Regardless of which lexicons we use, we still must decide what sorts of words we should examine in the Epistle to the Hebrews.

---

17. For more information on using these works for word study, see Bock, "Word Analysis."

Notes on the Vocabulary of Hebrews

The author of Hebrews used a very distinctive and "literary" vocabulary, compared with many of the other authors of the NT. Hebrews has 131 words (excluding proper names) not found anywhere else in the Greek NT and sixty-four more that are found in only one other NT book.[18] In addition, Hebrews has an incredible eight absolute hapax legomena (i.e., words that do not appear in any Greek writing prior to the Book of Hebrews),[19] which therefore have apparently been coined by the author.[20] Attridge rather tamely says of these facts: "The proportion of unique vocabulary is larger here [in Hebrews] than in the rest of the epistolary literature of the New Testament and bespeaks the author's sound literary education,"[21] but the presence of so many unique words says something much more significant. The author with whom we are dealing is boldly creative. Not only are several of his themes striking in their unique treatment vis-à-vis the rest of the NT and the whole early church as we know it, but his very language, while replete with well-known literary forms and vocabulary, is also impressively inventive.

More will be said in chapter 8 about rhetorical devices related to the vocabulary of Hebrews—flourishes such as alliteration and

---

18. Harold W. Attridge, *The Epistle to the Hebrews*, Hermeneia (Philadelphia: Fortress, 1989), 21, apparently loosely following Ceslas Spicq, *L'Épître aux Hébreux*, 2 vols., Études bibliques (Paris: Gabalda, 1952–53), 1:157 (who says there are 152), puts the number of NT hapax legomena at "some 150." I counted the hapax legomena listed in Kurt Aland, ed., *Vollständige Konkordanz zum griechischen Neuen Testament*, 2 vols. (Berlin and New York: Walter de Gruyter, 1978, 1983), 2:457–58, and got 131. Attridge, again probably following Spicq, puts the number of shared-once words at ninety; I counted them using Robert Morgenthaler, *Statistik des neutestamentlichen Wortschatzes* (Frankfort: 1958), to arrive at my figure of sixty-four.

19. Both Attridge (*Hebrews*, 21 n. 173) and Spicq (*Hébreux*, 1:157) list ten absolute hapax legomena, but εὐποιΐα and μετριοπαθέω are found in several places in non-Christian writers contemporary with the NT (e.g., Josephus *Antiquities* 2:261 for εὐποιΐα and 12:128 for μετριοπαθέω), so I did not include them in my count or list them in the table below (pp. 138–39).

20. Of course we cannot be absolutely sure that the author coined the terms; they could have been in current use and simply were not written down anywhere, or they may have appeared in one or more of the many thousands of books written in classical antiquity that are now lost to us. Nevertheless, it is a striking figure under any circumstances.

21. *Hebrews*, 21.

assonance—but it will suffice to say now that the vocabulary of Hebrews points to a readership that was relatively literate. Hebrews contains a high proportion of multisyllabic words and somewhat complicated grammatical forms, especially for the NT, and the high number of rare words seems to assume a widely read audience. As we shall see, the author draws on widely differing areas of experience for the metaphors he uses—including the spheres of education, agriculture, architecture, seafaring, law, athletics, and the cultus—though in fairness, most of these fields would not have been completely unfamiliar to the common folk. It is important to note that unlike many other ancient authors, he quotes no other work but the OT, which would of course have been familiar to even the most uneducated Jewish audience. Nevertheless, the sophisticated way in which he handles the OT and the very fact that he uses the LXX for his quotations points to the fact that at least some of his readership were educated people.

The following tables list some of the words in Hebrews that would reward further study. There are of course many more words in Hebrews worth studying, some more important than these. As you seek to interpret a passage, interesting words will stand out, and you will want to pursue them. I have put together these tables both because they contain information that is hard to obtain elsewhere and because I hope they will spark new ways to think about what sorts of words are worthy of study. The first table lists words that are important for the interpretation of Hebrews as a whole because of their frequency and their apparent interest to the author of Hebrews. The second table lists the words that were apparently coined by the author, with their location and translation. I then give some suggestions on their meanings in context.

Frequency Table of Key Words in Hebrews

Generally, this table lists the significant words that appear ten or more times in Hebrews. It does not list every word that appears that frequently, because many are not really significant for one reason or another. For example, the table omits all prepositions, articles, conjunctions, pronouns, and particles, as well as words that appear so frequently everywhere that they are not really meaningful for word study (e.g., the verb "to be" [εἶναι], θεός, etc.). Limiting the frequency to ten or more is admittedly arbitrary, and in fact in one case (τελειοῦν) I have broken my own rule because the word seemed worthy of inclusion in the list. Some interesting words get left out (e.g., ἅπαξ occurs eight times out of only fourteen in the whole NT!), but that shouldn't keep you from studying them too! The break had to be somewhere.

Greek Word	Translation	Occurrences in Hebrews	Occurrences in the NT
Ἀβραάμ	Abraham	10	73
ἄγγελος	angel	13	175
ἅγιος	holy	19	233
αἷμα	blood	21	97
αἰών	age, world	15	123
ἁμαρτία	sin	25	173
ἀρχιερεύς	high priest	17	122
γῆ	earth	11	248
διαθήκη	covenant	17	33
εἰσέρχεσθαι	to enter into	17	192
ἐπαγγελία	promise	14	52
ζῆν	to live	12	140
ἡμέρα	today	18	388
θάνατος	death	10	120
θυσία	sacrifice, offering	15	28
ἱερεύς	priest	14	31
καρδία	heart	11	156
κρείττων / κρείσσων	better, preferable	13	19
λαλεῖν	to speak	16	298
λαμβάνειν	to receive, take	17	259
λαός	people	13	141
λόγος	word	12	331

Greek Word	Translation	Occurrences in Hebrews	Occurrences in the NT
Μωϋσῆς	Moses	11	79
νόμος	law	14	191
οἶκος	house	11	112
οὐρανός	heaven	10	272
πίστις	faith	32	243
ποιεῖν	to do, make	19	565
προσφέρειν	to bring, offer	20	47
σκηνή	tent, tabernacle	10	20
τελειοῦν	to complete, fulfill	9	23
υἱός	son	24	375
χωρίς	apart from, separately	13	41

Words Coined by the Author of Hebrews

There are much fuller discussions of each of these terms in the commentaries. My comments here will simply explain what the author was trying to accomplish by coining a new word. As you will see, these words are not necessarily notable for their theological import, but they are sometimes important pointers to the author's style and to some of the rhetorical devices he uses in his letter.

Reference	Greek Word	Translation
7:3	ἀγενεαλόγητος	without genealogy
9:22	αἱματεκχυσία	blood-pouring, blood-sprinkling
12:1	εὐπερίστατος	easily besets
2:2; 10:35; 11:26	μισθαποδοσία	payment of wages, reward, penalty
11:6	μισθαποδότης	payer of wages, rewarder
11:28	πρόσχυσις	sprinkling, pouring

Reference	Greek Word	Translation
11:25	συγκακουχέομαι	suffer, be mistreated with (someone)
12:2	τελειωτής	perfecter, completer

The following discussions are not comprehensive; they are meant to provide some reasons why these particular words were coined and to give some guidelines on what is notable about them. Coined expressions sometimes make good preaching points because their meanings do often come directly from their etymologies. The problem is that in the sentence the *meaning* of the coined word or expression may be secondary. Often these expressions are brought in for stylistic reasons and contribute more to the sentence that way. Sometimes, of course, a coined word's etymological content is important. But even if it is not, stylistic significance can be every bit as interesting and helpful to a congregation as etymological information would have been. The fact that a word has been coined by the author, for whatever reason, can contribute a great deal to one's understanding of a sentence and should be included when teaching a passage.

ἀγενεαλόγητος (7:3)

This word appears in one of the most consciously rhetorical passages in the book, so stylized in fact that scholars often think there is some sort of hymn behind the passage. It seems to have been coined for alliterative purposes: ἀπάτωρ, ἀμήτωρ, and the present word appear in a list together and all emphasize the suprahuman nature of Melchizedek. This is a particularly effective device aurally and so demonstrates the sermonic quality of the text at this point.

αἱματεκχυσία (9:22)

This word refers to the sprinkling or pouring out of the blood onto the altar, not to the actual death of the animal as has often been implied (cf. NIV "the shedding of blood"). Rhetoric plays an important part here, too. The author had plenty of ways to say "pouring out of blood," but his coining of this term helped him create a rhythm in Greek that makes the clause a memorizable proverb. A rough English equivalent for the clause where the word appears (χωρὶς αἱματεκχυσίας οὐ γίνεται ἄφεσις) might be: "No sprinkling of the blood, no forgiving of the sin."

εὐπερίστατος (12:1)

This is a difficult term that defies easy translation,[22] in addition to being textually suspect (see table, p. 107 above). It seems to point to something that surrounds and constricts us, contrasting with the runner's need to be free of encumbrances. Sin is the source of "every weight" mentioned in the first part of the verse, and εὐπερίστατος might have been coined to avoid having to use an entire phrase as an adjective. It helps focus the reader's attention on the word ἁμαρτία (sin) as the weight that restricts the runner.

μισθαποδοσία (2:2; 10:35; 11:26)

This term seems to be a special favorite of the author since he coins it in chapter 2, uses it twice more later, and also coins a spin-off of it (the next word in this list, μισθαποδότης)! Commentators have made very little out of the fact that the word is used negatively in 2:2 and positively in 10:35 and 11:26, but the first is a remarkably ironic use of a very positive word etymologically to describe a very great evil in the author's mind. The word probably comes from combining μισθός (pay, wages) with ἀπόδοσις (payment, recompense), both terms that could be used negatively but were generally positive. In fact they are sometimes used together in Greek to express the idea of payment of wages.[23] "By coining the term μισθαποδοσία, 'punishment as reward,' the writer arrests the attention of his hearers and reminds them that carelessness and contempt for God's revelation under the old covenant brought in its wake just and appropriate punishment."[24]

In both 10:35 and 11:26, it is used in a positive way as one would expect. In 10:35, alliteration with the adjective μεγάλην aurally emphasizes the worthiness of the confidence the author is trying

22. Cf. F. F. Bruce, The Epistle to the Hebrews, rev. ed., New International Commentary on the New Testament (Grand Rapids: Eerdmans, 1990), 336.

23. Cf. Thucydides History of the Peloponnesian War 8.85.3.

24. William L. Lane, Hebrews, Word Biblical Commentary (Dallas: Word, 1991), 1:38.

to encourage his readers to hold on to. He uses the coined expression because of the power it gives the whole phrase in the hearing of his congregation, and he carries this over into the written form of his sermon.[25] In 11:26, Moses is said to have been willing to suffer abuse because "he was looking ahead to the reward." Here the word has the spiritual connotation of a "reward in heaven." Some think the author is drawing attention to the parallel between the experience of Moses and that of the community, which he describes in 10:32–39, since the word also occurs in 10:35.[26] This seems likely.

μισθαποδότης (11:6)

This word is a cognate of μισθαποδοσία and means something like "paymaster." It implies a trustworthiness on God's part to reward in accordance with OT promises (cf., e.g., Ps. 34:4, 10), but the word does not seem to be used with any special effect.

πρόσχυσις (11:28)

This noun is simply a substantive created from the verb προσ-χεῖν, frequently used in the LXX for the ritual of pouring or sprinkling the blood of a sacrificial lamb or goat on the altar (cf., e.g., Lev. 9:12). Here of course it refers to the sprinkling of the blood on the doorposts in Egypt so that the firstborn of the Israelites would be kept safe from the angel of death (Exod. 12:7, 22). Once again the coining of the word may have an alliterative purpose for rhetorical effect. The first four important words of 11:28 all begin with the letter π, and the effect of reading the first half of the verse aloud is quite striking.

συγκακουχέομαι (11:25)

This word is also often ignored by commentators but has an important etymology. The verb κακουχέομαι is known well enough in secular Greek and means "to suffer mistreatment, to be tormented." Our author uses it at 11:37 and again at 13:3, and it occurs interestingly in Greek papyri in marriage contracts, where the

---

25. Remember that these letters were often read aloud in the congregation, and many ancients, even when reading to themselves, read their books aloud.

26. Cf. Lane, *Hebrews*, 2:373–74, and James Moffatt, *A Critical and Exegetical Commentary on the Epistle to the Hebrews*, International Critical Commentary (Edinburgh: T. & T. Clark, 1924), 181.

husband takes an oath not to abuse his wife.[27] The prefix συγ-
(from the preposition σύν, "with") creates a term that emphasizes
the willingness of Moses to identify intimately with the people of
God in their suffering in Egypt (cf. NRSV "to share ill-treatment
with the people of God"). He does not shrink back from their
plight or only stand up for them from afar, but he shares their
plight with them as one of them.

τελειωτής (12:2)

This second hapax legomenon in two verses, and the sixth since
Heb. 11:6, is one of the most interesting of all. It is a simple sub-
stantivizing of the verb τελειοῦν which means "to complete, finish, accomplish, perfect, or fulfill." The author of Hebrews has
used this verb eight times already in the epistle, most recently in
the crucial summary statement of Heb. 11:40.[28] The noun derived
from it forms the second half of a remarkably concise and thought-
provoking double title for Jesus, "the pioneer (ἀρχηγός) and perfecter (τελειωτής) of our faith" (12:2 NRSV).

The noun seems to have been coined for at least two reasons.
First, it echoes a favorite verb of the author and one he uses particularly prominently in Heb. 11:40 to speak in an oblique way of the
perfection of Christians. Christ brings about that perfection by his
actions and is thereby able to bring his people to perfection as they
persevere in running the race with their eyes set on him. The substantive asserts that he is the very essence of that perfection, the
great perfecter who accomplishes perfection for his people
through his enduring of the cross.

A second, more subtle reason has to do with the other element
of the pair, ἀρχηγός. Ἀρχ- and τελ- form the roots of many words,
all having to do with "beginnings" and "endings," and the author
of Hebrews has juxtaposed these roots in several other places in
Hebrews for rhetorical effect.[29] "Taking a clue from the writer's in-

---

27. Cf. James H. Moulton and George Milligan, *The Vocabulary of the Greek New
Testament: Illustrated from the Papyri and Other Non-literary Sources* (1930; reprint,
Grand Rapids: Eerdmans, 1976), s.v. "κακουχέω."

28. See the statistical table above where it is noted that it occurs nine times in
Hebrews, out of a total of only twenty-three times in the whole NT.

29. Lane, *Hebrews*, 2:411, draws attention to 3:14 (τὴν ἀρχὴν . . . μέχρι τέλους)
and 7:3 (ἀρχὴν ἡμερῶν . . . ζωῆς τέλος).

terest in the notions of origin and completion, beginning and end, the predicates ἀρχηγός and τελειωτής suggest that Jesus is the initiator and head of the rank and file in the order of faith, just as he is the one who brought faith to its ultimate expression. . . . The predicates express the conviction that from first to last Jesus exercised faith in an essential sense and brought it to its triumphant completion."[30]

---

30. Ibid.

7

Grammar

In the last chapter, we began our study of the heart and soul of exegesis: the words of the text themselves. We started with what we might call the lifeblood of exegesis, vocabulary analysis. Blood left by itself, however, stagnates and dies; it requires the heart pumping it through the body's system to dispense its life-giving nutrients. The heart of exegesis, the mechanism that gives life, or meaning, to a text, is grammar.

Words do not stand alone in conveying their meaning. They are involved in several different kinds of relationships with other words—relationships that we call phrases, clauses, and sentences. Understanding the connections is crucial for our doing proper exegesis of any text. The study of word relations is the study of the grammar or, more precisely, the syntax of a text.[1] This chapter will be devoted to learning ways to grasp the grammatical relationships in a passage. Mastering them brings a clarity and a certainty to exegesis that preachers and teachers need in order to execute their calling faithfully. The next chapter will be devoted to the distinctive grammatical constructions, the style, of our author, a subject more subtle in some ways but important in its own right. We will look at this subject using categories that differentiate between *oral* stylistic devices and *written* ones, but since both involve grammar, the two are properly looked at together.

---

1. Syntax is technically a subset of grammar. For the most part we will be using the words syntax and grammar as synonyms in our discussion, since the other major subset of grammar, morphology, is not a concern of this volume.

Grammatical Study

No subject strikes fear into the heart of a student, or pastor or teacher for that matter, like being told that they need to understand grammar. Palms begin to sweat, eyes dart nervously from side to side, general internal mayhem is set loose. This ought not to be the case, because grammar is part and parcel of communication, and communication is essential to our functioning well as human beings. In other words, grammar has its rules, but they are merely descriptive of a deeper reality, the very structure of how we communicate, and that deep structure, those patterns of thought that bubble to the surface as language, are part of who we are. We should not fear grammar; in a sense we create and use it every day.

But that is not the grammar that bothers us. The grammar we deplore is that activity thrust upon us in our early teens—the memorization of rules about verb endings, relative pronouns, correlative clauses, and the like. It wasn't that grammar didn't make any sense or that it was particularly difficult. It was more that it seemed so useless and boring. We knew how to speak and how to write well enough. Why did we have to know that "his" was the "third person singular masculine possessive pronoun," when we knew instinctively that the word always referred to somebody other than ourselves, whom we were not addressing, that the person was one person and not a group, that he was male, and that we used the word "his" when we wanted to tell someone that this person owned or possessed something?

Well, we didn't have to know the grammatical name for "his," that's true, at least as long as we were using the language we grew up speaking. When it came time to understand a *foreign* language, however, it was a different story. Then all of a sudden the vocabulary of syntactical relations became very handy indeed. It became important, in fact essential, to know what a subordinate clause was in English so we could recognize a subordinate clause in French, Spanish, or German as the case may be. Even here, the better way to learn the language was to go to a country where it was spoken and to study it while talking with its native speakers. In the case of ancient Greek, though, this is not possible.

So we are stuck, needing to relearn in many cases what we should have learned so well in school that it would be second nature to us now. Nevertheless, as with the use of the vocabulary books we studied above, a little work can take you a long way.

Parts of Speech and Grammatical Categories

We will not spend a long time on the basics of grammar since very competent reviews of basic English grammar for those learning Greek are available.[2] Grammar begins by assigning a name to every possible function a word can have in a sentence. These names are collectively called the *parts of speech,* and consist of eight classifications:

1. noun—the name of a thing
2. pronoun—a word used in place of a noun
3. adjective—a word that qualifies a noun[3]
4. verb—a word that makes a statement, asks a question, or gives a command about some person or thing
5. adverb—a word that qualifies a verb, an adjective, or another adverb
6. preposition—a word joined to a noun or pronoun to show its relation to something else
7. conjunction—a word that joins two sentences, clauses, or words
8. interjection—an expression of feeling, bearing no syntactical relation to other words

There are many different subcategories within these that are helpful to know, but these will suffice to get you started in studying syntax, and it really is necessary to memorize them, if you are not yet familiar with them. An inability to place any word in one of these groups will keep you from doing even basic exegesis; con-

---

2. The very best review in an amazingly brief space is the first fifteen pages of J. W. Wenham, *The Elements of New Testament Greek* (Cambridge: Cambridge University Press, 1965). J. Harold Greenlee, *A Concise Exegetical Grammar of New Testament Greek,* 5th ed. rev. (Grand Rapids: Eerdmans, 1986) also explains English grammar in a round about way by defining the terms it uses, but it is so sparse in its presentation that it is not really a good way to review English grammar.

3. The article, in English classified as either *definite* ("the") or *indefinite* ("a, an"), is actually an adjective but is used so frequently that it sometimes receives its own classification.

versely, speed and facility in handling them will greatly increase your ability.

These parts of speech make up groupings of words (phrases, clauses, and sentences) by which we communicate with one another. Each of these groups has myriad subgroups, too, and defining them at even a basic level is difficult to do without introducing ever more complex categories. Fundamentally, the three groupings represent three different levels of completeness of thought. *Phrases* are the least complete; they may contain a verb, but only an infinitive or participle, types of verbs that are incomplete by themselves. A *clause* contains a finite verb and a subject, but it may be dependent on other clauses and phrases to make up a complete thought. The *sentence* expresses a complete thought and is the culmination of the syntactical chain. Larger groups of words (i.e., groups of sentences) form a *paragraph*, but a paragraph is a literary category more than a syntactical one. We will go no higher than sentences in this chapter.

How do we analyze sentences, then, in order to understand better the meaning of a passage? The first and most important skill to develop for that purpose is diagramming. We will discuss that first. The student should also know how to use the many grammatical tools that are available for investigating the text, and the second part of the chapter will be given over to developing that skill.

Diagramming

In the eighth grade, I had an English teacher who was dean of the junior high (this was before the days of "middle" schools). He was also the varsity track coach. He had one characteristic that carried over between all three vocations: he believed in the usefulness of discipline. Once, during a particularly rowdy study hall, when we had been warned several times to stop the noise, he took everyone in the study hall down to his office, lined us up in the hallway outside one office door, opened it and another door, and paraded each of us through his office for two applications of his "board of education" to our "seats of learning." The study hall was very quiet after that . . . at least for a few days. In track he was known for his brutal practices, but he was also loved for the time he spent with each team member, going over technique, analyzing, explaining, encouraging.

In his English class he believed in discipline, too, and his penchant for it came out in his insistence that we diagram sentences. Diagram, diagram, diagram. When we put the line in the wrong place, failed to put in the article, coordinated clauses when we should have subordinated them or vice versa, we did the assignment over. The problem was—as opposed to his spanking us when we were noisy or making the track team run more sprints at the end of practice—he never explained, as far as I can remember, *why* we had to learn diagramming in the first place. Who cares if a straight line separates the direct object from the verb, while a slanted line indicates a predicate nominative or predicate adjective? What difference will it make in fifteen years, if I put a prepositional phrase in the wrong place, having it modify an adverb when it should be modifying a participle? Do we really have to go again through the torture of eighth grade grammar, long forgotten for most of us or, for some of us with poorer teachers, never learned? The answer, with full sympathy for the unmotivated, is a qualified yes for three reasons.

First, diagramming forces us to think *closely* about the text. This is another way of saying that it makes us slow down to analyze a text and think about what part of speech each word is and how it is related to other words, where its major relationships are to be found, etc. When we are made to think carefully about every word and its function in the sentence, we come across surprising truths that we might have missed if we had not diagrammed the sentence. The very first words of Hebrews illustrate this well.

Hebrews begins with a stunning sentence, full of importance theologically, structurally, and formally. Its first two key words, πολυμερῶς and πολυτρόπως, are obviously a rhetorical device, powerfully getting the attention of the listener by the reduplication of the πολυ- prefix. But attention to this and other features of the words could cause us to miss the fact that both are adverbs modifying the participle λαλήσας, and as adverbs, they give us important information—not primarily about God or the prophets or the fathers (the nouns in the clause), but about the fact that God *spoke* in the past. They do not really tell us much about the ways in which he spoke. In fact, commentators are divided both about whether these words should be taken as telling us something positive or negative about the old way God spoke and about whether they describe the content or the forms of God's message. But they do emphasize the fact that God *spoke* and, by contrast with the next clause, that he has spoken in the lifetime of the author and his readers in a final and singular way in Christ. In preaching and teaching this passage, then, we could stress that this first part of the introductory sentence of Hebrews emphasizes the *activity* of God in Christ, whereas the second part emphasizes the *being* of God in Christ. There is a whole sermon on the act of revelation here, and all from knowing that these two words are adverbs pointing to the participle "spoke"!

Second, the act of diagramming a sentence forces us to think *cohesively* about a text. Not only does it help us to think of the part of speech that a word might be and therefore push us to connect that word with its particular function in the sentence, it causes us to think of the whole structure of a sentence at the same time. Diagramming answers questions such as what was most important for the author (usually the substance of the *main*, that is, most important, clause), what subsidiary things he has to say about this main thought, or what unusual grammatical structures he has used in order to emphasize something in the sentence. In short it helps us to bring order or priority to the thought of the author. Often the ideas to which diagramming leads us will become the major points of our sermon or teaching session, because using them in this way simply links what we say that much more closely with what the Word of God says.[4]

Third, diagramming can help us to think *connectedly* about a text by giving us a visual schematic that tells us immediately where the connections are in the sentence and how things are joined to one another. This is in many ways a restatement of our point about thinking cohesively, but it involves our ability to *visualize,* adding another weapon to our discursive arsenal as we attempt to persuade the passage to unlock its meaning for us. Seeing an entire sentence diagrammed aids us in finding where the au-

---

4. It is important to clarify that I am not advocating ascending into the pulpit and lecturing on gerundive participles! The key to using grammar in preaching is to use it illustratively, having based your main points on it.

thor has broken the "rules" of grammar or where we may have laid more stress on something in a sentence than we should have.

An excellent example again comes from the opening sentence of Hebrews. Should we consider the two halves of the sentence, the part about God speaking in Christ and the part about Christ's being and activity, as equal parts? The second part of the sentence is actually part of a lengthy subordinate clause; doesn't this imply that God's revelation having come in Christ is somehow more important for the author than who that revelatory Son is and what he has done? Diagramming at least makes us aware of the problem, whereas without diagramming and on the basis of the content of the sentence, we might have too easily divided the introduction into equal halves. We must now wonder whether or not the author intended us to give greater weight to the first part of the introduction.

If a last reason is needed for diagramming, there is the high degree of unanimity among those who should know that diagramming is an excellent and important tool for getting at the meaning of any passage of Scripture. Four volumes, for instance, as well as the introductory volume in this series, spend a great deal of time explaining how to diagram a NT sentence and advocating the process enthusiastically.[5]

A Diagram of Hebrews 4:12

The best way to learn how to diagram a sentence is simply to do it. There are several fairly thorough guides to diagramming, and I would suggest that, if you are not already used to it, you have one or more of these resources available for the more esoteric problems one sometimes runs into when diagramming a

---

5. See Scot McKnight, "New Testament Greek Grammatical Analysis," in *Introducing New Testament Interpretation*, ed. Scot McKnight, Guides to New Testament Exegesis (Grand Rapids: Baker, 1989), 89–94; Thomas R. Schreiner, *Interpreting the Pauline Epistles*, Guides to New Testament Exegesis (Grand Rapids: Baker, 1990), 77–96; Scot McKnight, *Interpreting the Synoptic Gospels*, Guides to New Testament Exegesis (Grand Rapids: Baker, 1988), 51–56; J. Ramsey Michaels, *Interpreting the Book of Revelation*, Guides to New Testament Exegesis (Grand Rapids: Baker, 1992), 89–94. Gary M. Burge, *Interpreting the Gospel of John*, Guides to New Testament Exegesis (Grand Rapids: Baker, 1992), does not do any diagramming but mentions very positively both grammatical diagramming and Schreiner's "argument diagramming" (cf. pp. 125 and 107, respectively).

passage.[6] We will diagram a well-known verse of Hebrews, just to illustrate how diagramming can help you make connections that enrich your understanding of a passage.[7]

4:12: Indeed, the word of God is living and active, sharper than any two-edged sword, piercing until it divides soul from spirit, joints from marrow; it is able to judge the thoughts and intentions of the heart (NRSV).

4:12: Ζῶν γὰρ ὁ λόγος τοῦ θεοῦ καὶ ἐνεργὴς καὶ τομώτερος ὑπὲρ πᾶσαν μάχαιραν δίστομον καὶ διϊκνούμενος ἄχρι μερισμοῦ ψυχῆς καὶ πνεύματος, ἁρμῶν τε καὶ μυελῶν, καὶ κριτικὸς ἐνθυμήσεων καὶ ἐννοιῶν καρδίας ·

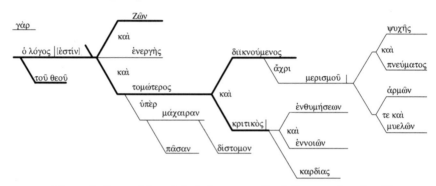

Though it would certainly be a worthwhile exercise, I will not go through a step-by-step analysis of how I came up with every detail of the above diagram. There are some basic rules to follow, however. First, always establish what the subject and predicate of the sentence are. In this verse, the subject is very brief and the predicate extensive, but in other sentences the roles could just as

---

6. For more detail and sophistication in diagramming than is possible here, see Grant R. Osborne, *The Hermeneutical Spiral: A Comprehensive Introduction to Biblical Interpretation* (Downers Grove, Ill.: InterVarsity, 1991), 27–35, and especially Gordon D. Fee, *New Testament Exegesis: A Handbook for Students and Pastors,* rev. ed. (Louisville: Westminster/John Knox, 1993), 65–80. Schreiner, *Pauline Epistles,* 79–94, does a very thorough job with examples from all over the NT. See also L. L. Kantenwein, *Diagrammatical Analysis,* rev. ed. (Winona Lake, Ind.: BMH Books, 1985), and the books mentioned in n. 5.

7. Hebrews 4:12 is actually just the first of two coordinate clauses in one full sentence encompassing all of Heb. 4:12–13. In the interest of brevity, we are only diagramming v. 12, but normally one should diagram complete sentences to get the full impact of what an author is saying.

easily be reversed. Second, establish what the primary noun in the subject is, if it has a primary noun, and what the main verb in the predicate is, if it has a main verb. After establishing these, one generally looks for direct and indirect objects and any other elements playing a key role in the sentence. After these steps, it becomes easier to find a place for the remaining elements in the sentence.

Before we look at some of the implications of this diagram, one last word of caution. There is nothing sacred about this diagram. As we shall see, there may be real cause for disagreement with some of its conclusions. Nevertheless, as we look at some of the diagram's implications, my hope is that you will see some of the benefits gained from going through this exercise.

The first thing to notice is that the main clause points us to the main thought of the author. As we said above, we should always start with the subject of the clause when thinking of what the author wants to emphasize. Sometimes the subject is not the author's focus; it may not even be stated in the sentence (i.e., the subject is sometimes understood and must be supplied from the obvious thought of the sentence or from the preceding sentence), but it is always the place to start. In this case, we have a subject: ὁ λόγος τοῦ θεοῦ. The author wants to say something about "the word of God." Notice that λόγος is the noun of greatest import; the author wishes to say something about a *word,* and a very particular word—the word *of God.* Notice that the article is used in both cases; is this significant?

Next, we look for what the author wants to say about his subject, and we will find this in the predicate of the sentence. The usual step is to focus on the main verb in the predicate to find out what the author is saying about the subject, but in our example the verb is weak. It is the verb "to be," a vague and basic verb in the first place, and it has so little prominence in the sentence that it is left unexpressed by the author. So right away we know that in this sentence the author is not talking about the word of God *doing* anything; he wants to focus on God's word *being* something. But what does he say that it is?

After identifying the subject and the predicate of the sentence, this verse could take one in so many different directions that it is difficult to suggest with any certainty what one should do next. In this case, knowing that the main verb is the verb "to be," one should look for adjectives or nouns or nominal forms (participles, noun clauses, etc.) that directly describe the subject. Immediately we find three: one participle and two adjectives. But look how much more is said about the third adjective![8]

In looking more deeply at this adjective, we find first that the word of God is sharper "than any two-edged sword," but the author foregoes any discussion about swords and goes on to describe how sharp it is. This is an important point for preaching and teaching: if the author did not dwell on swords at this point, why should we? Many sermons have been preached that have made much of the double-edged sword mentioned here, and there is nothing wrong with pointing out some of the parallel references to this sword in Scripture (cf., e.g., Rev. 1:16). But the lead of our author, as we can see from our diagram, is to go on to describe the word's sharpness in terms of two things: its piercing/dividing nature and its discerning nature. Here are two concepts (using three key words) that cry out for word study.

These are perhaps the most important points from our diagram for the exegesis of the passage, but there are many lesser points. For instance, the diagram helps us to see the two things we want to say about the sword: that no sword is sharper and that it is double-edged. We note that soul/spirit and joints/marrow form two parallel pairs, and we may think to look into what is going on in terms of literary convention to cause that odd occurrence. In addition, one might note that the "thoughts" and "intentions" are both connected with the heart, and one might look for a Hebraic kind of synonymous parallelism or perhaps a conceptual distinction between these two words. The relationship between κριτικός and καρδία is also worth pursuing: Does this combination occur anywhere else in Hebrews or elsewhere in the NT? What does it signify for the way God intends to judge us?

Questions about the precise meaning of the text are also raised by the diagram. In fact, some of the best lessons learned from diagramming come from having to figure out what is going on in a

---

8. In fact, one could argue that the participle ζῶν may rate a little more attention than the other two because the author has given it the prime place in the sentence by putting it first. Simple observation rather than diagramming makes this clear, however, but this conclusion must be balanced with what the diagramming does show about the importance of the other two adjectives for the sharp-sword metaphor.

passage well enough to diagram it. This passage, though fairly straightforward, is not without its difficulties. For instance, should the adjective κριτικός be subordinate to τομώτερος as it is in the diagram (qualifying the sharpness of the sword), or should it be promoted to an equal place with ζῶν, ἐνεργής, and τομώτερος (making it a fourth adjective directly describing the word of God)?

You may be saying to yourself, "I noticed many of the insights you just outlined when I last preached through Hebrews, and I never diagram sentences. Do I really need to learn this?" It's a fair question. But I would ask a question in return: Do you have a structure for gaining your insights, one that will yield results *each* time you approach a passage, or do you discover by trial and error, hit or miss? If you do have a structure, how much time does it take you to use it, and how comprehensive is it?

I admit that none of these insights is absolutely dependent on diagramming this clause. You could simply read the text very closely with a great deal of knowledge in grammar, looking for the kinds of connections we have found here, and you would quite likely find the majority of the connections and ideas we have found. But the process of diagramming helps train us to look for the right connections and provides a clear and relatively certain way of discovering what the text is really trying to say. The comprehensive nature of diagramming—requiring us to give *every* word its proper place in the diagram—helps to make sure that we don't miss something that could turn out to be just the point needing to be preached to the congregation that day. It does take time to master this technique, but as with anything worth doing, the rewards that it yields are worth the time. And as with any skill, the more you do it, the easier, quicker, and more interesting it becomes.

Using Greek Grammars

The size, depth, technical vocabulary, and academic look of Greek grammars sometimes puts off pastors and teachers who have no inclination to become professors of NT at Bigtime U. But to think of these valuable resources in this way is to give up on books that can be a great source of life and joy to your ministry. Even scholars don't regard them as something to be mastered, but rather as reference tools to be used in small bits to look up specific things. I learned this the hard way.

During the period when I was contemplating doing a Ph.D., I had occasion to get to know one of the great NT scholars of this century, Bishop Stephen Neill. He asked me what I was doing to keep up the Greek skills I had learned in graduate school (I was at that time teaching high school). Wanting to impress him, I told him I was working in Herbert Weir Smyth's *Greek Grammar*, a famous and standard advanced grammar for classical Greek.[9] It was, I am ashamed to say, a half truth at best. I was really using it only occasionally, certainly much more rarely than I led him to believe.

I will never forget the next words out of his mouth: "You foolish boy! Why waste your time on a massive tome like that? Unless your calling is something other than what you've told me (I had told him of my desire to teach the Scriptures to lay people), master the Scriptures *using* books like Smyth, but don't spend time mastering Smyth. He put all this stuff down in his book so that we might use it in interpreting texts, not reproduce grammar for its own sake. I, at least, have always only used it when I needed to understand a text."

I was properly chastened. I was using the book simply and easily as a reference tool with only my seminary knowledge of Greek to guide me, but thinking that the great scholars used grammars a different way, I lied in order to try to impress him, only to find out that he used it exactly as I did! That exchange was an important lesson for me in many ways, but the point for our purposes is clear: there is no other way to use these grammars than as reference tools for looking up grammatical points of interest, and anyone who has had even a year of Greek can use them to great advantage.

Now, how does one use them? First, you need to become familiar with some terminology. It is generally recognized that there are three levels of Greek grammar books: beginning, intermediate, and advanced. To lay out the distinctions in this way, however, is a little misleading. It implies that one begins the study of Greek with a beginning grammar (true), and then proceeds over an unspecified

9. Revised by Gordon M. Messing (Cambridge, Mass.: Harvard University Press, 1984).

number of years to use intermediate grammars (not true) until finally achieving some height of expertise where one can use the advanced grammar (certainly not true). One does normally begin with a teacher and a beginning grammar, but the categories of "intermediate" and "advanced" grammars are artificial and seem to be only terms of convenience, differentiating grammars that are less comprehensive and less lengthy (intermediate grammars) from ones that are more comprehensive and more lengthy (advanced grammars).

Which of these latter two types you should use depends on what you want to do with a text. Do you need a simple answer to a general question about some form? (Ah, yes, this commentator calls this construction a genitive absolute. What again is a genitive absolute?) Look it up in an intermediate grammar. There will often be a brief definition of the form and several examples. Are you interested in a usage in a particular passage that seems strange to you? (Hmm. Here I am reading Heb. 6:1, and I wonder why μετάνοια [repentance] appears in the genitive case? It looks like it is describing θεμέλιος [foundation], but is it somehow the source of the foundation? What does the author mean here?) Look it up in an advanced grammar. You may well find a discussion of the verse and of your particular problem.[10]

Using reference grammars has always been relatively easy and is even easier now that several books have been put together to help you know where to look for what you want. All the grammatical works we will mention below have both a subject and a Scripture index, so you can use them the way you would any index. But looking through every one of these grammars in hopes of finding a discussion of your particular passage can be time-consuming. Fortunately, two books have been compiled to help you bypass this process, and they can quickly tell you which grammars discuss your passage.

Robert Hanna. *A Grammatical Aid to the Greek New Testament.* Grand Rapids: Baker, 1983.

Timothy Owings. *A Cumulative Index to New Testament Greek Grammars.* Grand Rapids: Baker, 1983.

---

10. E.g., A. T. Robertson, *A Grammar of the Greek New Testament in the Light of Historical Research,* 4th ed. (Nashville: Broadman, 1934), 498, lists the phrase under the category "genitive of apposition."

Both of these works are arranged in canonical order; you simply look up the verse you are studying to find out which grammars refer to it. There are several minor differences between the two works, but the major difference is in content. Owings's book indexes more grammars and is comprehensive. As he puts it: "It [the *Index*] exhaustively includes the indices of eight major advanced and intermediate grammars used in colleges and seminaries today. It is in no way selective."[11] But it is simply a list of references to places in the grammars where a verse is mentioned, with no indication of how extensive the discussion in the grammar is. It could be anything from a passing reference to a full discussion, and one has no idea from looking at Owings's citation which it will be.

Hanna, on the other hand, is much more selective and comments on each reference, giving some indication of the extent of the discussion in the grammar. His index is in no way exhaustive. In fact he has only included what he believes to be the substantive treatments of NT texts in the grammars, so one is trusting the accuracy of Hanna's judgment. Time and necessity may demand that we sometimes make that choice, but it is something to keep in mind when using this book.

There is another problem with Hanna's work, though, besides its selectiveness. In his comments on the grammatical explanations of the various authors he has indexed, it is sometimes difficult to tell the difference between his comments and those of the authors of the grammars. He admits to rewording some of their comments, but he does have a mechanism for marking his own comments "when a contradiction or question arises."[12] Nevertheless, it is essential to look up the discussion in the grammar itself and not just depend on Hanna's gloss to prove a point. Hanna's intention of course is to move the reader to the grammars he has indexed anyway, so his method actually supports his purpose nicely.

---

11. Owings, *Index*, 9. Owings says *eight* grammars because he is counting the Moulton-Howard-Turner grammar as one work. He actually indexes eleven grammatical works, Hanna eight.

12. Hanna, *Grammatical Aid*, 7.

Useful Grammatical Works

There are too many useful grammatical works to comment extensively on all of them, so I will simply list some of the best ones, with brief comments on each. I have used the traditional categories of "intermediate" and "advanced" to refer to grammars that attempt to cover all aspects of syntax, but keep in mind the difference between intermediate and advanced grammars discussed above. The third category, Specialized Works, lists books that tackle one or more aspects of grammar either so comprehensively or with such a specialized focus on the use of NT examples that they are of value to pastors.[13]

Intermediate Grammars

F. Blass and A. Debrunner. *A Greek Grammar of the New Testament and Other Early Christian Literature.* Trans. and rev. by Robert W. Funk. Chicago: University of Chicago Press, 1961. The standard companion volume to the Bauer-Arndt-Gingrich-Danker lexicon. Always worth consulting. Its layout is somewhat cut and dried, and sometimes it is hard to locate the discussion of the reference you are investigating, but when you do find it, it often is very insightful. **O H**

James A. Brooks and Carlton L. Winbery. *Syntax of New Testament Greek.* Lanham, Md.: University Press of America, 1979. A very helpful grammar because of its many good examples. It is also laid out in a simple, direct format that makes the discussion of grammatical categories easy to find. Its brevity is its major drawback, but it is a useful quick-reference grammar. **O**

H. E. Dana and Julius R. Mantey. *A Manual Grammar of the Greek New Testament.* New York: Macmillan, 1927. Old and badly indexed, but it has a useful summary of each of the standard grammatical categories. If you get used to it, it can be a helpful quick-reference tool. **O**

Stanley E. Porter. *Idioms of the Greek New Testament.* Sheffield: JSOT Press, 1992. This work signals a real advance in intermediate grammar. It has not been around long enough to establish itself as a standard, but its logical classifications and its thoughtful,

---

13. An **O** at the end of an entry indicates that the book is indexed in Owings's *Index*; an **H** indicates that the book is indexed in Hanna's *Grammatical Aid.*

readable handling of difficult linguistic concepts may well make it the standard in years to come.

A. T. Robertson and W. Hersey Davis. *A New Short Grammar of the Greek Testament*. 10th ed. N.p.: Harper & Bros., 1958; reprint, Grand Rapids: Baker, 1977. As old as Dana and Mantey and not as helpful; listed because, though dated, it can still be of some use. **O**

Maximilian Zerwick. *Biblical Greek: Illustrated by Examples*. Trans. by Joseph Smith. Scripta Pontificii Instituti Biblici 114. Rome: Pontifical Biblical Institute, 1963. Less complete than other grammars, but good in the areas it discusses. Especially helpful when used in tandem with Zerwick's *Grammatical Analysis of the Greek New Testament*. Trans. and rev. by Mary Grosvenor. Unabridged, 4th rev. ed. Rome: Pontifical Biblical Institute, 1993. **O**

Advanced Grammars

James Hope Moulton. *A Grammar of New Testament Greek*. 3d ed. Vol. 1, *Prolegomena*. Edinburgh: T. & T. Clark, 1908. An extended discussion of general issues having to do with the writing of grammars. Fascinating if you have the opportunity to read it, but not very useful for actual exegesis of specific passages. **O H**

James Hope Moulton and Wilbert Francis Howard. *A Grammar of New Testament Greek*. Vol. 2, *Accidence and Word-Formation*. Edinburgh: T. & T. Clark, 1929. A specialized volume on morphology, or word formation. **O H**

James Hope Moulton. *A Grammar of New Testament Greek*. Vol. 3, *Syntax*, by Nigel Turner. Edinburgh: T. & T. Clark, 1963. This is the primary reference for the student interested in the syntactical aspects of the NT. It is extremely thorough, and with Blass-Debrunner-Funk and Robertson it serves as the most often consulted grammar in scholarly NT circles. **O H**

James Hope Moulton. *A Grammar of New Testament Greek*. Vol. 4, *Style*, by Nigel Turner. Edinburgh: T. & T. Clark, 1976. A helpful, though somewhat idiosyncratic volume, viewing NT Greek as having been "inoculated with Semitic influence and style" (p. 2). It is laid out according to the various authors of the NT and describes the distinctive elements of their individual styles. **O**

A. T. Robertson. *A Grammar of the Greek New Testament in the Light of Historical Research*. 4th ed. Nashville: Broadman, 1934. This huge book is the magnum opus of this great Baptist scholar. Sometimes it is extremely helpful; sometimes it just gives lists of references, but even the lists are often worthwhile. **O H**

Specialized Works

Ernest de Witt Burton. *Syntax of the Moods and Tenses in New Testament Greek.* 3d ed. Chicago: University of Chicago Press, 1900; reprint, Grand Rapids: Kregel, n.d. A standard work for many years, but some of its views are now being questioned by recent works like Fanning and Porter. It still offers many exegetical insights. **H**

Buist Fanning. *Verbal Aspect in New Testament Greek.* Oxford: Oxford University Press, 1990. A technical work dealing with the problem of what Greek tenses mean.

C. F. D. Moule. *An Idiom Book of New Testament Greek.* 2d ed. Cambridge: Cambridge University Press, 1959. Begun as a full-scale syntax, this long-standing work discusses in an unsystematic way some of the most interesting syntactical problems of NT Greek. It is a very clear, helpful book, if it discusses the problem you are addressing. **O H**

Stanley E. Porter. *Verbal Aspect in the Greek of the New Testament: With Reference to Tense and Mood.* Studies in Biblical Greek 1. Bern: Peter Lang, 1989. An extremely technical work, primarily for scholars of NT Greek. Like Fanning's book, it is a Ph.D. dissertation and assumes a very high level of competence in Greek. Nevertheless, it is an important corrective to the often simplistic view some have of the meaning of, for example, the aorist or perfect tense, and discussions of individual passages can still be helpful to the nonspecialist.

Nigel Turner. *Grammatical Insights into the New Testament.* Edinburgh: T. & T. Clark, 1965. The introduction says this book is primarily intended for those with no knowledge of NT Greek, but don't be fooled into thinking it is therefore simplistic. It is written in an accessible style, and the discussions are lively, often demonstrating how a knowledge of Greek grammar can solve problems of interpretation in the NT. **H**

I should also mention two works that are useful for identifying grammatical forms in the NT, though I do so with some reluctance. We should constantly work at being able to parse Greek

words in the NT without resorting to "crutches" like these, but it
is true that most of us need these sorts of books from time to time.

Barbara and Timothy Friberg, eds. *Analytical Greek New Testament:
Greek Text Analysis.* Grand Rapids: Baker, 1981.
Wesley J. Perschbacher, ed. *The New Analytical Greek Lexicon.* Pea-
body, Mass.: Hendrickson, 1990.

Having looked at how to tackle grammar through diagramming and the use of intermediate and advanced grammars—two
processes useful for the study of any NT text—let's look now at the
distinctive style of Hebrews so we will recognize the author's
unique grammatical choices as we read his book.

8

Style

S*tyle* refers to the distinctive elements in the vocabulary and grammatical constructions of an author. An author with a "flowing" style, for instance, may use more transitional words than other authors to move from thought to thought (as long as he uses them well and doesn't clutter up his sentences with them). An author with a "clipped" style may write everything in simple sentences with little use of adjectives, adverbs, prepositional phrases, and the like—a subject, a verb, an object, and on to the next sentence. An author with a "choppy" style may fluctuate between the two previously mentioned styles with no apparent logic. None of these styles are necessarily right or wrong; they are simply different ways authors use legitimate grammatical forms to get across their ideas.[1]

When we discussed the literary genre of Hebrews (chap. 3), we mentioned that the Greek of Hebrews is smoother and more polished than that of most NT books. While none of the books of the NT can properly be said to exemplify the elevated style of Attic Greek, some of them approach this classical standard (e.g., Acts, 1 Peter), and Hebrews is one. We noted, too, that this epistle exhibits a rhetorical flavor that makes it distinctive although not unique among the epistles of the NT. In chapter 3 we discussed some of the larger, genre-related stylistic elements that are apparent in Hebrews (diatribe, rhythm,

---

1. For an interesting discussion of the difference between grammar and style, see Nigel Turner, *Style,* vol. 4 of *A Grammar of New Testament Greek,* by J. H. Moulton (Edinburgh: T. & T. Clark, 1976), 1–2.

parallelism, etc.) to show that its author was well-versed in rhetoric. Now we will look at some of the smaller stylistic elements that also demonstrate the book's heavy dependence on first-century rhetorical devices and hence its quasi-classical nature.[2]

Before going to the specifics, the accurate and elegant summary of James Moffatt (and of W. H. Simcox before him) on the style of Hebrews, merits quotation and will serve as our guide as we look at this graceful book.

> To sum up. He has a sense of literary nicety, which enters into his earnest religious argument without rendering it artificial or over-elaborate. He has an art of words, which is more than an unconscious sense of rhythm. He has the style of a trained speaker; it is style, yet style at the command of a devout genius. "Of Hellenistic writers he is the freest from the monotony that is the chief fault of Hellenistic compared with literary Greek; his words do not follow each other in a mechanically necessary order, but are arranged so as to emphasize their relative importance, and to make the sentences effective as well as intelligible. One may say that he deals with the biblical language (understanding by this the Hellenistic dialect founded on the LXX, not merely his actual quotations from it) . . . as a preacher, whose first duty is to be faithful, but his second to be eloquent" (W. H. Simcox, *The Writers of the NT*, p. 43).[3]

Specific Rhetorical Elements in Hebrews

Discussion of the style of Hebrews properly begins with a discussion of rhetoric, the art of using language to impress or per-

---

2. Most of the stylistic elements we will discuss here were used in both oral and written situations. If this raises questions for the reader concerning the differences between written and oral flourishes, see the discussion above on the futility of finding the difference (chap. 3). Nevertheless, many of my observations on these rhetorical flourishes are as valid for *written* rhetoric as for *spoken*. This becomes even more apparent when one *reads* the passages, because in reading, the supposed "oral" stylistic elements still accomplish their purposes. If they work for a reader, then, how does one know they were originally fashioned for a listener? If we could determine that some were intended for oral performance, how could we distinguish them from devices created by a writer for readers? And of course, the last question is especially important for us as readers in the twentieth century: why is the distinction important? There are no simple answers to these questions, but I address some of these issues in this chapter.

3. James Moffatt, *A Critical and Exegetical Commentary on the Epistle to the Hebrews*, International Critical Commentary (Edinburgh: T. & T. Clark, 1924), lxiv.

suade hearers for or against a course of action. We will not go into great depth here on this vast subject, supremely important for understanding the high arts of argument and persuasion in the first century.[4] Nevertheless, the subject is so essential to understanding Hebrews that a brief introduction is in order.

As we said, the art of rhetoric in the ancient world was largely a matter of employing certain conventions and forms in order to persuade the hearer of one's argument. But as David Aune has pointed out, to classify these forms as if speakers simply sat down and plugged their ideas into a rigid pattern "is a little too neat."[5] Earlier, we looked at the rhythms of Hebrews, evidence that the author was consciously placing himself within the rhetorical tradition. Several other constructions illustrate that Hebrews can only be understood as a Greco-Roman sermon. Some of these constructions are merely interesting sidelights that fill in something of the background to Hebrews but that are not really crucial exegetical pointers, while others may be essential for understanding the passage in which they occur. Nevertheless, whether the construction is of major or minor importance, knowledge of the various distinctive stylistic elements of Hebrews will increase our ease in interpreting Hebrews.[6]

Alliteration

Alliteration, the repetition of initial consonants in words following one another in close proximity in a sentence, is a well-known de-

---

4. For a wonderfully readable and thorough treatment of the subject, especially as it relates to the NT, see George A. Kennedy, *New Testament Interpretation through Rhetorical Criticism* (Chapel Hill, N.C.: University of North Carolina Press, 1984). The portions of David E. Aune, *The New Testament in Its Literary Environment*, Library of Early Christianity 8 (Philadelphia: Westminster, 1987), devoted to the epistolary form (see esp. pp. 198–204, 212–14) are a very good introduction to the study of ancient rhetoric and its impact on the authors of the NT epistles.

5. Aune, *Environment*, 199. Cf. also William L. Lane, *Hebrews*, Word Biblical Commentary (Dallas: Word, 1991), 1:lxxix: "Hebrews cannot be forced into the mold of a classical speech."

6. Almost every one of the categories below could be illustrated copiously from the text of Hebrews, but one example of each should suffice for our purposes. Relatively complete lists of the rhetorical elements in Hebrews, at least most of the categories, are available in Harold W. Attridge, *The Epistle to the Hebrews*, Hermeneia (Philadelphia: Fortress, 1989), 20–21. See also Aune, *Environment*, 212–14; Turner, *Style*, 106–13; Lane, *Hebrews*, 1:lxix–lxxxiv; Moffatt, *Hebrews*, lvi–lxiv.

vice of preachers today, but many are not aware of how ancient this practice is and how well established it was at the time of the NT. In the modern world, alliteration is often denigrated, and sometimes rightly so, because the words chosen for alliterative effect are too often chosen simply because they begin with the right letter. Preachers sometimes forget that the alliterative words are supposed to bear some relation to the content of the text or the point being made! But to disregard alliteration altogether is to throw out the baby with the bath water. If employed with restraint and wisdom, it can be a useful means of making an idea memorable. Certainly, this device is not as needed in a world where people can read freely and more often than they could in the ancient world, where books were scarce. Since they couldn't just go look up something or listen to a tape, they needed "hooks" like alliteration to help them remember things. But as we today become more pictorially oriented in our approach to knowledge, we are losing our ability to listen well to talks and retain the content of what was said. Hence, the preacher's careful, thoughtful use of alliteration can be as helpful for today's listeners as it was for the ancients.

In many places, the author of Hebrews shows how effective alliteration can be as a communication tool. He often seems to order words, select vocabulary, and choose sentence constructions on the basis of their alliterative effect. The famous opening sentence of Hebrews is a clear example. Three of the first four words (πο-λυμερῶς, πολυτρόπως, and πάλαι) and five of the seven key words in the first clause (the same three plus πατράσιν and προ-φήταις) begin with π. It is dangerous to guess why an author or speaker chooses the words he does, but it seems likely that, with all the alternative forms of expression available to the author, all three of those first words were chosen for their alliterative effect. In addition, though the word of God being spoken through prophets is certainly a biblical idea, our author does not emphasize the prophetic role elsewhere in the letter[7] and might have been more likely to speak of the law or angels as the messengers of the divine word, but for the fact that προφήτης begins with π. Whatever his motives, the alliterative effect is there and indisputable.

---

7. Προφήτης occurs only one other time in Hebrews, in a list (Heb. 11:32), and προφητεύειν and προφητεία do not occur at all.

Anaphora

Anaphora is "repetition of a word or words at the beginning of two or more successive phrases, verses, clauses, or sentences."[8] In Hebrews 11 the author employs this well-known rhetorical device to draw attention to faith, the chapter's subject. The carefully constructed list of OT men and women of faith is reinforced in its effect by the constant repetition of the word πίστει ("by faith") at the beginning of each sentence. There is no missing the focus of the chapter—the straightforward and elegant opening and closing periods are powerful enough—but with the addition of no less than eighteen occurrences of πίστει opening many of the sentences of the chapter, the effect is even more impressive.[9]

Antithesis

Antithesis, the juxtaposition of contrasting elements, is a common device of philosophical argument and even forms a key element in the structure of Hebrews at one point.[10] The contrasts the author draws between flesh and spirit, earth and heaven, many priests and one priest, old covenant and new, and external and internal realities form the heart of his christological argument in chapters 7–10. Without antithesis, Hebrews would not be Hebrews. This technique accents the contrast by drawing out the differences between the items. For example, the law is portrayed as good, but Christ, the fulfillment of the law, is presented as something better—just as the reality is better than the shadow.

The author signals his contrasts by a variety of means: contrastive copulas, contrastive vocabulary, or a combination of the two. Thus, in Heb. 7:18–19 and again in 7:20–21 a simple μέν . . . δέ construction suffices. In 7:28 the language of weakness is contrasted with the language of perfection, and in 10:11–12 both methods are used: καθ᾽ ἡμέραν and πολλάκις being opposed to μίαν, and the μέν . . . δέ construction also emphasizing the anti-

---

8. *Random House Webster's College Dictionary* (New York: Random House, 1991), s.v. "anaphora."

9. Ceslas Spicq, *L'Épître aux Hébreux*, 2 vols., Études bibliques (Paris: Gabalda, 1952–53), 1:362, calls this "le plus bel exemple d'*anaphore* de toute la Bible et peu-têtre de la littérature profane" (the most elegant example of anaphora in the whole Bible, and perhaps secular literature as well).

10. See chapter 4 on the structure of Hebrews, and Attridge, *Hebrews*, 216.

thesis between the single sacrifice of Christ and the repeated sacrifices of the priests. All these devices create in the passage a
climate of illustration and proof that lends a strong note of per-
suasiveness to his arguments.

Assonance

Assonance is similar to alliteration in that it involves the repetition of letters in a string of words. The difference is that assonance
is word-internal: similar sounding vowels are not at the beginning
of words, but in the middle or at the end of them. Thus, at a crucial
point of warning in chapter 10, the author helps make his point by
beginning verse 26 with the repetition of a forbidding long *o*
sound (ἑκουσίως γὰρ ἁμαρτανόντων ἡμῶν) and then continues
by linking several words with a long *a* sound (τῆς ἀληθείας . . .
ἀπολείπεται). In the next verse (v. 27) he uses a short *o* sound followed by *s* (πυρὸς ζῆλος ἐσθίειν μέλλοντος). The latter particularly heightens the threatening sound of judgment that the author
wants to project, similar to our lengthening the *s* on the end of a
word to make a hissing sound when we want to make someone
feel uncomfortable.

Asyndeton

Asyndeton is stringing together successive parallel clauses
without using any conjunctions. The power and style of this device is obvious. Conjunctions can weigh down and emasculate the
impact of communication; nouns and verbs particularly, but even
adjectives and adverbs, convey the point much more forcefully. In
Heb. 11:33–34 the piling up of clauses describing the mighty acts
of faith of Gideon, Barak, Samson, Jephthah, David, Samuel, and
the prophets (and again of the "others" in 11:36–37) shows the rhetorical usefulness of this form. Stringing these impressive acts of
courage together with an "and" or two and making them into two
or three sentences, which could easily have been done, would
have robbed them of their cumulative power. One can almost see
the jaws drop in the congregation as they listen to this recounting
of the faith of these OT saints, building toward the dramatic conclusion that they were willing to die for only a promise of what is
now a reality.

Brachylogy

Brachylogy substitutes a simple shorthand expression or ellipsis for a longer one. It creates a shorthand image, verbally condensing and focusing it for the listener. In Heb. 12:24, where we would expect καὶ αἵματι ῥαντισμοῦ κρεῖττον λαλοῦντι παρὰ τὸ αἷμα τοῦ Ἄβελ ("and to the sprinkled blood that speaks a better word than *the blood* of Abel," so the NRSV, for instance), the clause instead ends παρὰ τὸν Ἄβελ ("than *Abel*"). The effect is to bring the audience up short by not fulfilling their expectations as they listen; they have completed the sentence in their minds, and when it is not finished in accord with their expectations, they are snapped back to attention.

Chiasm

Chiasm is a favorite device of many NT authors, and it is no less prominent in Hebrews. Chiasm reverses the order of parallel elements in successive clauses in order to draw attention to their importance. There are many examples of it in individual verses where contrasts are presented in chiastic arrangement to draw out the key elements for the reader/hearer.

An excellent but complicated illustration of this is found in Heb. 7:23–24. To facilitate analysis, scholars often use letters to designate the elements of a chiastic construction (e.g., *a* = one word; *a'* = the same or similar word to *a*, in another clause; *b* = a different word, in the same clause as *a*; *b'* = a word similar to *b*, in the same clause as *a'*; etc.). In Heb. 7:23–24, the author is contrasting the permanence of Christ's priesthood with the transience of the levitical priesthood. In the first clause, three key words appear in this order: *(a)* ἱερεῖς, *(b)* θανάτῳ, and *(c)* παραμένειν. In the next clause, their counterparts appear in the reverse order: *(c')* μένειν, *(b')* εἰς τὸν αἰῶνα, and *(a')* ἱερωσύνην. Thus, the formula looks like this: *abcc'b'a'*.

In Hebrews, chiasm is also found at higher structural levels. Many believe, I think rightly, that the order of words in Heb. 2:17 describing Jesus as a "merciful and faithful high priest" (ἐλεήμων . . . καὶ πιστὸς ἀρχιερεύς) is a programmatic device signaling, in chiastic order, the core themes of the next sections of Hebrews. Hebrews 3:1–4:15 declares Christ's faithfulness to be greater than that of Moses, moves to an exhortation urging his listeners to be faithful in their "testing in the wilderness," and ends with a strong statement of Christ's faithfulness under temptation (πεπειρα-σμένον δὲ κατὰ πάντα καθ᾽ ὁμοιότητα χωρὶς ἁμαρτίας, 4:15). The same verse is a transition into an explanation of the merciful nature of the perfect High Priest, and the discussion from there until 5:10 is dominated by this theme. So the programmatic statement and its development form an *abb'a'* pattern, the powerful, though subtle, chiasm working to communicate much.

Ellipsis

The rhetorical device we call *ellipsis* can be difficult to distinguish accurately from brachylogy, mentioned above. Both techniques omit words that the reader or hearer would expect, thus surprising them and drawing their attention even more closely to what is being communicated. The two forms are probably best distinguished by simple quantity: Brachylogy drops out individual words and combines with other figures of speech, such as synecdoche or metonymy, to communicate with simple, direct power. Ellipsis, on the other hand, omits larger phrases or whole clauses that must be mentally supplied by the reader. Its effect is cumulative and more subtle, but no less powerful in its rhetorical handiwork.

A striking example of ellipsis and the forceful result it can have is found at Heb. 12:25. Here the author is giving one of his stern warnings, building his argument on the earthly/heavenly contrast he enjoys so much. He has used condensation in the first clause of the sentence to give strength to his warning ("Look! Don't reject the Speaking One!"), and now in the third clause, he draws on the power of ellipsis to emphasize the words ἡμεῖς, ἀπ᾽ οὐρανῶν, and ἀποστρεφόμενοι. He avoids repeating that we shall not escape (ἐκφεύγειν) and that the Speaking One is warning us (χρηματίζοντα), in order to stress that (1) he includes himself with his readers ("we," not "you"), (2) the sin is rejecting God's warning, and (3) rejecting is perilous because this warning comes from heaven and is not merely part of the earthly law.

Hendiadys

Whereas most of the forms we have been discussing *condense* language for rhetorical effect, hendiadys is *expansive*. It uses two or more terms to express a single notion, usually by balancing nouns or participles alongside one another. Attention is thus drawn to the description in a fresh, arresting way.

At Heb. 5:2, the author states that because of his own weakness, the high priest is able to deal gently τοῖς ἀγνοοῦσιν καὶ πλανωμένοις ("with those who ignorantly go astray").[11] It is important to read this as an example of hendiadys, because it links the description to the OT prescriptions concerning those who sin without realizing it (e.g., Lev. 4:2; 5:17–18; Num. 15:22–31) and avoids misunderstanding the statement as referring to two classes of people (i.e., the ignorant and the wandering). If two different groups were in view, the verse would undercut the strong warnings against willful sin that the author gives just a few verses later (cf. Heb. 6:4–6); the ignorant would be excused, but so would the wayward, and he does not seem to want to say that. The hendiadys causes the expression to be understood as referring to one class of people: those who have sinned through ignorance.

Hyperbaton

Hyperbaton is a little-used device, but one that clearly identifies the author as rhetorically trained. It is the separation of words naturally belonging together, a form that only works because Greek, a highly inflected language, does not depend on word order to communicate basic meaning (as English generally does). Thus, Greek authors can change word order to suit their purposes. Our author uses hyperbaton by quoting OT passages and then reusing them in ways that draw special attention to the interpretations he gives them. The listener hears the OT passage coming again and expects to hear the rest, but gets something else instead, and so is alerted to it.

Heb. 2:9 is a clear example of this. There the author picks up two of the lines from Psalm 8, which he has quoted in vv. 6–8:

ἠλάττωσας αὐτὸν βραχύ τι παρ᾽ ἀγγέλους,
δόξῃ καὶ τιμῇ ἐστεφάνωσας αὐτόν,

But by separating the two lines with the words βλέπομεν Ἰησοῦν διὰ τὸ πάθημα τοῦ θανάτου, he concentrates attention

---

11. So Attridge, *Hebrews*, 144.

both on the name of Jesus and on the majesty of his suffering and death. It is through suffering and death that Jesus is crowned with glory and honor, not by wielding power, as the listener might have expected in hearing the portion of the psalm quoted. And it is Jesus, not anyone else, who is the one spoken of in the psalm. Both these points are made more forcefully in Greek than they can be in English, through the simple use of hyperbaton.

Isocolon

Balance is a cherished quality in Greek rhetoric, particularly in poetry, and Hebrews has no lack of it. Isocolon is the technical term for equally balanced parallel clauses, similar to balanced lines in poetry. Such parallelism and balance provides symmetry, and if done well and not just for show (which would draw too much attention to the form), it can provide depth and richness to a speech or a writing and impress its content upon the hearer.

The introduction to Hebrews contains a prime example of isocolon. The three participial phrases of 1:3, which work out better when translated as clauses in English, are controlled by the relative pronoun ὅς and nicely balanced in structure and content.[12] The first clause describes the essence of Jesus as a "reflection of God's glory and the imprint of his being," the second that he sustains all things by the word of his power, and the third that he made cleansing for sins. Each clause contains a participle (ὤν, φέρων, ποιησάμενος), an object of the participle (ἀπαύγασμα . . . χαρακτήρ, πάντα, καθαρισμόν), and an accompanying description (τῆς δόξης . . . τῆς ὑποστάσεως αὐτοῦ, τῷ ῥήματι τῆς δυνάμεως αὐτοῦ, τῶν ἁμαρτιῶν), and while each clause has some unique feature that makes the formal balance between the three clauses imperfect,[13] the form nevertheless holds well enough.

---

12. A fourth parallel participial phrase in 1:4 appears, for matters of content and transition, *after* the main verb.

13. For instance, the first clause contains two objects with accompanying genitives, the second an instrumental dative rather than a genitive as the other two, and the third differs from the other two clauses by putting the participle last rather than first.

Litotes

Litotes, or the affirming of something by negating its contrary, often uses the double negative, a grammatical expression far more common and accepted in Greek grammar than in English.[14] Litotes is an emphatic kind of double negative, however, that couples the negative form of a verb (or a verb that is inherently negative in meaning) with a negative particle (οὐ or μή) to express a particular truth more forcefully.

In Heb. 4:14–16, the author is attempting a double task. He exhorts his readers to enter the rest by holding fast the confession of Jesus (4:14) and drawing near to the throne of grace (4:16), and he reintroduces the sinless High Priest who has gone into heaven, looking back to the earlier introduction of him (2:17–3:1) and forward to a further explanation of his priesthood (5:1ff.). It is one of those transition passages in the epistle that calls for special handling. In 4:15, just where he states who Jesus is and how his temptation experiences enable him to relate to our weaknesses, the author uses litotes to express this ability elegantly: οὐ γὰρ ἔχομεν ἀρχιερέα μὴ δυνάμενον συμπαθῆσαι ταῖς ἀσθενείαις ἡμῶν. The litotes has the added effect of comparing the "real" Jesus to the figure who soared through the heavens, mentioned in the prior verse. This figure is of course the same Jesus, but our author wants to correct a possible misconception before it has time to take root: though Jesus is the Son of God, the High Priest who has passed through the heavens, he is nevertheless able to sympathize with us. So the "real" Jesus is neither exclusively the heavenly High Priest, high above us, nor exclusively the earthly high priest, just like us. He is both, and the litotes helps emphasize that fact.

Paranomasia

Paranomasia, or wordplay, is a favorite activity of biblical writers, OT and NT alike, though it is particularly common in the

---

14. Cf. Henry W. Fowler, *A Dictionary of Modern English Usage,* 2d ed., rev. Ernest Gowers (New York and Oxford: Oxford University Press, 1965), 384–86. Fowler makes the point that a double negative, though ungrammatical to educated ears, really almost never obscures meaning. I used to have a relative who, when asked to make a choice, would reply indifferently, "It don't make no nevermind to me." We never misunderstood him.

OT.[15] Hebrews uses it relatively often, again displaying the book's fondness for rhetorical devices that direct the hearer to attend more closely to its message. Paronomasia is what we know more commonly as a pun, a play on the etymology of a word in order to relate several meanings to the core meaning the speaker is trying to get across. Thus, in the famous Peter passage (Matt. 16:18), Jesus makes a play using the name Peter (Πέτρος) and the Greek word for rock (πέτρα) to signify the foundation upon which he will build his church. The meanings of (1) Peter's name and (2) a rock are used to speak ultimately of a third meaning, the foundation of the church, through the similar sound of the two words.

Analogously, in Heb. 5:8 the author uses the sound of ἔπαθεν to create interest in the word ἔμαθεν, making the hearer want to find out what could be learned through suffering. The answer: obedience. If said in a less arresting way, one of the most powerful statements in the epistle could have gone in one ear of his listeners and out the other. This is a clear example of the kind of rhetorical technique that preachers would use, especially when they wanted something to be particularly memorable.

Key Metaphors

In addition to the more technical rhetorical devices, our author utilizes a number of important metaphors, "many of which are part of the standard rhetorical repertoire."[16] Of course, the large scale ideas of the epistle are essentially metaphorical anyway. For example, there never was, nor did there later develop, a Melchizedekian priesthood. Jesus was not a Levite; the new covenant was not drawn up at a particular earthly locality with God and his people in attendance. The very reality of the priesthood of Christ and of the new covenant depends, in the mind of the author, upon the historical reality of the levitical priesthood and the covenant at Sinai, but in their present form, the priesthood and the covenant must be seen as metaphors as far as we are concerned. The whole structure of typology, by which heavenly realities are compared to their earthly shadows, is intrinsically metaphorical.

---

15. Cf. Grace I. Emmerson, "Paronomasia," in *Dictionary of Biblical Interpretation,* ed. R. J. Coggins and J. L. Houlden (London: SCM; Philadelphia: Trinity Press International, 1990), 511.

16. Attridge, *Hebrews,* 21.

But there are other metaphors used by our speaker, illustrations employed as aids to understanding, as any good preacher or teacher would. One of these is particularly noteworthy for us. He draws from the field of ancient education as he reproaches his readers for being like children in the classroom, needing still to be taught the ABCs of Christian truth when they ought by now to be teaching others (Heb. 5:11–6:2). In this stretch of just six verses, there are no less than seventeen different words or phrases used to speak of the classroom in ancient times. The metaphor is picked up again in Heb. 12:7–11, where the focus is on the discipline needed to learn holiness or righteousness, though here the picture is of the family "classroom" where the child is taught by parental discipline. Repeated use of the educational terms παιδεία, παιδεύ-ειν, and παιδευτής, while not enough in itself to prove a rhetorical background for the author, when added to the wealth of other indicators in the book, is a firm example of the author's tendency to draw from his own experience.[17]

Common Rhetorical Formulas

The introductions to some of the OT citations in Hebrews bear the marks of a rhetorical background, though this may be more Jewish than Hellenistic. In Heb. 2:6 the author introduces a quotation from Psalm 8 with a phrase that sounds curiously imprecise to our ears: διεμαρτύρατο δέ πού τις λέγων, "But someone has testified somewhere saying." The introduction does not reflect slack indefiniteness, however, for it has parallels in the Jewish philosopher Philo.[18] Our author seems to use it for two purposes. First, the formula indicates that the preacher does not want to dwell on the incidentals. It is as if he is saying to his hearers, "I cannot think of the source of this quotation right off the top of my head, but you know where it comes from, so let's go on to the really important thing: what the text says." Second, the formula "is consistent with the strong emphasis throughout Hebrews on the oracular character of Scripture. Precisely because it is God who speaks in the OT,

---

17. Attridge lists six spheres, in addition to that of education, from which the author draws his rhetorical images: agriculture, architecture, seafaring, law, athletics, and the religious cultus (*Hebrews*, 21).

18. For examples, see Attridge, *Hebrews*, 70 n. 19.

the identity of the person through whom he uttered his word is relatively unimportant. A vague allusion is sufficient."[19]

The use of certain kinds of transitional statements also betrays rhetorical influence. In Heb. 5:11 the author uses a common Hellenistic device to express the difficulty of the teaching that he is about to exposit. The two adjectives that describe his coming instruction, "much" (πολύς) and "hard to explain" (δυσερμήνευτος), are common enough in pagan authors, if not in the NT, and the excuse that the teaching will be difficult because the hearers are mentally dull is also found.[20] Even this attribution may be what Attridge calls "a rhetorical move . . . designed to elicit the response, 'no, we are not dullards, we are ready to hear what you have to say.' . . . Hence, rather than a precise indictment, what these verses offer is a challenge to the addressees to progress toward a truly mature faith. The author operates rhetorically, and his rhetoric is sensitive to the perceived condition of his audience."[21]

Genitive Absolute

A Greek genitive absolute is a clause containing at least a noun and a participle, both in the genitive case, that is independent of any grammatical relation with the rest of the sentence. Our author "uses the genitive absolute well, and varies the word-order considerably."[22] Whereas many NT authors use the genitive absolute in a flexible way,[23] intermixing elements that *do* connect with the rest of the sentence, the author of Hebrews uses it in the traditional classical way, a sign of his stylistic elegance and diversity. For instance, where a more boring author might have written Heb. 9:6–10 using a series of main clauses joined by simple copulas like "and" or "but," the author of Hebrews develops one long, elegant

---

19. Lane, *Hebrews,* 1:46. A similar formula is used at Heb. 4:4.

20. Cf. Attridge, *Hebrews,* 156. Attridge's discussion of this entire passage (pp. 156–58) is extremely clear and useful.

21. Ibid., 157–58. The rhetorical question in Heb. 11:32, followed by the statement that time would fail the author to speak of Gideon, etc., is another kind of standard rhetorical transition showing the homiletical nature of the epistle.

22. Turner, *Style,* 106.

23. Cf. F. Blass and A. Debrunner, *A Greek Grammar of the New Testament and Other Early Christian Literature,* trans. and rev. by Robert W. Funk (Chicago: University of Chicago Press, 1961), §423.

sentence, using no fewer than three genitive absolutes and without a single copula.[24]

Variety in the Style of Hebrews

As W. H. Simcox noted in his summary of the style of Hebrews (quoted near the beginning of this chapter), the author is relatively free of the failing that separates Hellenistic writers from classical ones: monotony of style.[25] Though style variation is also a function of Greco-Roman rhetorical style and could be treated as a subcategory of it like the other devices listed above, it is so pervasive and applies to so many elements within the style of Hebrews that it deserves to be treated with its own set of subcategories. Variety in the style of Hebrews is evident in the larger aspects, like the general tone of the discourse and the well-known alternation of exhortatory and explanatory passages, and in the smaller aspects, like sentence structure.

Variety in the General Tone of the Discourse

Harold Attridge points to three different tendencies in the mood of Hebrews, stating that it ranges from "solemnly festive, quasi-poetic passages through serious logical or quasi-logical argument to playfully suggestive exegesis."[26] As we saw in chapter 3, our author has paid great attention to rhythm in penning his "word of exhortation," and the most lyrical of these could certainly have been used in religious feasts and ceremonies. The exalted statements about Christ in Heb. 1:2–3; the majestic affirmation of the Word, coupled with a solemn reminder of judgment in Heb. 4:12–13; the elegant statement of the nature of the priesthood of Melchizedek in Heb. 7:1–3, a statement for which the reader has been primed so often in the earlier part of the epistle and that, when it comes, even elicits a worshipful response from the author

---

24. Of course a sentence this long in English would be impossible, but just for comparison's sake, it is interesting to note that the NRSV translates Heb. 9:6–10 using four copulas in three sentences.

25. See chap. 3 for examples of various rhythms used in Hebrews, and Attridge, *Hebrews*, 20.

26. Attridge, *Hebrews*, 20.

(θεωρεῖτε δὲ πηλίκος οὗτος, "See how great he is!" Heb. 7:4
NRSV)—all these border on the liturgical.

There is the rational argumentation of the philosopher as well.
In Heb. 4:1–9, for instance, we see an extended argument, carefully
applying the historical experience of Israel to his readers. The οὖν
of Heb. 4:1 leads to a series of γάρ clauses in Heb. 4:2–5,[27] and
again in 4:6, ἐπεὶ οὖν leads to the πάλιν of 4:7. Perhaps even more
clear as a philosophical argumentative device is the anticipation of
an objection and its answer in Heb. 4:8. There the author assumes
that someone will say, "Yes, but they *did* enter their rest when
Joshua led them into the promised land." The author, sticking
close to the text of Scripture, the only "proof" he needs, says that
this cannot be so, otherwise David would never have spoken
much later than Joshua's time of another day yet to come. In Heb.
4:9–10, the argument is summarized and conclusions drawn: the
possibility of entering God's rest still remains, where believers
cease from their labors as God did from his. Therefore we must
work to enter that rest. Other examples of this type of argument
abound in Hebrews (see Hebrews 7 and 10 particularly).

The variety in tone sometimes approaches what Attridge calls
"playfully suggestive exegesis."[28] An example is the intimation in
Heb. 7:9–10 that Levi and his heirs paid tribute to Melchizedek by
virtue of the fact that they were "in the loins" of Abraham when
he rendered his tithe to this king of Salem. Such tentative speculation is rare in our author, and probably displays an "argument
weak, shout louder" feeling on his part. He shows a hesitancy of
belief in the power of his own argument by the comical introduction he gives it, blending the paronomasia of a stock Philonic
phrase (ὡς ἔπος εἰπεῖν) with only the briefest mention of the idea,
and then dropping it. Of course, if he had carried it out much farther, he might have run up against the problem that some have

---

27. Within the structure of the larger argument is a clear example of the rabbinic method of argument known as *gezerah shawah*, which uses the meaning of a
term in one place in Scripture to interpret its meaning in another place. Cf. H. L.
Strack and G. Stemberger, *Introduction to the Talmud and Midrash*, trans. Markus
Bockmuehl (Edinburgh: T. & T. Clark, 1991), 21. This form has a parallel in Greek
rhetoric, the σύγκρισις πρὸς ἴσον; cf. Kennedy, *Interpretation*, 89.

28. Attridge, *Hebrews*, 20.

suggested: by this logic, Jesus, being a descendant of Abraham, also paid tithes to Melchizedek!

Variety in the Alternation of Exposition and Exhortation

One of the most important aspects of the structure of Hebrews is the alternation between lengthy *expositions* of themes (drawn from Scripture and centering on the superiority of Christ) and dramatic *exhortations* (also based in Scripture and delivered with almost equal doses of encouragement and warning). This alternation is a major factor in varying the content of the epistle, and it includes brief interludes as well as longer structural movements, where the author's attention shifts not for just a moment but for a lengthier, more focused period.[29] So, for instance, the first of five warnings in the book comes at Heb. 2:1–4, between the longer expositions about the Son being superior to angels (Heb. 1:5–14) and the necessary humiliation of the Son, which qualifies him to be a merciful and faithful high priest (Heb. 2:5–18; cf. also the briefer exhortations at 5:11–6:12 and 10:19–39). Examples of longer, more focused exhortations are the one on faithfulness and entering into God's rest (Heb. 3:1–4:16) and, of course, the last two chapters of the book, which are almost entirely paraenetic. For a schematic of this alternation, see the end of chapter 4 above.

Variety in Sentence Structure

Hebrews has many long, complex sentences. We have already looked at Heb. 1:1–4 from several different angles. It is probably the most famous of Hebrews' long periods, but it is by no means the only one. The sentence contains two coordinate clauses and eight subordinate clauses in seventy-two words. Eight other sentences stand out alongside this one as worthy of note for their length and complexity (Heb. 2:2–4, 8c–9, 14–15; 5:7–10; 7:1–3; 9:6–10; 10:19–25; 12:1–2). Each of these periods is remarkable in its construction. Though there are some elements that make the passages memorable,[30] for the most part these rhetorical flourishes resist precise memorization.

---

29. Attridge, ibid., notes that there is even variation between imperatives and hortatory subjunctives within the paraenetic sections, so interested in variety is the author.

30. E.g., the alliteration and isocolon of Heb. 1:1–4 (see above under these headings).

Our author does not depend wholly, or even predominantly, on long involved sentence structures, however. He uses shorter forms as well. Sometimes his sentences bear an almost inscriptional character. The description of the people who were not able to enter into rest is short and arresting: καὶ βλέπομεν ὅτι οὐκ ἠδυνήθησαν εἰσελθεῖν δι᾽ ἀπιστίαν (3:19).[31]

Another less common form that he employs to great advantage is the brief, staccato question. The three verses just prior to Heb. 3:19 consist of a series of rapid-fire questions intended to shock the audience by their directness and conclusiveness. The variety in cadence is never more apparent than here, where five quick questions come immediately after one of the longest periods in the book (Heb. 3:12–15), which contains four coordinate clauses (counting the OT quotation) and eight subordinate clauses in sixty-eight words.

Semitic Style in Hebrews?

Before finishing our discussion of the style of Hebrews, we should take some account of the views of Nigel Turner, who claims that there are Semitisms in the Greek of Hebrews. Though he states quite clearly that "if the author was a Jew . . . , he has at least succeeded in eliminating many of the characteristic features of Jewish Greek,"[32] he nevertheless devotes an entire section of his chapter on Hebrews to what he calls "underlying traces of Jewish Greek."[33] We have suggested that the author's style demonstrates the heavy influence of Greek rhetoric.[34] Does it also show Semitic influence?

Of course, I am not asking whether or not the author was a Jew. A Jew would not necessarily have to write in a style that shows Hebraic or Aramaic influence. Nor am I assuming that Hebraic in-

---

31. Heb. 2:16; 4:9; 7:19; 9:16; 10:4, 18, 31; 11:1; 12:29; 13:1, 8 also contain examples of this brief, pithy form.

32. Turner, *Style*, 108.

33. Ibid., 108–12.

34. Allen Wikgren supports the rhetorical background of the epistle while not addressing the question of Semitisms at all. See his "Some Greek Idioms in the Epistle to the Hebrews," in *The Teacher's Yoke: Studies in Memory of Henry Trantham*, ed. E. Jerry Vardaman and James Leo Garrett, Jr. (Waco: Baylor University Press, 1964), 145–53.

fluence cancels out Greek influence; a style could show both influences at the same time. Also, I recognize the difficulty of pinning
down a definitive answer to this question. It is important to attempt an answer, though, for at least two reasons. First, if we
could answer this question, it might shed light on the age-old
question of who wrote Hebrews. Second, it will be helpful to know
if there is Semitic influence since this knowledge may affect how
we translate certain passages.

Turner uses two kinds of evidence to argue for traces of Semitic
style. He divides his data into two sections: "Semitic Quality in
General" and "Semitisms." It is not important to discuss Turner's
arguments in detail here. We shall confine ourselves to an analysis
of the elements mentioned under the first heading. The evidence
put forth in the second section is more technical but can be dealt
with adequately in a few sentences.

Turner speaks of "general" Semitic qualities such as the fact
that Hebrews is a "homily, a literary genre of which there were
many Jewish examples," listing Philo's commentary on Genesis,
1 Clement, James, the Epistle of Barnabas, the Shepherd of Hermas,
parts of the Didache, and the "Exhortation" from the Zadokite
Damascus Rule. Quite apart from the fact that only two of these
documents are Jewish, let alone examples of Jewish homilies, he
does not offer any criteria for distinguishing between a "Jewish"
homily and a secular speech. If he means to do so on the basis of
content, then he undercuts his argument, because he is supposed
to be talking about form, not content, since style is primarily a
matter of form. Of course, Hebrews is "Jewish" in the sense that
much of the content it expounds is Jewish, but this is simply because it is also Christian. But the document takes most of its formal
elements from secular rhetorical training.

Allegorizing is also said to be evidence of the general Semitic
quality of the epistle. "Like the Epistle of Barnabas, Hebrews is
given to allegorizing. Its oratory therefore is probably Hellenistic
or Palestinian rabbinical rather than secular Hellenistic, and its
nearest parallel may be in Hellenistic synagogue addresses, such
as 4 Maccabees."[35] Not only is it wrong to limit allegorizing to
Jewish writing, since the Jews learned it from the Greeks in the

---

35. Turner, Style, 108.

first place, but there simply is not the allegorizing tendency in Hebrews that Turner suggests. The author of Hebrews certainly uses typology liberally, and the difference between allegory and typology is admittedly difficult to define, but it is a clear distinction that should be maintained nevertheless.

Another general Semitic quality to which Turner refers is the writer's heavy use of the Pentateuch and the Psalms. This is said to indicate that Hebrews may be a Hellenistic Jewish homily rather than a Palestinian one, but again, Turner makes the mistake of arguing on the basis of content rather than form. I suppose it could be argued that the author of Hebrews had many texts from which he could have chosen, and therefore it is significant that he chose so many texts from the Pentateuch and Psalms, but the argument does not appear very strong in light of the fact that Melchizedek, the centerpiece of the author's priestly arguments, is only mentioned in those two sources. In fact, the more germane argument tends against Turner, since when discussing the covenant—a subject mentioned often in Scripture—the author does not use the covenants of Genesis, Exodus, Deuteronomy, or Psalms as his mainstays. Rather, he chooses one of the prophets, Jeremiah (see the use of Jer. 31:31–34 in Hebrews 8–10).

It is also curious that Turner mentions possible parallels with 4 Maccabees as evidence of Semitic influence in Hebrews. The two documents are similar in some ways and dissimilar in others. But the problem for Turner's argument is that 4 Maccabees is recognized by many to be a good example of a work done by a Jew following classical Greek rhetorical principles.

> He is unquestionably a Jew. But he is no less certainly a Jew profoundly influenced by Greek philosophical thought and thoroughly at home with the Greek language. His work is conspicuously devoid of semitisms, and citations from the Old Testament consistently follow the Septuagint. The images, symbols, and metaphors employed as well as the antitheses, climaxes, and apostrophes that abound all clearly exhibit his skill in the craft of the Greek rhetorician. His Greek is free and idiomatic, indicating that he thinks in that language; it is his native tongue.[36]

_____

36. James H. Charlesworth, ed., *The Old Testament Pseudepigrapha*, 2 vols. (Garden City, N.Y.: Doubleday, 1983–85), 2:532.

So 4 Maccabees hardly seems like a good example of a synagogue homily, at least one trying to distinguish itself from secular Greek rhetoric, and its likeness to Hebrews makes Turner's argument about Semitisms that much weaker.

Turner offers more evidence of a general tone of Jewish influence in Hebrews, but it does not prove his claim at all. For example, that the author uses ἐπ᾽ ἐσχάτου τῶν ἡμερῶν τούτων at the beginning of the letter (Heb. 1:2) is said to point to the age of the Messiah having come. It is also said to be a "Septuagintism." Both things may be true, but neither of these facts, like the parallel with 4 Maccabees above, proves the point. Someone who is trained in Greek circles is *likely* to use the LXX, so all Septuagintisms only point away from Jewish style. And that the author points to the Messiah only says that he and his audience are Jewish Christian, not that he is using a Jewish style of writing.

The rest of the grammatical and stylistic items to which Turner points in this first section exhibit the same fallacy of illegitimate parallelism. The impersonal "he says/has said" (8:5; 4:4; 13:5), the use of *a minore ad maius* argument (for which there are parallels in rabbinic writings and Philo), the tendency of the author to model some sentences "on OT poetic sense-parallelism" (11:17; 4:15–16)—all are either not exclusively Jewish or are not sufficiently justified by examples to prove the point.

The same can be said for the evidence put forth in Turner's section on Semitisms in Hebrews. He claims that the epistle is full of Septuagintisms, but what does that prove? That the genitive follows the noun is claimed to be evidence of Semitic thinking, since that is the word order of the construct state, but Hebrews also places the genitive before the noun sixteen times in the epistle. Even Turner admits that classical writers like Thucydides and Philostratus put the genitive after the noun as often as before it. He also tries to base his case on the author's use of particles, but his own statistics deny his point. He claims that the author "is drawn by the Semitic tendency to seek only first-place particles or to place the others in first-place, as in Biblical Greek,"[37] but he offers as evidence three particles that appear a total of only four times in the

---

37. Turner, *Style*, 111.

whole epistle, while the ninety-one occurrences of γάρ (never first, of course) are passed over in silence.

Turner does point out a few expressions in the section that could be accepted as legitimate Semitisms, including the famous explanation of Matthew Black that a Hebrew circumstantial clause underlies the grammatical problem at Heb. 11:11 on Sarah's barrenness, but these examples are neither frequent nor clear enough to warrant the claim that Hebrews was written in something Turner calls "Jewish Greek." He does admit that the author could have been a proselyte, but the style of Hebrews demonstrates something stronger than that. It seems to have been written by someone who was trained in classical rhetoric and who used Greek with the ease of a native-born speaker and writer.

9

Theology

If the study of vocabulary, grammar, and style form the life-blood of exegesis, theology is the body in which that blood moves. But each exegete's "body" is unique: the theology you bring to the text, or to any experience of life for that matter, is unique to you. It is the duty of every exegete to recognize the theology we bring to the text and to allow that theology to be shaped by the text while engaged in the exegetical task. This process of moving back and forth between firmly holding our conclusions and allowing the text constantly to challenge them forces us to recognize our presuppositions about the theological content of the text.

Nontheologians sometimes think that exegesis is exempt from the influence of presuppositions; nothing could be farther from the truth. When Rudolf Bultmann some fifty years ago wrote an essay entitled "Is Exegesis without Presuppositions Possible?" he rightly answered no and proceeded to enumerate what he thought the presuppositions of a NT exegete should be.[1] Although we cannot take time to explore that question now, students of Hebrews should not think that they can approach passages like Heb. 1:1–14 without some preconceived notions about what sort of Christology they'll find there or read Heb. 6:4–6 without some soteriological presuppositions.

Having said that, a limited objectivity can still be attained while investigating the theology of Hebrews, if we constantly work at

---

1. Rudolf Bultmann, "Is Exegesis without Presuppositions Possible?" in *Existence and Faith*, trans. Schubert M. Ogden (New York: World, 1960), 342–51.

basing the investigation on the grammar, syntax, vocabulary, and literary structure of the text—in other words, on the essentials of exegesis. Rigorously questioning our own biases while doing exegesis as well as when applying the fruits of that exegesis to form our theological understanding of the text, is the best way to develop a theological portrait of any biblical book.

And it is enough. The text is supposed to shape our lives, to give us thoughts and motives on which to base our belief and our behavior, so there is no reason to apologize for our subjectivity. Indeed, we should embrace it gladly but recognize it for what it is— *our* subjectivity. Humility that admits its own subjectivity and, while unashamedly arguing for its positions, acknowledges that its views are simply well-considered opinion is essential to a theology that is useful to the church. Anything else is driven by hubris. Though subjective, forming this theology is basic to our Christian growth. It is how the text is translated into our lives; it is what we communicate to others in preaching and teaching. As frustrating as it may be to have to admit that we can only begin to understand the mind of God, rather than exposit it fully and exhaustively, it is nevertheless incumbent upon us to begin and, in our attempt, to rejoice at the truth that is to be found in the biblical text.

Two Approaches to the Theology of Hebrews

To do full justice to the theology of Hebrews would require a full-scale theological commentary on the text, an undertaking well beyond the parameters of this book. But it is possible to open a window into the theology of Hebrews by giving a brief introduction to the main theological themes of the book. This exercise will enable us to read the text "theologically," that is, to be aware at all times of the underlying thoughts that give the author his purpose, that drive him to write what he does. Without a basic understanding of this structure, we will see Hebrews as a series of isolated pericopes, a mistake with any piece of literature in the NT, perhaps most of all with the Epistle to the Hebrews.

Two ways of summarizing the theology of any NT book have become popular in recent years. We will try to follow a combination of the two, but first let me introduce you to them. I call the first the *authorial theology* of the book, the second *reader-response theol-*

ogy. Many names have been given to these two approaches down through the years; these two names reflect my own understanding of who sets the theological agenda when a text is read.

Authorial Theology of Hebrews

This approach to the theological enterprise attempts to allow the author's theological agenda to set the direction of the theological investigation. What issues concerned him most deeply? How does he answer the questions he raises? How does he rank these questions? What are the secondary and tertiary concerns he addresses? In short, what is his primary doctrinal and/or ethical concern? Is he writing about God's character? Human unbelief? Christ? Rebellion against authority? Salvation? The nature of the church? A problem with immorality? Eschatology?

This method of theological investigation is often called Biblical Theology, a term that came into common use in this century.[2] The name can be misleading to the theological novice, however, because it implies that the theological method it replaces is not based on the Bible. Indeed, its early proponents boldly stated that dogmatics had departed from the text of Scripture and Biblical Theology was needed to save the church from excessive philosophical speculation.[3] Dogmatic, or systematic, theology (what we will describe below as reader-response theology) is no less biblical than authorial theology. It simply approaches the Scriptures in a different way.[4]

Reader-Response Theology of Hebrews

A second way of looking at the theology of Hebrews is determined by us, the readers of the text. It reflects *our* questions, *our* theological interests, the passions that drive *us* to the holy text to understand God, the meaning of our own existence, our salvation, and so forth. The name reader-response theology is thus self-

---

2. See the excellent article on the history of this movement by G. E. Ladd, "Biblical Theology, History of," in *International Standard Bible Encyclopedia*, rev. ed., ed. Geoffrey W. Bromiley et al. (Grand Rapids: Eerdmans, 1979–88), 1:498–505.

3. Ibid., 1:498–501.

4. See Donald Guthrie, *New Testament Theology* (Leicester, England: InterVarsity; Downers Grove, Ill.: InterVarsity, 1981), 21–74 (esp. 27–34), for a good discussion of the problems involved in doing NT theology, including the difference between Biblical and systematic theology.

explanatory; it reflects our response to reading the book with our questions in mind and not necessarily those of the author.[5]

Traditionally, in fact at least since the time of Thomas Aquinas, users of this theological method have come to the text with a certain set of questions in logical order that they wished to ask of the text.[6] Some theologians asked these questions with little reference to the historical, cultural, literary, and sometimes even the linguistic and grammatical background of the text. The meaning of the text was assumed to lie on the surface. The influence of presuppositions was too-little recognized, and correlating the meaning of one text with the meaning of others to form a coherent or "systematic" theology was thought to be a tedious process but one that was not necessarily exegetically problematic.

Whatever we may think of the strengths or weaknesses of these two theological approaches, exclusively embracing one over the other will imperil our souls. To believe that we can do authorial theology without incorporating the insights of reader-response theology is to deny that we have any biases or presuppositions that will color our judgment. This is myopic. No matter how much we *think* that we are asking the author's own questions, we are always (rightly) wondering in the back of our minds, "So what does this text mean to me now in my situation?" Unless we recognize this fact, we are likely to elevate certain questions to a higher status than they actually had for the original author.[7] In addition, of course, our own questions about the text are important in their own right. While we may prefer the methodology of authorial theology, we are wise to

---

5. This is not to be confused with a newer form of criticism called reader-response criticism, which regards the reader's response to the text as the chief category for understanding how to interpret the text. See Grant R. Osborne, *The Hermeneutical Spiral: A Comprehensive Introduction to Biblical Interpretation* (Downers Grove, Ill.: InterVarsity, 1991), 377–80, for a brief description of this form of criticism.

6. See Thomas C. Oden, *The Living God*, vol. 1 of *Systematic Theology* (San Francisco: Harper San Francisco, 1987), 1–5, 322–406, for a discussion of the historical roots of this endeavor and for a superb discussion of the importance and legitimacy of doing systematic theology.

7. Perhaps a modern example of this is the present discussion of 1 Timothy 2–3, which is so often framed in terms of the good and important question of the role of women in ministry that we sometimes lose sight of the fact that the author was primarily concerned with describing the character traits necessary for worship and leadership in the church.

ask our own questions regularly in the process. Moving back and forth between the two sets of questions lets us continue to see the text in the way we should, as the Word of God that both confronts our lives, telling us what to believe and do, and clarifies our lives, answering our doctrinal and ethical questions.

Four Doctrinal Discussions in Hebrews

How, then, do we proceed to read the text theologically? Briefly, one simply asks questions like the ones we suggest above. But which questions? I propose the following.

The first question is subtle and dangerous because it allows the subjectivity of the exegete to run wild. It nevertheless must be asked, and the answer must be understood in order to proceed. What subjects does the author assume his first readers understood that may be misunderstood by a modern reader and require further explication? As a control, I suggest that there must be good and sufficient reasons arising from the text itself to spend time studying the subject. It will do no good to say that the author presupposes an understanding of this or that doctrine, when there is no evidence from the text for the claim. In Hebrews this turns out to be a crucial question because, for example, the author clearly presupposes an understanding of how to interpret the OT that is basic to understanding anything else he has to say. Hence, that will be our first topic of investigation.

There are other questions to ask, however, that will help us set the agenda for discovering the theology of Hebrews. The most obvious approach is to pursue the subjects about which the author wrote most extensively. This can be determined to some degree simply by asking a statistical question: What subjects appear most often in the text? But the answer to that question does not give the whole story. We should also ask, What subjects does the author discuss most fervently and prominently by using the most engaging language or the most persuasive arguments or by placing the discussion in a particularly prominent place? Another question to ask is this: What subjects directly encourage or warn the readers to change their belief or behavior? These subjects must surely have been important to the author as he wrote. These four questions can get us started in our investigation of the theology of Hebrews by pointing us to the right topics. Once we are underway, other questions will arise from our own experience and from the text itself that will enable us to do the theological thinking necessary for the text to do its work on our lives.

Having asked these questions of the text, I will now present the four topics that seem to me to have been most urgent in the mind of the author. After discussing the foundational question of how the author used the OT Scripture, the remaining topics will be treated alphabetically. With as much space as the Book of Hebrews devotes to each of these topics and the interweaving of them with each other, it is impossible to decide which was most important to the author. Handling them in alphabetical order prevents us from having to decide between them.

The Doctrine and Use of OT Scripture in Hebrews

A chapter on the theology of Hebrews should begin with a serious investigation of the author's understanding and use of the OT. This is true for a number of reasons, two of which should be readily apparent: (1) the author bases much of his carefully worded argument on OT texts and their authority, and (2) he uses distinctive methods to interpret the OT. The first gives us the author's understanding of epistemology and his sources of authority, two categories that generally belong to the prolegomena of any theological system. Understanding his methods for interpreting the OT is important, too, so that we may be better able to interpret his arguments. It will also help us answer the secondary question of whether he, being an author of inspired Scripture, used interpretive techniques that are illegitimate for us to imitate. Thus, some comments are in order on (1) the author's theology of Scripture, (2) his interpretative method, and (3) its application for us today.

The Doctrine of Scripture in Hebrews

There is no doubt that the author of Hebrews regarded the Scriptures as in every sense the Word of God. He states as much in Heb. 1:1, when he says that *God* spoke to the fathers through the prophets in diverse times and ways (πολυμερῶς καὶ πολυτρόπως πάλαι). This certainly means the spoken word, and probably the acted parables of prophets like Ezekiel as well, but it must also include the written word. The OT itself gives evidence everywhere of the importance of the written word, especially the Torah, and of its prophetic nature, and first-century Jewish groups bear abundant testimony to this same view. It is certain that the reference to God speaking "long ago and in many ways" includes written Scripture.

But there is an even more direct statement in Heb. 4:12, where the author says that "the word of God (ὁ λόγος τοῦ θεοῦ) is ... able to judge the thoughts and intentions of the heart" (NRSV). The author's understanding of the phrase "word of God" should be dynamic enough to include the preached word, but it should also include the written Scriptures.[8] Lest we be unclear on this point, the author insists that the Scriptures are the Word of God's Holy Spirit (cf. Heb. 3:7; 10:15). The author's insistence on the divine element in Scripture is so great that, while "human instrumentality is of course recognized," it is also true that "the humans involved are often ignored" by the author.[9]

This Word of God, however, is no static, dull book; it is "living and active" (ζῶν ... καὶ ἐνεργής, Heb. 4:12). It is a word that should strike fear into our hearts, because of its sharpness and power to judge us, but it is also a word that brings us the comfort and clarity of God speaking in history. Indeed, the key to understanding and applying the Word of God and its true significance lies in recognizing that it has been fulfilled finally and completely in the person of God's Son, Jesus Christ (Heb. 2:3). It is to him that God has bequeathed the full inheritance of his creation and through him that God has spoken definitively to humans (Heb. 1:1–2). Probably no book of Scripture gives a clearer and more forceful proof that the NT authors regarded the OT as the very Word of God.

Methods of Interpreting Scripture in Hebrews

The methods our author uses to interpret Scripture is a complex subject that is treated well in the commentaries. William Lane lists nine categories of "principles guiding the writer in his approach to the OT text."[10] While these categories overlap somewhat, they are a good way of approaching this subject, and we will use them here.

---

8. See William L. Lane, *Hebrews*, Word Biblical Commentary (Dallas: Word, 1991), 1:102–3.

9. Harold W. Attridge, *The Epistle to the Hebrews*, Hermeneia (Philadelphia: Fortress, 1989), 24.

10. Lane, *Hebrews*, 1:cxix. In the following pages, I am heavily indebted to the fine, succinct discussion of these methods found in 1:cxix–cxxiv of his commentary. Lane's comments are based on the research of George H. Guthrie, who presents his findings in an article titled "The Uses of the Old Testament in Hebrews," in *Dictionary of the Later New Testament and Its Developments*, ed. Ralph. P. Martin and Peter H. Davids (Downers Grove, Ill.: InterVarsity, forthcoming).

1. **Dispelling Confusion.** At many points in his sermon, the author of Hebrews attempts to clarify passages of the OT text. A good example of this is found in Heb. 2:8–9, where discussing Ps. 8:4–6, he seems to anticipate an objection that the reader might have about his use of the text: Though the Scripture predicts that all things will be subject to the Messiah, we do not yet see everything in subjection. In response, he points to Jesus, who is now "crowned with glory and honor" (Heb. 2:9), who is now ruling over all things, but it is not yet (οὔπω) the time when he will rule over them finally and completely (2:8; see the discussion of eschatology below). More subtly, our author also teaches that the one to whom all things would be subject is Jesus rather than humankind in general, contrary to what a casual reader of Psalm 8 might have thought. Jesus, as the representative of his people and the head of the church, is often regarded by the NT writers as the fulfillment of OT promises that seem to have been made to either the nation of Israel or humankind in general.[11] Jesus is the one "in whom the human vocation finds its true expression."[12]

2. **Reinforcement.** Perhaps the most common use of Scripture in the modern day, and a very important use of Scripture throughout the history of the church and Judaism as well, is citing it to support one's argument. The author of Hebrews is no exception. In Heb. 6:13–15, for instance, his claim that through faith and patience we inherit the promises is supported by reference to the story of Abraham and a quote from Gen. 22:17. The author believed that his readers would not fall away, and as part of his warning to them, he emphasized that Abraham was able to believe and have patience and ultimately inherited God's promise to make of him a great nation.

Similar reinforcement appears in the warning of Heb. 10:19–39, where Hab. 2:3–4 is loosely quoted to support his exhortation to endure because the Messiah is coming back, and the righteous one who lives by faith will not be lost when he returns.

3. **Explaining Implications.** Biblical exposition has always included the drawing out of the text's implications for the life of the

---

11. Cf., e.g., William L. Kynes, *A Christology of Solidarity: Jesus as the Representative of His People in Matthew* (Lanham, Md.: University Press of America, 1991), passim.

12. Lane, *Hebrews*, 1:cxx.

community. In Heb. 8:8–13, the author quotes the famous covenant passage of Jer. 31:31–34, and focuses on one aspect of that passage, the newness of the new covenant. Unlike category 1 above, where confusion is dispelled, here the author assumes his readers understand the passage, and he applies it to the covenant God has made through the person and work of Jesus Christ. He draws out the implications of the word *new* by saying "In speaking of 'a new covenant,' he has made the first one obsolete" (Heb. 8:13 NRSV). The author then goes on to explain in some detail that the old covenant has been superseded and will shortly disappear, calling it a shadow of the reality that has now replaced it. The implications of OT Scripture are expounded in many other places in Hebrews as well.[13] It is one of our author's most common techniques.

4. **Literal Sense of a Word or Phrase.** An appeal to the "literal meaning" is a common practice of NT writers. Perhaps the most famous example is found in Gal. 3:15–18, where Paul makes a great deal of the fact that the word for "seed" in Gen. 12:7 is singular rather than plural. The author of Hebrews argues in a similar fashion when he quotes Ps. 95:7 and focuses on the word "today" (cf. Heb. 3:13, 15; 4:7–8). In Heb. 3:13, he instructs his readers to exhort each other "as long as it is called 'today,' " to emphasize that this passage is relevant to them. He repeats and strengthens that warning in 3:15–18, using five rhetorical questions to convince his readers that the quotation is as relevant to them as it was to the people in Moses' day.

The literal sense is even more important for a second point that the author wants to make. He states that the promise of entering "the rest of God" is still open and that we who have believed enter that rest. In Heb. 4:7, he speaks of "a certain day" (τινὰ ἡμέραν), stressing that David used the word "today" with reference to his own day, many days after Moses, and that "today" continues to be available to them. As he puts it: "A sabbath rest still remains for the people of God. . . . Let us therefore make every effort to enter that rest . . ." (Heb. 4:9–11 NRSV). The literal sense of the word "today" is being played with here, to be sure, but it is essential to the meaning of the passage that his readers regard "today" as the time

---

13. Cf. Heb. 2:8; 3:16–19; 4:6–10; 7:11–12; 10:8–9; 12:7–10, 26–29.

in which they were living. Other instances in Hebrews of this kind of literalism show how important the method was for the author. In Heb. 7:23–25, for example, the word "forever" from Ps. 110:4 is essential to his argument.

5. **Other Early Rabbinic Principles of Interpretation.** The four categories we have just mentioned were commonly used in rabbinic writings in the post-NT era.[14] Two of the seven better-known rules of interpretation laid down by Hillel in the early first century A.D. are also used by our author. They were referred to as *qal wa-ḥomer* and *gezerah shawah*. *Qal wa-ḥomer* was another name for the *a fortiori* argument of lesser to greater: what is true in a less important case applies all the more in an important case.

This type of argument is used in the crucial passage at Heb. 2:2–4. Using γάρ and a conditional clause, the author argues that if the OT message declared through angels was valid and significant, how much more the "great salvation" (τηλικαύτης σωτηρίας) that had now been declared to them by the Lord and those who heard him. And if every transgression or disobedience against the angelic message received "a just penalty" (ἔνδικον μισθαποδοσίαν), how much more serious will the punishment be for those who reject the message God confirmed "by signs and wonders and various miracles, and by gifts of the Holy Spirit, distributed according to his will" (Heb. 2:4 NRSV). Our author uses this kind of appeal also in 9:13–14, 10:28–29, and 12:25.

The *gezerah shawah* argument establishes a relationship between two passages of Scripture on the basis of similar wording, allowing one passage to expand the meaning of the other. This way of thinking is largely foreign to twentieth-century Westerners, but it was common in biblical times. In Heb. 4:3–5 the author uses the statement that God rested from all his work on the seventh day (Gen. 2:2) to elaborate on the quotation from Ps. 95:11. The Genesis passage shows that God's rest has been available from the beginning of creation, but God's people failed to share in it because of their disobedience. The writer goes on to tell more about the kind of rest from which the Israelites were excluded: not a rest from physical work, but a rest from sin and its effects. The usefulness, then, of Gen. 2:2 in clarifying Psalm 95 hangs on the fact that the

---

14. Cf. Lane, *Hebrews*, 1:cxix–cxx.

word "rest" occurs in both passages, the verb καταπαύειν in Gen. 2:2 LXX being cognate with the noun κατάπαυσις in Ps. 95:11 (Ps. 94:11 LXX). *Gezerah shawah* is also found in Heb. 5:5–6, where the author links Ps. 2:7 with Ps. 110:4 on the basis of the shared word "you" (σύ).[15]

6. **Chain Quotations.** Most students of the NT will be familiar with the practice of citing several quotations from several different places in the OT in support of a point that the NT author makes. While this is not done with great frequency in the NT, it is done at very important points in order to create the impression that Scripture everywhere teaches whatever point the author is trying to make. Perhaps the best-known example of this occurs in Romans 3 near the end of Paul's great argument that all human beings are under sin. Having established that the immoral pagan, the Jew, and the moral pagan are all nevertheless sinful, Paul then nails the coffin shut in Rom. 3:10–18 with a string of quotations from at least five different OT passages.

The author of Hebrews does the same thing, albeit only in one place. In Heb. 1:5–13, we find him quoting from seven separate sources. In 1:5, he cites two verses concerning sonship from Ps. 2:7 and 2 Sam. 7:14 (=1 Chron. 17:13). This pair of quotations, linked together by a simple καὶ πάλιν, establishes the sonship of the Messiah Jesus, who is "as much superior to the angels as the name he has inherited is superior to theirs" (Heb. 1:4 NIV). The next quotation seems to stand on its own, linking the Son to the Father in a position above the angels because the angels "worship him" (προσκυνησάτωσαν αὐτῷ). The next quotation also mentions angels and calls them "servants" (λειτουργούς). The author then moves into a lengthy quotation from Ps. 45:6–7, a well-known passage about the Messiah having a throne that will last forever and ever. He is the one who loves righteousness and hates wickedness, who has been set by God "beyond your companions" (παρὰ τοὺς μετόχους σου, Heb. 1:9). This text is then loosely joined by καί to another quotation, this time from Ps. 102:25–27. This quotation continues the theme of the Messiah being higher than the angels, or, as the author had called him in 1:3, "the radiance of God's glory and the exact representation of his being"

---

15. See Lane, *Hebrews*, 1:cxxi.

(NIV). Now he is referred to as the Lord who "laid the foundations of the earth," whose handiwork is the heavens, and who stands changelessly above these with years that "will never end." The created order, by contrast, will perish. The last quotation is from a psalm that the author will use frequently throughout the epistle, making its first appearance here: "Sit at my right hand until I make your enemies a footstool for your feet" (Ps. 110:1 NIV). The string of quotations occurs early in the book because the theme of the superiority of Jesus is a dominant interest of the author (see below under Christology).

7. **Example Lists.** Another method of OT interpretation that the author uses effectively is the example list, a long string of examples from the OT to prove a point. The famous "Hall of Fame of Faith" in Hebrews 11 dramatically demonstrates this practice. There the writer, beginning from creation and Abel and continuing all the way through OT history to the later prophets, describes for his readers what it means to be people who live "by faith" (πίστει). The author does this to show his readers that they continue in a tradition of salvation that began by faith and continues by faith to the present age. Their faith differs from that of the OT faithful in that the Messiah has come; they have "received what had been promised" (Heb. 11:39–40).

8. **Typology.** Perhaps no other element of biblical interpretation has been as often identified with the Book of Hebrews as typology. Typology views a place, person, event, institution, office, or object in the Bible as "a pattern by which later persons or places are interpreted due to the unity of events within salvation-history."[16] Generally, typology consists of two elements: a *type*, which is the original element, and an *antitype*, which is the later element that serves as the final expression of the original type. These two are in a temporal relationship, a crucial factor for the understanding of typology. The type is important in the flow of salvation history in and of itself; its historicity and usefulness within its contemporary context is never doubted and is often affirmed by the later author. But the type takes on a significance beyond its historical reality when it is viewed as a picture or pattern of a more important anti-

---

16. G. R. Osborne, "Type; Typology," in *International Standard Bible Encyclopedia*, rev. ed., ed. Geoffrey W. Bromiley et al. (Grand Rapids: Eerdmans, 1979–88), 4:930. This article is a brief, extremely useful summary of biblical typology.

type that follows. Thus, typology must be seen in a temporal context, for the type gathers significance in relation to the antitype only from its being recognized later as a pattern. Therefore, it is better to think of typology as a hermeneutical principle that discovers subsequent correspondences between antitype and type than as a prophecy/fulfillment dynamic that regards such correspondences as consciously anticipated by the OT authors.

The writer of Hebrews makes use of typology from the outset. His opening sentence makes quite clear that something happened in the past, and now has happened again in a definitive and final way in the readers' own time. "Long ago God spoke to our ancestors in many and various ways by the prophets, but in these last days he has spoken to us by a Son . . ." (Heb. 1:1–2 NRSV). This ringing opening statement, so heavy with rhetorical emphasis as we have seen (see chap. 8 above), in fact has this forcefulness because of the newness of the event of Christ. The strong eschatological emphasis at the beginning of the epistle creates a context for understanding the OT as a book consistently looking forward to Christ and builds that expectation in the reader.

The list of types and antitypes discussed in Hebrews is quite lengthy and need not be repeated here. Suffice it to say that the long central section of Hebrews (Heb. 8:1–10:18) is dominated by the notion of typology, and the vast majority of those types apply directly to the person of Jesus Christ. For instance, while the author earlier stressed that Jesus is "a priest forever, in the order of Melchizedek" (Heb. 7:17 NIV), he now presents him as the antitype of the levitical high priest in the OT who ministers in a heavenly sanctuary (Heb. 8:1–6). He offered his sacrifice once for all, in contrast to the frequent offering of the blood of bulls and goats by the levitical priests, and is the mediator of a new covenant that is the antitype of the old covenant found in OT Scripture (Heb. 8:6–13).

The heavy typology related to the sacrificial system continues in Hebrews 9. Now we see that the tabernacle and all of its particulars correspond in detail to NT realities, though the author claims that "of these things we cannot speak now in detail" (Heb. 9:5 NRSV). The crucial point for the author is that the sacrificial system of worship carried on in the earthly tabernacle—which included the lampstand, the table, the consecrated bread, etc.—is a type of the ministry that Christ now carries on for us in the heavenly tabernacle. The blood of the animal sacrifices is clearly a type of the blood of Christ, and the elements of the tabernacle, symbolic of God's judgment upon sin, are evidence that Christ's sacrifice for us has satisfied divine justice (Heb. 9:27–28).

Not only is Christ typified in the details of the sacrificial system, but the law itself, perhaps the most important element of Jewish life, is directly stated to be a "type" (τύπος, Heb. 8:5) of the reality that is Christ. "Since the law has only a shadow of the good things to come and not the true form of these realities, it can never, by the same sacrifices that are continually offered year after year, make perfect those who approach" (Heb. 10:1 NRSV). Here we see that not just some of the ritual activities were understood to be typical of Christ, or only certain passages in the OT and certain teachings, but in fact the whole law—the entire focus of the Jewish mind and probably the whole OT—points to Jesus Christ. This is confirmed in Hebrews 10, where Jesus is said to be the one who "sets aside the first to establish the second" (Heb. 10:9 NIV), meaning that he set aside the law in order to establish himself as the sacrifice that would definitively cover the sins of the people.

All of this is finalized quite clearly by the once-for-allness of Christ's sacrifice. This is what makes typology so important for the author of Hebrews; we have reached the "end of time" in regard to the action of God in salvation. It is about Jesus that the author states, "when Christ had offered for all time a single sacrifice for sins, 'he sat down at the right hand of God,' and since then has been waiting 'until his enemies would be made a footstool for his feet.' For by a single offering he has perfected for all time those who are sanctified" (Heb. 10:12–14 NRSV). The author then follows this with two quotations (not typological) emphasizing the permanence of the law written upon the minds and hearts of the people and the certainty that their "sins and lawless acts" will not be remembered any more (Heb. 10:15–17). Then in the next section, on the basis of this three-chapter typological argument, the author encourages his readers to "draw near to God with a sincere heart in full assurance of faith, having our hearts sprinkled to cleanse us from a guilty conscience and having our bodies washed with pure water. Let us hold unswervingly to the hope we profess, for he who promised is faithful" (Heb. 10:22–23 NIV). Typology, then, is a major interpretive method for the author of Hebrews, which he uses to clearly instruct his readers that Christ is sufficient and the basis for encouragement to draw nearer to God. A more important hermeneutical foundation for the warnings and encouragements of Hebrews cannot be found.

9. **Homiletic Midrash.** There is so much debate about the meaning of the word *midrash* in modern theological usage and the idea of midrash with reference to Hebrews is so comprehensive that we must proceed with caution and be very brief in our explanation. Midrash is simply a Hebrew noun meaning " 'inquiry,' 'examination,' or 'commentary.' "[17] It was a method of applying the Scriptures so as "to bring the text into the experience of the congregation. It involved making the Scriptures contemporary so that they could no longer be regarded as a record of past events and sayings but a living word through which God addressed the audience directly."[18]

An example of this is found in Heb. 12:5–13. When our author wants to encourage his readers to continue in their struggle against sin, he scolds them for forgetting the "word of encouragement that addresses you as sons" (Heb. 12:5 NIV). He then quotes Prov. 3:11–12, which describes the Lord's discipline of his children, punishing "those whom he loves, and chastis[ing] every child whom he accepts" (Heb. 12:6 NRSV). With this family metaphor in his mind, the writer then expands upon what it means to be disciplined as a son: "for what child is there whom a parent does not discipline?" (Heb. 12:7 NRSV). The author states that those who are not disciplined are illegitimate children and, using a lesser-to-greater *(qal wa-ḥomer)* argument, says that if we submitted to the discipline of our human fathers, how much more should we submit to the discipline of the "Father of our spirits" (Heb. 12:9 NIV). This Father "disciplines us for our good, in order that we may share his holiness," and the discipline that he administers "always seems painful rather than pleasant at the time, but later it yields the peaceful fruit of righteousness to those who have been trained

---

17. C. A. Evans, "Midrash," in *Dictionary of Jesus and the Gospels*, ed. Joel B. Green, Scot McKnight, and I. Howard Marshall (Downers Grove, Ill.: InterVarsity, 1992), 544. This article is an excellent introduction to the whole complicated discussion of midrash, though it is limited to a discussion of the Gospels as far as the concept applies to the NT.

18. Lane, *Hebrews*, 1:cxxiv.

by it" (Heb. 12:10–11 NRSV). Therefore, we are to pursue peace and holiness and accept the discipline that God gives us as our Father. All of this material is an extension and application of the original OT quote, a text that is relatively simple and compressed. The notion of God's parental discipline from Prov. 3:11–12 is expanded and applied more concretely by the author of Hebrews. This constitutes his midrash on the text.[19]

Does Hebrews Use Methods We Cannot?

We will look only briefly at whether or not the author of Hebrews uses methods that we cannot legitimately use. Not only is it not a question that particularly relates to our exegesis of the text of Hebrews (but rather, the exegesis of OT texts), but also it more properly belongs in a systematic theology text. Although the subject is difficult and complex, it boils down to this question: Are we able to use the biblical texts in the same manner that the biblical writers did? Some would say yes, without hesitating. The Bible is a book that uses human language in human circumstances to discuss very human thoughts about God. His inspiration of those thoughts, and even the words chosen to express them, is not in question, but the techniques that he moved them to use are purely human, and therefore open for us to use as well in our exegesis of the text. Others would say no. The inspiration of Scripture includes not only the words the authors chose but the very techniques they used to interpret other texts of Scripture. Just as Jesus was able to say certain things because he was God and man at the same time, so Scripture can interpret itself in unique ways because it is both written by humans and divinely inspired. Therefore, there are techniques open to the biblical writers that are not open to us.

As one might expect, the answer lies somewhere in between. Surely, Hebrews is a human book, and we must understand it as such. Therefore, the interpretive techniques used are humanly devised, and it should not surprise us to find that many of the methods used by the author of Hebrews were widely used by other

---

19. Lane, ibid., lists the following passages as containing examples of homiletic midrash, though they are also listed as fitting some of the other categories above as well: 2:5–9; 3:7–4:13; 6:13–20; 7:11–25; 8:7–13; 10:5–10, 15–18, 35–39; 12:5–13, 25–29.

biblical expositors in the first century. This legitimizes any interpretive technique we find in Scripture, as long as the text is handled in a manner consistent with the author's intent.

But therein lies the rub. The author of Hebrews is often accused of doing exactly the opposite. Some say that he has twisted certain OT texts in order to relate them to Christ, manipulating not only their interpretation but the words of the texts themselves. Is this true? If so, what does that say about our ability to use the text in a similar way? Can we also manipulate it in support of new spiritual insights? Certainly not. We can use human techniques as long as they are in line with the intent of the author, but to contradict an author's original intent by giving the words a meaning that they do not bear is certainly wrong. But did the Holy Spirit inspire the author of Hebrews to do so? That is the bone of contention. However, I think it is accurate to say that the author of Hebrews did not contradict any earlier Scriptures, but made their original intent clear to his readers and applied them clearly and forcefully to the historical reality of Jesus of Nazareth. Rather than mishandling them, he applied them properly to the coming of the Messiah and the ramifications of that event for us.

But does that mean that we can similarly apply and extend the Scriptures to refer to present-day events? The answer is yes and no. Yes, as long as you are willing to say that it is *your* interpretation and *your* application of the Scriptures to *your* situation. This is doing nothing more than applying the Word of God to our life, which is not only permissible but necessary. The Bible is a living book and intended for living people and real situations. We must apply it to our lives everyday to be able to live according to its teachings. But it is another matter to claim that we are offering a definitive interpretation that is true for all people at all times. To say that is to step over the line between divine illumination in our study of the biblical text and divine inspiration of our own new text that, if it were divinely inspired, should be printed in our Bibles alongside Hebrews, Matthew, and Habbakuk. The church has steadfastly resisted this temptation for ages, and we must continue to resist it.

There is much more to be said about the theology and use of the OT in Hebrews, but the above discussion may be summarized as follows. The author of Hebrews accepts the OT fully and finally as the Word of God, though he is willing to regard the LXX and even text-types currently unknown to us as accurate expressions of the Word of God. Based on his theology of Scripture, he is free to use the OT text in a number of ways that seem strange and difficult for us to accept but that were recognized as legitimate within their first-century context. Knowing how the author uses the OT will help us as we seek to be faithful interpreters of the Book of Hebrews.

Christology

Systematic theologians have traditionally separated the discussion of Christology into two categories, the *person* of Christ and the *work* of Christ. The first discusses the questions of his deity, his humanity, his role within the Trinity, etc.; the second discusses the purposes for which he became incarnate, his miracles, preaching, death on the cross, etc. These categories have proved convenient down through the years for answering certain questions of reader-response theology, but as the agenda for our theology has become formed more by the biblical texts themselves, this way of dividing Christology has been increasingly less able to satisfy the needs of interpreters. In the NT, the person of Christ is generally not separated from his work, and they are certainly not separated in Hebrews, so we will proceed to discuss both together.

But at this point we face another problem. On what aspect of Christ does our author focus? There seem to be two possibilities: the sonship of Jesus and his priestly office. The first is clearly the focus of the ringing introduction to the epistle (Heb. 1:1–4). There our author focuses on the fact that God has a Son through whom he has revealed himself to humankind and who is of a certain character and accomplishes a certain set of tasks. However, beginning in Hebrews 5 and stretching through to the end of Hebrews 10, the author rarely departs from the idea of Jesus as a high priest after the order of Melchizedek and superior to the levitical priesthood. This theme is so important in this central section of the epistle that it is hard to argue against its prominence in the mind of the writer. Ultimately, the question of priority between these two foci in the mind of the author is unimportant. Both themes are so crucial to his epistle and so interwoven with each other that the question can be left unanswered as we discuss the Christology of the epistle.

Jesus the Superior Son

The epistle begins with the sonship of Christ, and so shall we. From the opening phrases, we understand that the sonship of Jesus is a sonship to the Father/Creator of the entire universe. This is the God who has "spoken" (λαλήσας) in the past, revealing himself to his people, and who has "spoken" (ἐλάλησεν) now to us in his Son, who is his heir and through whom he created. This Son "is the reflection (ἀπαύγασμα) of God's glory and the exact imprint (χαρακτήρ) of God's very being (ὑποστάσεως)" (Heb. 1:3 NRSV). This ontological statement about Christ will be demonstrated functionally throughout the epistle, but never outside the context of the fact that Jesus is the ἀπαύγασμα and the χαρακτήρ of God himself.[20] The author's focus on the sonship of Jesus does not stay purely ontological for long, however. He immediately describes a number of Jesus' activities that demonstrate his divinity: he (1) "sustains all things by his powerful word," (2) "made purification for sins," and (3) "sat down at the right hand of the Majesty on high" (Heb. 1:3 NRSV). These three functions point to three elements of Jesus' nature: he is (1) God, who sustains all things; (2) the perfect sacrifice, who made purification for sins; and (3) the High Priest, who at the right hand of the divine majesty performs the priestly function in the heavenly tabernacle. Thus, ontology and function, Christ's person and work, are completely joined in the description of Jesus' sonship and priesthood in Hebrews 1.

The sonship of Jesus then becomes a dominant motif for establishing the superiority of Jesus to several other possible rivals in the minds of the readers of Hebrews. The writer begins by showing Jesus' superiority to angels (Heb. 1:5–2:18). The next major block of teaching (Heb. 3:1–6) shows Jesus' superiority to Moses, "as the builder of a house has more honor than the house itself" (Heb. 3:3 NRSV). This naturally leads into a clear statement of the superiority of Jesus to Joshua who led the people into the promised land, since Jesus now leads believers into the greater sab-

---

20. See the commentaries for the important role these words played in the later Christological formulations of the church and for the depth of meaning they had for ancient readers.

bath that "still remains for the people of God" (Heb. 4:9 NRSV). In each of these sections—showing Jesus superior to the angels, Moses, and Joshua—the writer focuses on the sonship of Jesus, though he mentions the high priesthood of Jesus as early as Heb. 2:17.

The prologue to the epistle introduces a notion that is crucial to understanding these contrasts. It states that Jesus is as much superior (κρείττων) to the angels as the name he has inherited is superior to theirs. Κρείττων describes someone who ranks above others by virtue of a qualitative difference; Jesus is qualitatively above the angels, Moses, and Joshua. How Jesus is superior to these other parties is variously described. Jesus is superior to the angels as the unique, divine Son of God. Angels are common spiritual beings, but only Jesus is uniquely begotten of the Father. As Heb. 1:3 makes clear, this unique Son is equal to the Father in every respect and is in no way a created being or to be placed on a par with the angels. God the Son is superior to the angels even while temporarily made lower by his suffering and death (Heb. 2:7, 9–15), because "it is not to angels that [God] has subjected the world to come" (Heb. 2:5 NIV) but to Jesus (Heb. 2:8). At the end of this comparison between Jesus and the angels, the motif of priesthood is introduced, beginning to make the point that though Jesus is the High Priest, he is also the unique, Divine One who is superior to angels (2:14–18).

Jesus' superiority to Moses, described in Heb. 3:1–6, is also heavily freighted with theology. "Jesus has been found worthy of greater honor than Moses, just as the builder of a house has greater honor than the house itself" (Heb. 3:3 NIV). Moses is described as a faithful servant in God's house, perhaps most importantly as the giver of the law (since he testified "to what would be said in the future"),[21] whereas Jesus was "faithful as a son over God's house" (3:5, 6 NIV). In this brief segment, the writer also refers to Jesus as "the apostle and high priest whom we confess" (3:1 NIV), but he does not emphasize the high priesthood at

---

21. As the giver of the prophetic law, Moses is ranked among the prophets through whom God spoke in former times and who are superseded by Christ (Heb. 1:1–2). Cf. Paul Ellingworth, *The Epistle to the Hebrews: A Commentary on the Greek Text*, New International Greek Testament Commentary (Grand Rapids: Eerdmans, 1993), 208–9.

this time as he moves into a description of Jesus' superiority to Joshua.

Jesus is presented as superior to Joshua, though this comparison is the least explicit of them all. The point that the author wants to make—warning the people not to be like the people of Israel in the wilderness—dominates his thinking, and the comparison between Jesus and Joshua is almost lost. Nevertheless, at the end of this segment of teaching, the comparison is made explicit (Heb. 4:8). The writer seems content to leave largely in the background the theme of Jesus as the one who leads God's people into rest. The strong statements about his leading many "to glory" (Heb. 2:10) and his freeing "those who all their lives were held in slavery by their fear of death" (Heb. 2:15 NIV) is enough to sustain the comparison with Joshua throughout the two chapters. He does make an explicit statement about Jesus, the Son of God, going through the heavenlies (4:14) to end this series of comparisons and move into the priesthood motif.

Jesus the Great High Priest

In a transitional section, at least as far as the Christology of Hebrews is concerned, our author, while continuing to call Jesus "Son," begins to focus upon the central typological teaching of our book: the priesthood of Jesus in the order of Melchizedek. In Heb. 4:14, we see Jesus called "a great high priest," but also referred to as "Jesus the Son of God." The high priestly motif is mentioned again in the following verse, emphasizing the humanity of Jesus and his ability "to sympathize with our weaknesses," where the author describes him as "one who has been tempted in every way, just as we are—yet was without sin" (Heb. 4:15 NIV). The theme of Jesus' high priesthood is then developed further, though the author briefly returns to the sonship motif by quoting Ps. 2:7: "You are my Son; today I have become your Father" (Heb. 5:5 NIV). The juxtaposition of the two ideas in the author's mind is once again apparent, however, as he immediately follows his quotation of Ps. 2:7 with the central quotation of the book, Ps. 110:4: "You are a priest forever, in the order of Melchizedek" (Heb. 5:6 NIV).

In the next four verses, the author shifts the focus clearly and eloquently from sonship to priesthood by describing Jesus' days on earth as a testing period: "Although he was a son, he learned obedience from what he suffered and, once made perfect, he became the source of eternal salvation for all who obey him" (Heb. 5:8–9 NIV). These verses, so important for establishing Jesus not only as a perfect high priest but also as a perfect sacrifice—and later as a perfect example of one who learned through suffering (cf. Hebrews 12)—lead clearly to the pinnacle statement of this transitional section: Jesus "was designated by God to be high priest in the order of Melchizedek" (Heb. 5:10 NIV).

After the aside containing the famous warning about not being able to repent again once one has fallen away (Heb. 5:11–6:20; see below under "Sanctification and Perseverance"), our author begins the central section of the epistle on the priesthood of Jesus. Much has been written about Jesus' priesthood, and one can consult the commentaries for an extensive theological exposition of this motif, but four things must be mentioned in even the briefest description of this crucial theological motif in Hebrews.

First, the comparison is made with Melchizedek in order to emphasize the uniqueness of Jesus' high priesthood. Though the author will later describe Jesus' priesthood largely in levitical terms, the comparison must begin with a priesthood that is separate from the Levites in order to emphasize its uniqueness. Melchizedek is mentioned only twice in the OT, both in rather strange and unique circumstances, and his priesthood was ideal for describing how Jesus' priesthood was similar to and yet different from the levitical priestly system.

Second, the argument that Melchizedek is more important than Abraham (Heb. 7:1–10) ranks him higher than even the highest Jews. Abraham tithed to the king of righteousness and peace (Heb. 7:2, 4–8), demonstrating his subservience to Melchizedek, even though Abraham had defeated other kings (Heb. 7:1). Abraham was the father of the Jewish nation. Even Moses was not ranked higher than he by first-century Judaism. Thus, presenting Jesus as a Melchizedekian priest reinforces the claim that Jesus is superior to Moses and Joshua and to other major OT Jewish leaders.

Third, Melchizedek seems to be a theophany, which enables the writer to point once again to Jesus' sonship. Melchizedek is said to have had no father or mother, to be without genealogy, and to be without beginning of days or end of life, and, significantly, the writer mentions that this is "like the Son of God" (Heb. 7:3).[22] This makes not only his person but also his priesthood perpetual and indestructible (Heb. 7:3, 15–17).

Fourth, that Jesus' priesthood is in the order of Melchizedek emphasizes the perfection of it. This motif dominates Hebrews 8–10 because it blends easily with the idea that Jesus' priesthood fulfills the typological elements of the OT levitical priesthood, but it is introduced in the summary section at the end of Hebrews 7. In 7:11, the argument is made that "if perfection could have been attained through the Levitical priesthood . . . , why was there still need for another priest to come—one in the order of Melchizedek, not in the order of Aaron?" (NIV).

The idea of "perfection" (τελείωσις) is not emphasized as strongly in this transitional section as it is in Hebrews 8–10, but it underlies the text. The law "made nothing perfect" (οὐδὲν γὰρ ἐτελείωσεν ὁ νόμος, Heb. 7:19), but Jesus' priesthood is "permanent" (ἀπαράβατον, Heb. 7:24), "holy, blameless, pure, set apart from sinners, [and] exalted above the heavens" (ὅσιος ἄκακος ἀμίαντος, κεχωρισμένος ἀπὸ τῶν ἁμαρτωλῶν καὶ ὑψηλότερος τῶν οὐρανῶν, Heb. 7:26 NIV). In the last verse of this transitional passage, the underlying idea becomes explicit: "the oath, which came after the law, appointed the Son, who has been made perfect (τετελειωμένον) forever" (Heb. 7:28 NIV). In describing Jesus' priesthood, the author now shifts his focus from its relationship to Melchizedek to its superiority to all aspects of the old covenant. Since we have discussed this in some detail above, while looking at how our author used the OT, it is time to move on to the topic of eschatology.

Eschatology

Eschatology, like Christology, is a topic of such breadth and depth in NT studies that it is impossible to do justice to even one NT writer's notion of it in the short space allowed here. The reason for this is that, while systematic theologians usually focus narrowly on events at the end of time in their study

---

22. We must be careful not to make too much out of this theologically, however, because of the highly rhetorical nature of the statements about Melchizedek (cf. pp. 178–79 above).

of eschatology, most NT scholars include the whole sweep of what is called "salvation history," or God's redemptive action in human history. We will briefly sketch the importance of this topic for the author of Hebrews.[23]

As with other aspects of the theology of Hebrews, the importance of eschatology is demonstrated in the first few verses of the book. The writer contrasts former days (πάλαι) with "these last days" (ἐπ' ἐσχάτου τῶν ἡμερῶν τούτων).[24] The prologue catalogs what has happened in Jesus in a historical progression of events moving from his role as Creator to Redeemer to heavenly intermediary for his people. This has all happened in human history in fulfillment of what had been taught in different ways and at various times through the prophets of old. Setting the work of Christ in the sweep of cosmic history could give the impression that the sermon will be full of abstract philosophical speculation; these first four verses—and, indeed, the whole first chapter of the epistle—do not seem aimed at the practical needs of a typical NT congregation.

Of course the author of Hebrews is never abstract, but rather these deep truths form the foundation for the message he wants his audience to heed (Heb. 2:1ff.). The eschatological mind of the author of Hebrews is seen in his desire to bring the past into the present so that it will affect the future. We spoke about this above when we looked at how the author makes the OT relevant to his readers' current situation. In the eschatology of the epistle, he uses a device known in NT circles today as the "already, but not yet" aspect of biblical history. Jesus is the one who now sits at the right hand of the Father, superior to the angels, but he is also the one to whom all things have "not yet" (οὔπω) been made subject (2:8).

The occurrences of this little word οὔπω in the book are instructive in this regard. In the first reference (Heb. 2:8), the focus is on the cosmic aspect of Christ as king of the universe subjecting all

---

23. Many have written on this topic, but perhaps most prominent in the discussion of the eschatology of Hebrews is the article by C. K. Barrett, "The Eschatology of the Epistle to the Hebrews," in *The Background of the New Testament and Its Eschatology: In Honour of Charles Harold Dodd*, ed. W. D. Davies and D. Daube (Cambridge: Cambridge University Press, 1964), 363–93. For further bibliography on this subject, see Attridge, *Hebrews*, 27 n. 211.

24. Of course, the Greek word for "last" is ἔσχατος, from which we get our word eschatology, "the study of last things."

things to himself, showing the author's interest in the larger questions of human history. The second occurrence (Heb. 12:4) shows the author's interest in the part his readers play in this cosmic history. In their specific circumstances in space and time, they have not yet resisted to the point of shedding blood. Nevertheless, their persecution is seen as part of God's larger agenda in human history. Christ, the mediatorial High Priest, serves both the larger needs of humankind and the people of God worldwide, and the smaller needs of the particular community to whom the author of Hebrews is writing.

Eschatology figures prominently in several other ways in the epistle. The discussion in Heb. 3:6–4:11 about the "rest" of God is clearly eschatological and points not only to the past history of the Israelites but also to the present and future of the believing community to whom our author writes. The author begins his discussion by warning "If we hold firm the confidence and the pride that belong to hope" (Heb. 3:6 NRSV), we shall be counted as part of his house and will be found to have passed the test of the wilderness.[25]

Hope is another theme that runs throughout the epistle and demonstrates its eschatological focus. Already eschatological by definition, this hope is nevertheless bolstered in its futurist orientation by a cluster of concepts. In Heb. 3:6, the readers are asked to "hold firm" (κατάσχωμεν) their confidence and hope. In 6:11, it is the "full assurance of hope" (τὴν πληροφορίαν τῆς ἐλπίδος) that the author wants to be realized "to the very end" (ἄχρι τέλους) in the lives of his readers, and only a few verses later he encourages them "to seize the hope set before us" (κρατῆσαι τῆς προκειμένης ἐλπίδος, Heb. 6:18 NRSV), a reference that has both spatial and temporal connotations. At the same time, 6:19–20 makes clear that this hope is "a sure and steadfast anchor of the soul, a hope that enters the inner shrine behind the curtain, where Jesus, a forerunner on our behalf, has entered" (NRSV), indicating that the hope is not only future oriented but brings present benefits through the work of Jesus in heaven. This idea is essentially repeated in Heb. 7:19, where Jesus introduces "a better hope, through which we approach God" (NRSV). In perhaps the most integrative of all the pas-

---

25. For more on this theme, see Barrett, "Eschatology," 366–73.

sages on this theme, the writer encourages his readers to "hold fast to the confession of our hope without wavering, for he who has promised is faithful" (Heb. 10:23 NRSV). They are to do this by considering how to stir up the Christian community to love and good deeds and by meeting together and encouraging one another, doing this "all the more as you see the Day approaching" (Heb. 10:25 NRSV). "Day" here is a clear reference to the future judgment of God (cf. 10:27).

Finally, the warnings in the Epistle to the Hebrews, which will be prominent below in our discussion of sanctification and perseverance, are essential to the eschatological thrust of the epistle. The threat of God's future judgment gives these warnings their solemn tone, as does the present fearful prospect of falling into the hands of the living God (Heb. 10:27, 30–31). In Heb. 6:4–12, this theme comes to the fore as well. The author assures his readers that God will not be unjust so as to overlook their work in the day of judgment, but he wants them to continue to show "diligence so as to realize the full assurance of hope" and "inherit the promises" (6:10–12 NRSV). They will obtain these promises by continuing in their salvation, which began in the past, as the author reminds them when he says that they "have once been enlightened, and have tasted the heavenly gift, and have shared in the Holy Spirit, and have tasted the goodness of the word of God and the powers of the age to come" (Heb. 6:4–5 NRSV). Whether or not this salvation will continue into the future is a question that is perhaps best discussed under our next topic, sanctification and perseverance.

Sanctification and Perseverance

No topic has created more controversy among theological analysts of Hebrews than the epistle's teaching regarding whether or not one can lose one's salvation.[26] The discussion involves many complex exegetical issues. In each of the relevant passages, the definitions of many key terms are disputed, a variety of grammatical possibilities exist, and one must make assumptions

---

26. See Scot McKnight, "The Warning Passages of Hebrews: A Formal Analysis and Theological Conclusions," *Trinity Journal* 13 (1992): passim (esp. 21 n. 1 and 22 n. 2), for its extensive bibliography of recent articles on this topic in Hebrews. This article provides an excellent model of how to deal with theological issues in a biblical text of some size.

concerning the nature of the original problem in the community—and these are just a few of the problems that plague interpreters approaching this thorny issue. The difficulty even
extends to the category under which we should discuss this issue. While perseverance is clearly an issue in Hebrews, it is ques-
tionable whether *sanctification* or *justification* is the proper term to
describe the aspect of soteriology under dispute. The question,
particularly when discussing passages like Heb. 6:4–12 and
10:19–39, is whether the author is speaking of initial salvation or
of continuing to grow in holiness within the sphere of salvation.
Why I have titled this section as I have will become clearer as we
proceed. It can be said now, however, that Hebrews seems at the
very least to have been written to those who claim to have already had an experience of justification. We will approach the
subject from that standpoint, viewing the salvation discussed as
pertaining to the Christian's growth in Christ. I have chosen to
discuss this theological problem because it illustrates the need to
think in terms of both authorial and reader-response theology at
the same time, but it is impossible to do more than outline the issue in its most basic form (though even this may prove to be easier than restoring an apostate to repentance!).

At the heart of this discussion are four passages, known commonly as the "warning passages." While there is some dispute as
to the relative importance of these passages, there seems to be general agreement that in Heb. 2:1–4, 3:7–4:13, 5:11–6:12, and 10:19–39
the author addresses the need for faithfulness in holding on to the
gospel.[27] In 2:3, the author asks "How can we escape if we neglect
so great a salvation?" (NRSV), a rhetorical question that demonstrates his profound worry that this salvation can be lost and that
the judgment of God in the eschaton will be inescapable. At Heb.
3:12, the author clearly warns his readers to "take care, brothers
and sisters, that none of you may have an evil, unbelieving heart
that turns away from the living God" (NRSV). This is followed immediately by another command, to encourage one another daily
"so that none of you may be hardened by the deceitfulness of sin"

---

27. Others have included 12:1–29 and a number of the exhortations in chapter
13. While these certainly have a warning character to them, they seem distant
enough from the question of losing one's salvation (i.e., perseverance in the face of
apostasy rather than persecution), that they are not included here.

(Heb. 3:13 NRSV). Once again in Heb. 4:1, the readers are exhorted to "take care that none of you should seem to have failed to reach it [i.e., the rest of God]" (NRSV). At the end of the passage, the author wraps it up with another exhortation: "Let us therefore make every effort to enter that rest, so that no one may fall through such disobedience as theirs [i.e., Israel in the wilderness]" (Heb. 4:11 NRSV).

The two most difficult and most often cited passages on this question are Heb. 5:11–6:12 and 10:19–39. They too make it quite clear that the author is concerned with perseverance and the sanctification of the believer. The first passage in fact contains the only direct accusation found in the epistle of the readers' lack of faithfulness. The author scolds them for needing "someone to teach you again the basic elements of the oracles of God. You need milk, not solid food," though by this time they ought to be teachers (Heb. 5:12 NRSV). An exhortation is implied as well in 6:11, where the author declares that he wants "each one of you to show the same diligence [as they had previously shown] so as to realize the full assurance of hope to the very end" (Heb. 6:11 NRSV). Hebrews 10:19–39 begins in a much less confrontational manner by encouraging the readers to approach the throne of God "with a true heart in full assurance of faith" and to "hold fast to the confession of our hope without wavering" (Heb. 10:22–23 NRSV). Another exhortation follows: "And let us consider how to provoke one another to love and good deeds, not neglecting to meet together . . . but encouraging one another . . ." (Heb. 10:24–25 NRSV). This, however, leads into a strong warning about those who "willfully persist in sin" and "have spurned the Son of God, profaned the blood of the covenant . . . , and outraged the Spirit of grace" (Heb. 10:26, 29 NRSV). All of these warnings certainly show the importance of this issue for our author; sanctification and perseverance were subjects about which the writer of Hebrews was deeply concerned.

We will now briefly examine the four passages, outlining some of the questions that one must face in trying to think theologically about Hebrews. Since these issues are complex and involve many different variables, our review will seem somewhat superficial. Nevertheless, a summary of some of the relevant issues will help us get a clearer overall picture of the debate and its importance.

Hebrews 2:1–4

Hebrews 2:1–4 follows hard upon the author's long discussion of Christ's superiority to angels (Heb. 1:5–14). Key terms in dispute in the passage are "escape" (ἐκφεύγειν), "salvation" (σωτηρία, Heb. 2:3), and "drift away" (παραρρεῖν, Heb. 2:1). The rhetorical question in Heb. 2:3 surely seems to refer to escaping the judgment of God. Two factors call for this conclusion. First, the passage follows hard upon two OT quotations in chapter 1 that allude to judgment by the Messiah (Ps. 102:25–27 = Heb. 1:10–12; Ps. 110:1 = Heb. 1:13). Second, the meaning of the rhetorical question in Heb. 2:3 depends upon the contrast with the law spoken of in Heb. 2:2. There the description of the law ends by stating that "every violation and disobedience received its just punishment" (NIV), connecting the escape in Heb. 2:3 with the idea of punishment. Thus, the salvation which is announced by the Lord in Heb. 2:3 must have to do with salvation from the wrath of God, his punishment of evildoers at the end of time. More difficult is a definition of the verb "drift away" (παραρρεῖν, Heb. 2:1). The vagueness of this rare verb is noted by many commentators,[28] but it introduces in a general way the issue of believers being able to lose their salvation, which is all that the author intends at this moment. Much fuller and more explicit warnings come later, so little can be gained from trying to define the term more fully here. We will discuss this issue further in later passages. At this point, we can say with Harold Attridge that "although ... the community addressed is perceived to be in danger, the vagueness of the imagery and general character of the warning shed no light on the causes or nature of that danger."[29]

Hebrews 3:7–4:13

The major question in this passage is of course what the idea of the "rest" (κατάπαυσις) of God means (cf. Heb. 3:11). Whatever the precise meaning of this phrase, it has something to do with salvation from sin, for the warning in 3:12–13 cautions members of the community not to become "hardened by the deceitfulness of sin" (ἵνα μὴ σκληρυνθῇ τις ἐξ ὑμῶν ἀπάτῃ τῆς ἁμαρτίας). The

---

28. Cf., e.g., Attridge, *Hebrews*, 64.
29. Ibid.

idea of hardening also appears in Heb. 3:8, a quotation from the OT that is directly applied to the readers of Hebrews. Further definition of the idea of hardening may come in 3:18–19, where the Israelites are said not to have been able to enter God's rest because of "disobedience" (ἀπειθεῖν) and "unbelief" (ἀπιστία). These two elements are reinforced in 4:2 and 4:6, where faithlessness and disobedience are again linked to this issue.

Whatever else can be said about Heb. 3:7–4:13, we can at least conclude four things.

1. The section is certainly about sanctification. In Heb. 3:16 and 4:1, the wilderness journey of the people of Israel is used as an example for the readers of Hebrews. The notion of entering the rest dominates the passage and clearly refers to a journey that the readers are taking. The analogy only makes sense within the context of a spiritual journey here on earth.

2. The references to hardening can only refer to a time of sanctification as well. Logically, the readers' hearts would first have to be soft toward God for them to be able to harden them, but there is more than just logic to support this statement. In Heb. 4:2 we read that "the good news came to us just as to them" (NRSV), and again in 4:3 that "we who have believed enter that rest" (NRSV). Therefore, the author is certainly writing to those who have already come to faith and have believed the promises. What is now required is a persevering faith in those promises, and this can only be a relevant motif within the theological framework of sanctification, not justification.

3. According to this passage, those who do not enter God's rest are left outside the realm of God's grace. In Heb. 4:11, we read that we are to "make every effort to enter that rest, so that no one may fall (πέσῃ) through such disobedience (ἀπειθείας) as theirs" (NRSV). The use of πίπτειν and ἀπείθεια make it certain that the author is talking here about final unbelief. These terms are always used in the NT with this finality. In addition, the metaphor of anger, used so often in the passage to describe God's response to the Israelites who fell in the wilderness, implies that such

anger will be extended to any readers who might fall away. The wrath of God directed toward any person indicates that they are outside the reach of the grace of God; it is one of the most common metaphors for judgment of sin used in the NT (cf., e.g., 1 Thess. 5:9). So any reader who might engage in this falling away is very clearly said to "have an evil, unbelieving heart (καρδία πονηρὰ ἀπιστίας) that turns away (ἀποστῆναι) from the living God" (Heb. 3:12 NRSV). There is no doubt that this refers to those who, having turned away from the living God, are no longer in relationship with him.

4. This passage also declares that persevering to the end of the journey is essential to salvation, to becoming "partners of Christ" (μέτοχοι ... τοῦ Χριστοῦ, Heb. 3:14). Readers are to exhort each other "every day, as long as it is called 'today' " (Heb. 3:13 NRSV), and there would be no need for this exhortation if there were no need for perseverance. Also, the rest remains "open" (Heb. 4:6, 8–9, 11); it is something that still waits to be entered. Lastly, there is an effort to be made (Heb. 4:11), to "hold fast to our confession" (Heb. 4:14), a further indication that perseverance is in view. The metaphor of holding fast cannot imply anything else.

Much of what has been said in the preceding paragraphs seems obvious, but it must be restated because so many have questioned the reality of the need for the warning passages in Hebrews. There can be no doubt that, while the author of Hebrews considers the readers to be firmly in God's hand at present, he is concerned that they persevere to the end in order to be clearly in God's hand at the time of judgment. The question of whether they only *appear* to be in God's hands—only appear to be Christians, while in reality not being so—is simply not addressed. This passage gives us no help in answering the fundamental theological question about the nature of the salvation of the readers of Hebrews and whether they are able to lose a "real" salvation that they already possess or only able to lose an "apparent" salvation that by every human measuring stick seems to be theirs, but is in fact not really theirs.

We will look at the next two warning passages in an attempt to find an answer to that question.

Hebrews 5:11–6:12

Perhaps no passage in Hebrews has been more discussed than Heb. 5:11–6:12, particularly Heb. 6:4–6.[30] Hebrews 5:11–6:12 has so many difficulties and can be approached in so many different ways, that it presents a formidable challenge to the interpreter. Although our evaluation must of necessity be brief and somewhat superficial, we can still observe how some of the major elements in this passage fit within the authorial theology of Hebrews as this pertains to the issue of sanctification and perseverance.

Four terms or groups of terms cause the main difficulty within the passage, all of them falling within Heb. 6:4–6. Perhaps the most important is the redundant phrase in Heb. 6:6 "to restore again to repentance" (πάλιν ἀνακαινίζειν εἰς μετάνοιαν, Heb. 6:6, cf. 6:4 in NRSV). The meaning of παραπίπτειν (Heb. 6:6) is the second crucial factor in the passage. The third element in the passage is the phrase that is translated "since on their own they are crucifying again the Son of God and are holding him up to contempt" (ἀνασταυροῦντας ἑαυτοῖς τὸν υἱὸν τοῦ θεοῦ καὶ παραδειγματίζοντας, Heb. 6:6 NRSV). As with πάλιν ἀνακαινίζειν, so also here we have the problem of the prefix ἀνα- being used to speak of an activity that has happened once and is now happening again, but it is the definition of the activity that creates the difficulty for interpreting this verse. Fourth, the meaning of the word "impossible" (ἀδύνατον, Heb. 6:4) and of the string of terms beginning in Heb. 6:4 and extending through 6:5 are crucial to understanding what the passage is about. We must look briefly at each of these now.

1. Though ἀνακαινίζειν and καινίζειν could be used interchangeably (see *Epistle of Barnabas* 6.11), it is difficult to miss the idea of redundancy that is found in the use of the prefix ἀνα- and the use of πάλιν to reinforce the idea of repetitive action. This is especially true since πάλιν echoes its use in 5:12 and ἀνα- is echoed

---

30. Many feel that this passage vies mightily with Heb. 10:19–39 as the NT passage that most clearly reflects the possibility of a believer falling into apostasy. Although it would be difficult to argue with this assessment, deciding between these two passages is a question of little significance.

three words later in 6:6 by ἀνασταυροῦντας. The author is clearly addressing whether this act that has already happened once can be repeated. The act he regards as unrepeatable is *being restored unto repentance,* a clear reference to a state of salvation. As Ellingworth puts it: "The 'impossibility' of a second repentance is thus not psychological, or more generally related to the human condition; it is in the strict sense theological, related to God's saving action in Christ."[31]

2. The verb παραπίπτειν is a hapax legomenon in the NT. It does occur in the LXX and other early Christian literature with a variety of meanings, including "to fall beside, go astray, miss."[32] It also, however, commonly means to fall away from salvation (cf., e.g., Wisdom of Solomon 6:9; 12:2; and esp. Ezek. 22:4). Perhaps as important as the verb itself, is its cognate, παράπτωμα, which occurs often in the NT, almost always describing some sort of apostasy (cf. esp. Rom. 5:15–20). Judging by the context, the serious sin of apostasy is probably the meaning of the participle here. Of course this is dependent upon the meaning of the phrases in Heb. 6:4–5, which we will discuss below, but the clear link between παραπεσόντας and πάλιν ἀνακαινίζειν εἰς μετάνοιαν, pretty well decides the case. This "falling away" is the opposite of faith, which enables one to hold fast.

3. Although there is some question whether the word ἀνασταυροῦν means "to crucify" or "to crucify again,"[33] the context demands that it mean "crucify again." Πάλιν reinforces this idea. The sin here is a further crucifixion of Christ in addition to his real, historical crucifixion. Jesus Christ has died once for all; to crucify Jesus *again* carries with it a stigma so great as to be unconscionable.

It is clear enough that complete apostasy is the author's meaning, but just to reinforce the point, he declares that those who recrucify Jesus "are holding him up to contempt" (παρα–δειγματίζοντας). There is an ironic twist in the author's use of this term. It alludes to Jesus' crucifixion and the shame he endured

---

31. Ellingworth, *Hebrews,* 323.

32. Walter Bauer, *A Greek-English Lexicon of the New Testament and Other Early Christian Literature,* trans. and adapted by William F. Arndt and F. Wilbur Gingrich, 2d ed. rev. and augmented by F. Wilbur Gingrich and Frederick W. Danker (Chicago and London: University of Chicago Press, 1979), s.v. "παραπίπτω."

33. Cf., e.g., the references to commentators in Ellingworth, *Hebrews,* 324.

from the Romans, both as a Jew and as a supposed criminal. But this sort of public humiliation was also administered by Rome in the political sphere to its conquered enemies. Thus, there is a double condemnation for those who committed this sin. The author writes to those who knew how offensive any Roman humiliation was to a Jew, having tasted it themselves (cf. Heb. 10:32–34), so he writes that one who crucifies Jesus in this way not only humiliates him but humiliates him as a pagan would.

4. The fourth important element in the passage is the word "impossible" (ἀδύνατον, Heb. 6:4). This adjective is found in three other places in Hebrews (6:18; 10:4; 11:6). The neuter gender of the adjective is significant. It indicates that his readers cannot be renewed again to repentance objectively, not that they themselves are incapable of repentance.[34] Ellingworth therefore asks whether the implied subject of ἀδύνατον is God or some human agency. He suggests that according to Heb. 10:26–29 even God is rendered powerless in this situation, because in Christ he has offered the perfect sin offering and it has been rejected. Therefore there remains no sacrifice for sins.[35] This is surely correct.

A discussion of the string of descriptions found in Heb. 6:4–5 could occupy much more space than we have to give, but it is instructive at least to lay out the parameters of the discussion. There are two major differences of opinion about the terms. On the one hand, some say that the terms describe something very close to salvation, without actually mentioning it, and refer to those who have not really believed. On the other hand, there are those who say that these terms are clear and powerful rhetorical descriptions of a "real convert" and only lack direct propositional character in the interest of literary power.

The question is a moot one because it requires knowledge of the author's view on an issue he does not address: whether he thought that all those whom he *addressed* as Christians were in fact Christians. In either case, the author of Hebrews gives a *real* warning concerning a *real* falling away. He states this warning in the strongest of language, so that even if what he describes is purely hypothetical as far as his readers are concerned (cf. Heb. 6:9), his

---

34. Cf. F. F. Bruce, *The Epistle to the Hebrews*, rev. ed., New International Commentary on the New Testament (Grand Rapids: Eerdmans, 1990), 144 n. 35.

35. Ellingworth, *Hebrews*, 319.

warning would affect those who think they are Christians and are not. Therefore, these warnings do describe a *real* situation in their literary context; falling away is viewed as a *real* possibility and its consequences are viewed as a *real* danger. Whether such a situation is a real possibility theologically is a question for other texts at other times. As far as the author of Hebrews is concerned, people who at least appear to be Christians (genuine or not) have fallen away. This is all that matters. The true state of their hearts prior to that falling away is irrelevant.

Several other things need to be mentioned about this passage. First, the author does not believe that his readers are guilty of the things that he has described in Heb. 6:4–5 (cf. Heb. 6:9–12), so the question of whether someone who has truly believed can fall away is a hypothetical one. The warning to the readers of Hebrews is sincere. Nevertheless, the author takes some of the edge off that warning by declaring that he does not believe his readers are of the company of those who would fall away.

Second, the illustration of ground being evaluated by its fruit (Heb. 6:7–8) can be seen as favoring either side of the debate about the readers' spiritual state. One could say that the author of Hebrews is looking purely at fruit and cannot know the true character of the land. The rain falls equally on all the land. If God blesses the land, it produces a crop; without his blessing it produces thorns and thistles. This would indicate that the land can be the same but that the blessing of God is what makes the difference. On the other hand, especially as one compares this with similar statements by Jesus (cf. Matt. 7:17–20 = Luke 6:43–45), one could conclude just the opposite: that the land is not all the same; a difference in fruit indicates a difference in the quality of the land. So the one view says that the land is, as it were, neutral (i.e., able to accept or reject the gospel at any time depending on God's blessing), while the other view says that the land is not neutral but rather determines the kind of fruit that will be produced. If we read Heb. 6:7 in light of the statements of encouragement that follow (Heb. 6:9–12), the illustration is essentially positive. His readers are good land and he expects them to yield good fruit. Yielding bad fruit (i.e., apostatizing and recrucifying Jesus) will show that they were bad land after all. Further discussion will move us into categories that go beyond exegesis, so we will leave the illustration here.

Lastly, there is no doubt that the passage as a whole moves toward Heb. 6:19–20, which encourages us to seize the hope that is ours in Christ, a hope that is "an anchor for the soul, firm and secure" (ἄγκυραν . . . τῆς ψυχῆς ἀσφαλῆ τε καὶ βεβαίαν, Heb. 6:19 NIV). This indicates that while Hebrews 6 is certainly a warning, it can be read as much as an encouragement to persevere as a warning of what happens if one does not. We should read it in this positive light and not entirely in the negative light of reader-response theology with its question of whether or not it is possible to lose one's salvation. For the author, the question is rather, How do we hold on to our salvation? And the answer, of course, is that we hold on to Jesus.

Hebrews 10:19–31

This passage is often held up as the most difficult passage in Hebrews for those who wish to defend the position that one's salvation cannot be lost. As with previous passages, so here as well there seems to be no doubt that the persons described are Christian as far as that can be determined. First person plural pronouns in 10:19–26 set the tone for the passage that describes the falling away, clearly reflecting the author's belief that he and his readers share a common faith. It is important to note, however, that the author moves to the more general "anyone" (τις) and "one who" (ὁ + participle) in Heb. 10:28–29, where he describes the person who apostatizes. Nevertheless, in 10:30 he returns to addressing his readers directly and seems to connect them with the hypothetical person mentioned in Heb. 10:28–29.

The second thing to be said about the passage is that it describes divine judgment. The sentence in Heb. 10:26—"there no longer remains a sacrifice for sins" (οὐκέτι περὶ ἁμαρτιῶν ἀπολείπεται θυσία)—cannot be read as referring to anything other than a final judgment. This conclusion is supported by what follows: "a fearful prospect of judgment, and a fury of fire that will consume the adversaries" (Heb. 10:27 NRSV). Κρίσεως, πυρός, and τοὺς ὑπεναντίους are terms that refer to God's final judgment of unbelievers, both in the rest of the NT and in the Book of Hebrews.[36] The men-

---

36. Cf., e.g., Lane, *Hebrews*, 2:293: "The consequence of apostasy is terrifying, irrevocable judgment."

tion of punishment, vengeance, and judgment (Heb. 10:29–30) reinforce the conclusion that this is the final judgment of God.

Lastly, as serious as this passage is in its warning against apostasy, it nevertheless focuses once again on hope. Not only is the
warning broken up by the author's strong exhortation to recall the
earlier days when his readers were acting more in accord with
their responsibility as Christians (10:32–34) but he ends the whole
passage on a confident note by saying "we are not among those
who shrink back and so are lost, but among those who have faith
and so are saved" (Heb. 10:39 NRSV). He also makes the confident
assertion that perseverance will bring reward (Heb. 10:35–36).
Nevertheless, the warning is a real one and appears even in this
exhortatory wrap-up: God will not be pleased with those who
shrink back (Heb. 10:38).

Hebrews 10:26–27 is perhaps the strongest statement in the
book warning first-century readers of the danger of apostasy. The
inclusive "we" and the present tense forms reinforce the impression that this poses a real threat to his readers and is not merely a
hypothetical situation. Besides using the present tense to create a
sense of the vividness and continuous nature of the danger they
faced, adding ἑκουσίως emphasizes that it takes repeated and
willful sin against God to lose one's salvation. Yet the author's use
of "we" implies that he saw apostasy as a real possibility even for
himself. Nevertheless, this is the only statement in all of these
warnings that could answer positively the question "Can one lose
salvation after receiving it?" Perhaps we should not hang too
much on such a slender thread.

If one first accepts the idea that here the author views apostasy
as a real possibility, then many other passages in Hebrews can be
understood as pointing in that direction. But that is just what we
are trying to avoid: making theological suppositions and then going to the text to prove them. As one looks objectively at these four
warning passages in Hebrews, one sees only the author's constant
encouragement to his readers and his confidence that they will not
fail him or their Lord but will persevere to the end. Second, one
sees a great hope that the warnings will have their intended effect,
driving them closer to Christ and the life of faith. There is ultimately no way to tell whether the author believed in the theological distinction between real and apparent believers when he

uttered these warnings. The seriousness of salvation necessitated that the author use the strongest possible language to describe believers who had fallen away, because he believed they really were believers. Whether or not our author would have concluded that those who ultimately remained apostate were never truly believers must remain a mystery to us.

Conclusion

Each of the four theological issues we have examined highlight the importance of first seeking out the author's understanding before asking our own questions of what we have determined is in the text. We must derive our theology of Hebrews from the author's own questions and concerns, for we will do him a great disservice if we try to impose our theology upon him. At the same time, our concerns are real and important, and it is to be hoped that the text as it was originally written and understood will have something to say about those concerns. But as we saw in the last section, for instance, the text may not say anything about whether it is possible for true believers to lose their salvation, and we must be willing to leave such questions open. Nevertheless, our text has said much that we can grasp and incorporate into a theology that warns of apostasy, recognizing that the warnings are sincere and passionately aimed at believers, whether apparent or real.